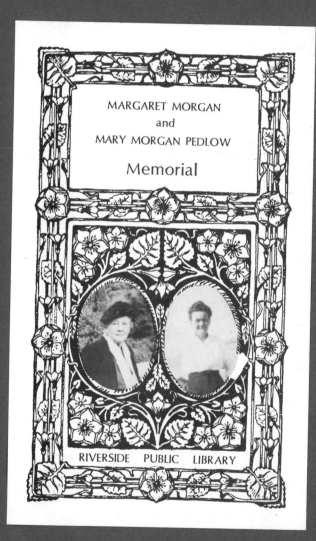

MARGARET MORGAN
and
MARY MORGAN PEDLOW

Memorial

RIVERSIDE PUBLIC LIBRARY

WITNESS TO APPOMATTOX

"With Fate Against Them" *(from the painting by Gilbert Gaul)*

WITNESS
TO
Appomattox

☆

☆

RICHARD WHEELER

1817

HARPER & ROW, PUBLISHERS, New York

Cambridge, Philadelphia, San Francisco, London

Mexico City, São Paulo, Singapore, Sydney

FIRST EDITION

Designer: Sidney Feinberg

Library of Congress Cataloging-in-Publication Data

Wheeler, Richard.
  Witness to Appomattox / Richard Wheeler.
    p.   cm.
  Bibliography: p.
  Includes index.
  ISBN 0-06-016078-0
  1. Appomattox Campaign, 1865.   I. Title.
  E477.67.W48 1989
  973.7′38—dc19   88-45532

---

89 90 91 92 93 CC/RRD 10 9 8 7 6 5 4 3 2 1

For my Aunt Marie Addington

Contents

List of Illustrations

MAPS

Preface

Witness to Appomattox is a companion book to *Witness to Gettysburg,* published in 1987. Both of these Civil War topics have maintained a strong appeal among readers of history, Gettysburg because of its significance and high drama, and Appomattox because of its unique combination of significance, drama, and poignancy. Like *Witness to Gettysburg, Witness to Appomattox* is history told as largely as possible in the words of participants, both military and civilian, both male and female. The accounts have been linked together so as to form a chronological narrative. Although the book is intended for the general reader rather than the Civil War scholar, it is offered as a veracious study. The technical statements have been checked against the official records, and the personal episodes have been analyzed for credibility. Although most of the book's ellipses indicate the employment of condensation, some were used to eliminate details that appeared to be faulty. It was occasionally necessary to include clarifications enclosed in brackets. Some of the quotations were extracted from the Appomattox Campaign's better-known eyewitness records, but many others represent material that never achieved more than transient notice. Numbers of the illustrations, all of which were taken from *Battles and Leaders of the Civil War* and other publications of the postwar decades, are adaptations of sketches or photographs made while the campaign was in progress.

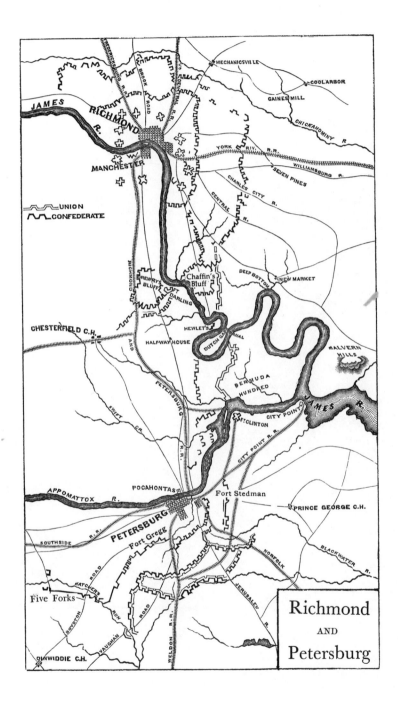

Richmond
AND
Petersburg

1

Events Foretell an Ending

B y the beginning of 1865 the war between the Union and the Confederacy, which had been raging for nearly four years, was entering its final months. Union prospects were flourishing in all theaters. The west had already seen its last major battle, that of Nashville, a decisive victory for Northern commander George H. Thomas. In Georgia, a great blue army under William T. Sherman had steamrolled its way from Atlanta to the sea and was preparing to march northward through the Carolinas, where the foe was modestly numbered. In the key state of Virginia, Union cavalry leader Philip H. Sheridan had broken the Confederate hold on the Shenandoah Valley, the backdoor route between Washington and Richmond; and the North's commander in chief, Ulysses S. Grant, in personal charge of the combined Armies of the Potomac and the James, was besieging Richmond and Petersburg from the east and was eroding the forty-mile arc of defenses held by the diminished Army of Northern Virginia under Robert E. Lee. The capture of Richmond, the Confederate capital, had been a Union goal since the outset of the war, and events were finally shaping in a manner that promised success. Confederate President Jefferson Davis, however, hoped to find a way to end the war before Richmond fell, and he now tried negotiations.

As explained by the Union's General Grant: "On the last of January, 1865, peace commissioners from the so-called Confederate States presented themselves on our lines around Petersburg, and were immediately conducted to my headquarters at City Point [northeast of Petersburg at the junction of the Appomattox and James Rivers, a spot

1

Ulysses S. Grant

from which the army maintained water communication, by way of the Chesapeake Bay, with Washington]. They proved to be Alexander H. Stephens, Vice President of the Confederacy; Judge [John A.] Campbell, Assistant Secretary of War; and R. M. T. Hunter, formerly United States Senator and then a member of the Confederate Senate.

"It was about dark when they reached my headquarters, and I at once conducted them to the steamer *Mary Martin,* a Hudson River boat which was very comfortably fitted up for the use of passengers. I at once communicated by telegraph with Washington and informed the Secretary of War and the President of the arrival of these commissioners and that their object was to negotiate terms of peace between the United States and, as they termed it, the Confederate Government. I was instructed to retain them at City Point until the President, or someone whom he would designate, should come to meet them. . . .

"I had never met either of these gentlemen before the war, but knew them well by reputation and through their public services, and I had been a particular admirer of Mr. Stephens. I had always supposed that he was a very small man, but when I saw him in the dusk of the evening I was very much surprised to find so large a man as he seemed to be. When he got down on to the boat I found that he was wearing a coarse gray woolen overcoat, a manufacture that had been introduced into the South during the rebellion. The cloth was thicker than anything of the kind I had ever seen, even in Canada. The overcoat extended nearly to his feet and was so large that it gave him the appearance of being an average-sized man. He took this off when he reached the cabin of the boat, and I was struck with the apparent change in size, in the coat and out of it.

"After a few days, about the 2nd of February, I received a dispatch from Washington directing me to send the commissioners to Hampton Roads [near the mouth of the Chesapeake Bay] to meet the President and a member of the cabinet. Mr. Lincoln met them there and had an interview of short duration. It was not a great while after they met that the President visited me at City Point. He spoke of his having met the commissioners, and said he had told them that there would be no use in entering into any negotiations unless they would recognize, first: that the Union as a whole must be forever preserved; and second: that slavery must be abolished. If they were willing to concede these two points, then he was ready to enter into negotiations and was almost willing to hand them a blank sheet of paper with his signature attached for them to fill in the terms upon which they were willing to live with

Robert E. Lee

us in the Union and be one people. He always showed a generous and kindly spirit toward the Southern people, and I never heard him abuse an enemy. . . .

"Right here I might relate an anecdote of Mr. Lincoln. It was on the occasion of his visit to me just after he had talked with the peace commissioners at Hampton Roads. After a little conversation, he asked me if I had seen that overcoat of Stephens's. I replied that I had. 'Well,' said he, 'did you see him take it off?' I said yes. 'Well,' said he, 'didn't you think it was the biggest shuck and the littlest ear that ever you did see?' "

(This anecdote—in which Lincoln, of course, was comparing Stephens to a cob of corn and its covering—eventually got around to the diminutive Southerner himself, and he found it hilarious.)

Many people of the Confederacy, civilians and soldiers alike, had pinned a fervent hope on their government's peace initiative. In a letter to his wife, his "Sally of the Sunset Eyes," young Major General George E. Pickett of Gettysburg fame (and a prewar friend of his present enemy, Abraham Lincoln) described the effect of the failure on the defenders of Richmond and Petersburg: "On every side gloom, dissatisfaction, and disappointment seem to have settled over all, men and officers alike. . . . The anxious, despairing faces I see everywhere bespeak heavy hearts. Our commissioners knew that we were gasping our last gasp and that the peace conference was a forlorn hope. Because of the informality of the conference and my knowledge of Mr. Lincoln, his humanity, his broad nature, his warm heart, I did believe he would take advantage of this very informality and spring some wise, superhuman surprise which would, somehow, restore peace and, in time, insure unity. Now, heaven help us, it will be war to the knife, with the knife no longer keen, the thrust of an arm no longer strong. . . ."

The deterioration of Lee's proud Army of Northern Virginia had begun after the Battle of Gettysburg in July 1863 and had grown critical during the spring of 1864 when Grant, with his Wilderness Campaign, had driven Lee southeastward from the Rapidan River and placed him at bay in his present position east of Richmond and Petersburg. Lieutenant J. F. J. Caldwell, a member of the 1st Regiment, South Carolina Volunteers, explains the circumstances behind the army's decline: "It had suffered large casualties in battle, it had been exhausted by toil and want, and it had received no reinforcement worth mention. . . . Indeed, it had been so trusted and neglected, it had been so called upon to perform so much, and it had so bravely executed its task that . . . it did not number sixty thousand men in all arms of the service. Yet we had to hold our forty miles of line against an army of considerably more than a hundred thousand men.

"But this conducts us to the saddest feature in the condition of the Confederacy. A majority of the people were wearied out with war, and of those who were still willing that it should be prosecuted, the smallest number were at all willing to contribute their persons or their means. They certainly suffered. The ports were blockaded, so that they could procure most articles of manufacture at only exorbitant prices and in exceedingly small quantities at that; there was no outlet for cotton, the staple of the country; the currency had become almost worthless; an immense debt had accumulated; the leading men of the nation were in dissension with the government and with each other; the whole world was either avowedly hostile or supremely indifferent.

"And against this weakened and necessitous people were arrayed a nation who counted over twenty million inhabitants, while we could not pretend to more than seven millions; whose productions were almost entirely sufficient for their wants; who had access to every part of the globe for munitions of war and for troops [i.e., soldiers of fortune]; who, finally, were terribly united in the determination to subdue us or perish themselves. There is little room for wonder at the decline of ardor under these circumstances.

"But it did not stop there. . . . The people not only did not reinforce us with soldiers, not only did not supply us with decent food and clothing, but they refused us the small comfort which our deeds wrung even from our enemies—admiring and sympathetic words. . . . Thousands of citizens went even beyond hopelessness, beyond indifference, and encouraged every shirking of duty in soldiers, encouraged discontent with our leaders, encouraged actual desertion. I heard it frequently remarked in our army that scarcely a man had deserted but he could be proved to have been urged to it by his family at home.

"The very women began to fail us, those women who had blessed our banners when we went forth to battle; who had cheered us with their affection in all our toils; who had tended us when wounded and diseased; who had rewarded us with their favor when we acted well, and incited us to fresh exertion; who had made even death tolerable by the tenderness of their regret and by the sublimity of the self-denial with which they gave us to our country. The bloodshed had sickened them; their losses and their wants had become irritating to them. They began to complain, they lost heart, and, as a class, they finally sat down and left us to ourselves.

Confederate cavalryman and foot soldier

"Thus Lee's army stood . . . with a government unable, and a people unwilling, to sustain it . . . girdled by a cordon of Federal arms . . . its own numbers reduced to less than half of the force immediately before it; without enough of the coarsest food and clothing to ward off hunger and cold; with only its glorious memories to cheer it. . . .

"Lee's lines extended from the Chickahominy [north of Richmond] across James River below Chaffin's Bluff, along the outskirts of Petersburg to a short distance north of Hatcher's Run. . . . Our wings extended somewhat beyond the front of Grant's army. . . . The chief occupations of the troops were picketing and building breastworks. The picket line [which was out in front] ran about parallel with our works, and on an average of five hundred yards from them. In some places this line [of pickets] had regular intrenchments, but, as a rule, we had only strong rifle pits. . . . The enemy's picket line varied in distance from ours, but, opposite the right of our brigade picket, was not more than two hundred and fifty yards off. There was no firing between the lines, and sometimes the men were allowed to converse with each other, although that was generally forbidden. The Federal line of battle was about a mile in rear of their picket at this point.

"The men were required to keep on their accoutrements and remain in the pits all the time; and at night at least one man in every pit was required to be awake, with his rifle in his hand. As a general rule, a third or a half of the men were allowed to sleep. . . . But there was little rest to be had, for we lay on a perfectly bare ridge swept by every wind, and we could get wood with only the greatest difficulty. Long before the winter passed, we had cut every tree between the picket line and the breastworks, and we had finally to haul wood from a considerable distance in rear of the army.

"There was a growth of small pines between the greater part of our brigade line and the enemy. These we cut somewhat; but they ran so much nearer the enemy, usually, that we had to manage very carefully to prevent a collision. I remember once taking a party under my command to the very vidette line of the Federals, where we cut wood and carried it off. Occasionally a Federal officer would object to this, and once we were informed that future woodcutters would be fired upon. Preparations were made by us the next day to test the matter. But the objections were withdrawn, and we had no fight.

"This picket was very hard duty; for wind, rain, snow, and sleet had to be met without a particle of shelter, and with the scanty supply of wood I have just spoken of. . . . I frequently walked the whole night to keep from freezing.

"The sharpshooters of the brigade performed the brigade picket every third or fourth day, as a rule. These performed the only active service done on the picket line. . . . When a few prisoners were wanted (and they were sometimes our only chance for information of the enemy's movements), General [Cadmus M.] Wilcox would order one or more of his battalions of sharpshooters to capture some. . . . They would move out of our picket line a little before day, creep close to the enemy, form, rush in, generally by the flank, and sweep up and down the works. They always captured some prisoners and a good deal of plunder, and sometimes killed a few of the enemy; but I never heard of a single casualty among them. At dawn they would return to our lines. . . .

"The other important employment of the brigade was intrenching. We not only erected a strong line of works in our front, but we assisted in throwing up powerful field fortifications some two miles below our camp. . . . These works would conceal troops marching behind them, would afford perfect protection from small-arms and ordinary field artillery fire, and they could scarcely be stormed, on account of the ditch and the brush abatis in front. This was hard work; for we had to walk at least two miles over ground almost always either shoe-deep in mud or frozen hard and rough, and we had to dig up earth frequently frozen to the depth of a foot, and at other times running streams of water.

"It was at this work that I had the strongest evidence of the exhaustion of the troops. Some men dug and shovelled well; but the majority, even of those who looked strong and healthy, would pant and grow faint under the labor of half an hour. This was most strikingly the case when our meat ration failed. A pint of cornmeal could hardly keep men hearty in the winter. . . .

"Now we experienced a greater suffering for food and clothing than we had ever known before. . . . The most pitiful shifts were employed to procure us meat. Canned beef . . . was issued a few times, and at other times small bits of poor, blue beef were doled out. Sometimes we had coffee, and now and then a spoonful of sugar. Tobacco of the worst quality was issued. . . . Once we had half a gill of whiskey issued to each man. It was amusing, as well as sad, to see the delight of the troops over this drop of comfort.

"All this time the enemy drank coffee, ate fat fresh beef and good bread, and drank quantities of whiskey, as their roarings at night testified.

"Clothing was sparely issued, and what we received was coarse and flimsy. . . . Shoes were scarce. More than once a soldier left a bloody

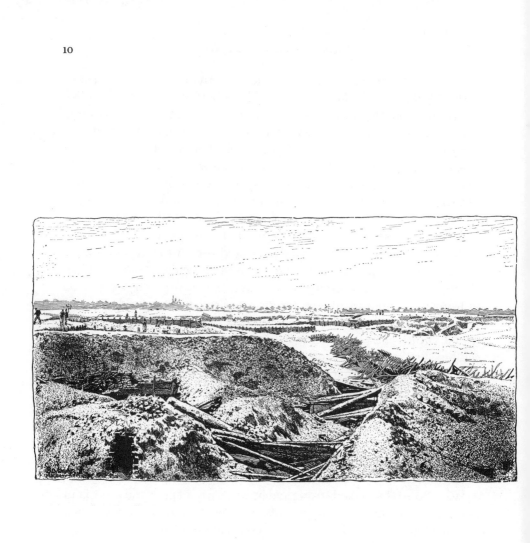

Interior view of Confederate defenses

track on the frozen picket line. . . . We drilled very little, and what we did was not creditable. The truth is, the men were worn out in mind and in body, and every effort had become painfully irksome.

"The unpleasant question of desertion presents itself very naturally in this connection. . . . The first desertion I remember was that of a soldier in the 1st Regiment, who was soon followed by another of that regiment. Then . . . [about a dozen men of other regiments] deserted. . . . Finally, twenty-six men of the 13th Regiment marched from their post on the picket line, at a signal. All of these went to the enemy. The last party were fired upon by their comrades, but I do not know whether with any effect.

"Eleven men of the 1st Regiment quitted the camp . . . and started for home. But five of them were captured next morning and brought back to us. They were tried before the corps court-martial, sentenced, and four of them shot on the following day. The fifth was respited on account of his youth and the temptation supposed to have been offered him by the rest. It was a sad spectacle, and its sadness was increased by the fact that one of these four had been an excellent soldier, and bore that day the scars of three wounds received in battle. The whole number of deserters in the brigade reached a hundred and four.

"We looked our condition in the face, and we saw that the war was rapidly drawing to an issue more or less disastrous to us. The conviction everywhere prevailed that we could sustain but one more campaign. . . . We were not confident that the Confederacy would be subjugated, for there was at least a possibility of interference on our behalf by that mysterious Providence we had been taught to trust, or by the almost equally mysterious powers of Europe [who had an economic interest in the South's cotton] which we should have been taught never to trust. But whatever the end was to be, and whether it was to come soon or late, we knew that our duty was to stand to our arms and fight the battle through.

"Therefore, though we were cold and ragged and hungry; though we were abandoned by that country for which we had suffered so long and so terribly; though thousands of the enemy held high revel before us, waking the echoes far and near with shoutings and the strains of bands and bugles—we lay in grim repose and expected the renewal of the mortal conflict."

2

Conditions in Richmond

Although it was true, as the foregoing account indicates, that the impotence of the Southern military at the start of 1865 was well understood by the soldiers themselves, it was different with the Confederates outside the military. "The populace of Richmond," says the outspoken and often captious associate editor of the capital city's *Examiner*, Edward A. Pollard, "was but little aware of the terrible decrease of General Lee's army; and, indeed, the people of the Confederacy were studiously kept in the dark as to all details of the military situation. So reticent had the Government become that the newspapers were forbid publishing anything of military affairs beyond the scanty doles of information and the skeleton telegrams furnished to the reporters by an official authority, and copied at the desks of the War Department.

"It thus happened that while there was a general despondency in the public mind, there were few outside the severe official circles of Richmond who knew the real extremities to which the arms and affairs of the Confederacy had fallen. There was a dull expectation of what was next to happen; there was a vague condition of the public mind in which, although not able to discover any substantial and well-defined ground of hope, it yet plodded on under the shadow of old convictions, and with a dim anticipation of something favorable in the future. While everyone affirmed that the affairs of the Confederacy were in a bad way, and while everyone appeared to have a certain sense of approaching misfortune, there were very few who knew the real condition and numbers of the armies of the Confederacy, and realized how far had been undermined its system of defense.

"It was difficult indeed to believe that the Army of Northern Virginia—that army whose name had been for four years as the blast of victory—had declined to a condition in which it was no longer capable of offensive operations. It was difficult indeed to abandon altogether the idea that the happy accident of a victory somewhere in the Confederacy might not, after all, put a new aspect on affairs. Even if the conclusion of subjugation had become probable, its day was at least uncertain, distant; and the opinion of General Lee was quoted in the streets of Richmond that in any event the Southern Confederacy was likely to last another year's campaign. . . . The idea of Independence was yet in the loose conversations of the people; and a favorite cantatrice of the Richmond Theater sung to nightly plaudits, 'Farewell forever to the star-spangled banner!'

"Then there were those rumors of extravagant fortune, always indicative of a weak and despairing condition of the public mind, among them endless stories of peace negotiations and European recognition. A few weeks before Richmond fell, the report was credited for the space of three or four days by the most intelligent persons in the city, including some of the editors of the newspapers and President Davis's pastor, that a messenger from France had arrived on the coast of North Carolina and was making his way overland to Richmond with the news of the recognition of the Southern Confederacy by the Emperor Napoleon!"

Adds another of Richmond's citizens, Mrs. Sarah A. ("Sallie") Putnam: "If there was no foreboding of the coming wreck of our coveted independence, we could at best only look forward to an indefinite continuation of the dire evils which had shrouded our land in sorrow and misery. Day by day our wants and privations increased. The supply of provisions in the city of Richmond was altogether inadequate to the demand, and generally of a quality that would have been altogether unappetizing in seasons of plenty. Every fresh encroachment of the enemy increased this scarcity, and, in a proportionate ratio, the prices at which articles of food were held.

"There was also a great want of fuel. Those formerly accustomed to well-heated houses, where comfort and luxury presided, now parsimoniously economized with a single ton of coal, or a single cord of wood, to insure its lasting as long as possible, lest, when the last lump or the last stick was consumed, no more could be obtained at any price.

"In addition to our other miseries, robberies were fearfully on the increase. The fortunate possessor of a well-stocked larder or coal house was in constant danger from burglary. It finally became an almost uni-

versal fashion in Richmond to permit 'every day to take care of itself.'
It was useless to lay up for the morrow, or to anticipate the rise in prices
and provide against it, for the cunning housebreakers were still better
at calculation, and would ever upset the best laid schemes by their
successful midnight depredations.'"

Housing itself was an acute problem in the city, whose population
at this time was about 100,000. Virginia E. Dade, a temporary resident
who was known, for an unexplained reason, as "Miss Lucy," says that
she and her younger sister, Fanny, "were room-keeping . . . in the same
house [with] twelve or fifteen other ladies and a few gentlemen, mostly
wounded and discharged soldiers, or men otherwise incapacitated for
duty in the field, and who were now serving in the various Government
departments in the city. As 'room-keeping' is a term and mode of life
which had its origin in the war, some explanation may be necessary.

"Richmond was so crowded by the women and children who had
sought refuge there when their homes were taken possession of by the
advancing Federal forces, that rents soon became incredibly high, and
it was rarely the case that a single family [of refugees], even of large
means, could afford to occupy a whole house to themselves, and even
the mansions of the rich were pointed at with indignation and con-
tempt if they were known to have one unoccupied chamber while so
many homeless refugees were begging for shelter. Consequently a
house of average size would usually contain from two to six families,
each occupying one, two, or three rooms, and each having their own
private table, but all using a common parlor when the guests to be
entertained were not intimate enough to be brought to the family
room. . . .

"Usually there would be but one cook for the entire household, a
colored woman who would cook often for five or six different families,
and it was wonderful how she would keep the different lots of provisions
separate, always making for each family a loaf of bread hot for breakfast
every morning, and sending up to each the exact quantity of flour or
number of potatoes sent down to her.

"I remember, though, one very ludicrous mistake which occurred
in this connection. I had given out for dinner for my sister and myself
two slices of ham, two large sweet potatoes, and a cup of rice. Our
dinner was served, and my sister had just helped herself to one of the
potatoes and broken it open when a little mulatto girl came running in,
in eager haste, exclaiming, 'Aunt Chany say how dat Miz Brown's tater
you got!' And sure enough, on looking at the smoking tuber which

Fanny was at that moment raising to her mouth, I found that it was a red-skinned 'tater,' while all that I had bought were yellow. However, the mischief was quickly remedied, the pieces placed together and carried to Mrs. Brown; and in the one which she sent back I readily recognized . . . my own golden 'sweet.' "

A further look at conditions in Richmond at this time is given by Kate Burwell Bowyer, the wife of one of Lee's officers: "Any lingering tendency towards following a fashion had long since been beaten out of the female mind, and women now aspired to nothing beyond the mere *wearing of clothes*, irrespective of style, shape, or texture. Large women appeared squeezed into garments of smallest proportions— small women floating about in almost limitless space; while women of tall stature dangled below circumscribed skirts, and others trailed about in fathoms of useless material. To all these eccentricities of costume the Confederate eye had become inured, as well as to the striking effect of blue bonnets with green plumes, red dresses with purple mantles, etc., etc., until these extraordinary modes failed to offend even the most fastidious.

"Indeed, expedients of the most desperate sort had now to be re-sorted to in all directions. The flooring of our country meat houses, saturated with the salt drippings of years, was dug up and prized as a salt substitute in horse food. The ashes of corncobs were much esteemed in lieu of soda. Sorghum . . . was the received substitute for sugar, while wheat, rye, chestnuts, sweet potatoes—in short, anything in the vegetable kingdom—was found to supply the place of coffee, and so on *ad infinitum*.

"For a Virginian of the old regime, who had always lived on the choicest of edibles, to smack his lips and relish a decoction of burnt chestnuts, sweetened with sorghum, was considered—especially by himself—as highly patriotic! It was at once amusing and pathetic when these cavalier old Virginians would meet and innocently endeavor to assist each other in sustaining our various Confederate delusions. . . .

"I am reminded of a severe test to which one of this esteemed class was brought during the winter I describe in Richmond. This lady, having two friends to dinner, relied chiefly upon the rarity of a mince pie for their regalement, which pie failing to appear in a reasonable time, the lady sustained light conversation as long as she could control her feelings, and at last excusing herself from the table hurried to the kitchen and exclaimed, 'Mary, where *is* the pie?' Mary answered desperately, 'Miss Jane, I dun *eat* de pie. I ain't see no pie for so long, an' it smell dat good, I couldn't help taceing it; an' arter I tace it I was *blice* to eat it!'

". . . The lady returned to her guests and described the disaster so cleverly that one of the gentlemen present . . . declared he would not have had it fail to happen, as the joke was far richer than the pie could possibly have been."

Returning to narrator Sallie Putnam: "During the war the 'rebel capital' became famous for the large number of beautiful ladies who belonged to the city, or who found within its friendly walls refuge and security. While the god of war thundered from its ramparts, not less busy was the artful boy-god [Cupid]. . . . The gossips thoroughly acquainted themselves with Cupid's victories. Ever and anon, these *quidnuncs* [the gossips] whispered of interesting *affaires de coeur*, in which were associated the names of gallant officers and soldiers of our army and of the fair and beautiful belles of the capital. . . . [An] unusual number of weddings . . . were celebrated during this winter. St. Paul's seemed to be the fashionable church for the solemnization of these happy bridals. . . . Of the numerous marriages which served as fruitful digressions from the war topic . . . we will mention particularly only one, rendered of thrilling interest from all the associations connected with it. In January, the brave, gallant, and chivalrous young . . . General [John] Pegram, of Richmond, led to the altar the fairest of the fair—the universally acknowledged queen of society—the beautiful and accomplished . . . [Hetty Cary, of Baltimore]. A dense throng crowded the church to witness the nuptials of the popular young officer and his magnificent bride. Sincere congratulations were pressed upon them, and they set forth on their matrimonial route with the brightest prospects for happiness, and sustained by the prayers and best wishes of numberless friends."

Weddings were not the only social assemblies Richmond saw that winter. A diarist named Judith McGuire (she was fifty-one years old, a clerk in the Commissary Department, and a hospital volunteer) reported in a January entry: "Some persons in this beleaguered city seem crazed on the subject of gayety. In the midst of the wounded and dying, the low state of the commissariat, the anxiety of the whole country, the troubles of every kind by which we are surrounded, I am mortified to say that there are gay parties given in the city. There are those denominated 'starvation parties,' where young persons meet for innocent enjoyment, and retire at a reasonable hour; but there are others where the most elegant suppers are served—cakes, jellies, ices in profusion, and

St. Paul's Church and Washington Monument

meats of the finest kinds in abundance, such as might furnish a meal for a regiment of General Lee's army. I wish these things were not so, and that every extra pound of meat could be sent to the army.

"When returning from the hospital, after witnessing the dying scene of a brother whose young sister hung over him in agony, with my heart full of the sorrows of hospital life, I passed a house where there were music and dancing. The revulsion of feeling was sickening. I thought of the gayety of Paris during the French Revolution, of the 'cholera ball' in Paris, the ball at Brussels the night before the Battle of Waterloo, and felt shocked that our own Virginians, at such a time, should remind me of scenes which we were wont to think only belonged to the lightness of foreign society. It seems to me that the army, when it hears of the gayety of Richmond, must think it heartless, particularly while it is suffering such hardships in her defense."

Actually, the army—in the person of its younger officers—was well represented at the city's dances. According to one observer, a citizen named Thomas Cooper DeLeon, the military dancers responded to critics such as Mrs. McGuire in this manner: "We do the fighting; we are the ones who are killed; and if we don't object, why in the deuce should you? Cooped up in camp, with mud and musty bacon for living, and the whistling of Miniés and whooing of shells for episode, we long for some pleasure when we can get off. This is the sole enjoyment we have, and we go back better men in every way for it."

These words, says DeLeon, comprised a "rather unanswerable argument; and the younger ladies were all willing to back it; so . . . the dancing went on."

Certain Richmonders, it must be noted, were still willing to make special sacrifices for the Southern cause. Youthful Mary Tucker, a refugee from the war-ravaged Shenandoah Valley, was one of these. "A few weeks before the close of the war a large audience assembled in the Negro Baptist Church on Broad Street, Richmond, to hear some patriotic addresses upon the situation. A gentleman spoke most eloquently and forcibly upon the emergencies of the times, and fired my patriotic heart to the very core. Amongst other things, he said, 'When the women of the South are ready to do as the matrons of Rome did—throw their ornaments of gold and silver into the treasury and redeem the Confederate bonds—the Confederacy will be safe.'

"I at once turned over in my mind a list of my treasures. Sadly small it was. Of jewels, not one was left. But I had two beautiful pieces of silver, a legacy from my grandmother. Surely they could not be better applied, so the next morning I sent them down to the treasurer. . . ."

(When the war ended so soon afterward, Mary could not help but feel regretful over her sacrifice. Some months after peace had been established, she chanced to meet the orator. "I told him the circumstances, how his eloquent tongue had wiled away my treasures, and he promised that he would consider it a debt from him to me—and [so] it . . . continued. . . .")

3

A Winter Maneuver

The first substantial fighting of 1865 was done on February 5, 6, and 7 as Grant sought to extend his left flank southwestward, or farther around Lee's right at Hatcher's Run. About 35,000 Federals took part in the maneuver. Among the 14,000 Confederates who were rallied to meet this emergency was a Captain Morrow (first name unknown) who relates: "We were in pretty good winter quarters, behind a line of low earthworks which extended continuously to and around Petersburg. On a cold, bleak morning in February the long roll started me from a sound sleep just before daylight. I seemed to hear the rattle of the drum for some seconds before I could awake—at least that was my thought as I bounded off my bunk and felt around in the darkness for my clothing, sword, and belt. As I stepped out of my hut, half clad and shivering with the cold, I heard my orderly sergeant storming at the men to fall in.

"In a few seconds the company was formed, and we took our place in the regiment. It was too dark to see, but the colonel's voice could be heard as he gave the command, 'Forward, march!' and we moved off in rear of the earthworks in the direction of Petersburg. It was an intensely cold, misty morning, and it seemed as if daylight would never come. We stumbled on for half an hour in the darkness, over stumps and logs, until there were some signs of daylight, when the regiment was halted at a narrow opening in the works. Here we found some pieces of [our] artillery, the horses harnessed and the artillerymen sitting motionless in their saddles and on the caissons.

"In a few minutes we filed through the works into the open field beyond, where there were other bodies of troops waiting in silence,

Confederate works at Hatcher's Run

apparently for orders. As these were passed, one of the men said to a comrade, 'So we're to be the advance, it seems.' 'Of course,' replied the other, 'ain't it always so?' 'Fold up your tongue, Williams, and pack it away till next summer. Where's your thirst for glory?' 'I thirst now for a warm bed and a good breakfast later,' answered Williams.

" 'Don't you know Mars' Bob [Robert E. Lee] can't make a mistake?' 'That's so,' replied Williams, 'but some of his couriers made a whopper in waking us up too early.'

"With such chaffing, we passed out of the open into a wood. The talking ceased, and the silence was broken only by the hurried tread of the men and the clanking of the canteens. A few hundred yards further on, and the column is again halted. 'Load your guns, men,' is the order, and the ramrods are ringing in the Enfields as the cartridges are pressed home. The first command to load always gave me a slight shiver. The order is suggestive of blood. I have known of but few jests circulating among the men while obeying it, and now the wag of the company is as solemn as a judge.

"A short distance further, and the line of battle is formed. Scarcely a word is spoken, save the quick, sharp word of command as the companies file into their places. Some of the men seem confused (though all are veterans), and appear to have partially forgotten the usual company commands. 'Skirmishers to the front!' is passed down the column, and the thin line of sharpshooters trot away and in a few seconds are lost to sight.

"It is a solemn moment, and I find it necessary to keep my teeth clenched to keep them from chattering with something else besides the cold. I also have an involuntary catch of the breath. . . .

" 'Forward!' is the order, loudly repeated down the line, and the long double column, neither end of which can be seen, moves rapidly to the front. Soon it is broken and in disorder from the obstruction of the trees and leafless undergrowth, and the order is passed to halt and reform. As the ranks are closed up, scattering shots are heard in front and to the right and left, which, by the time we are again moving forward, have rapidly increased in number. Our skirmishers have struck those of the enemy. We press on, and in a few minutes our sharpshooters [the skirmishers] are in sight, popping away at the bluecoats, who seem disposed to stand their ground. Minié balls are whistling about us by this time, and the men involuntarily dodge.

"An opening in the distance can be seen through the trees as we hurry on, crowding . . . upon the skirmishers, who, with a yell, charge the opposing line [of skirmishers], which, seeing our column, retreat.

. . . A gray-coated skirmisher passes through our line to the rear, with blood streaming from a wound in his face, over which both hands are pressed; and I step over a fallen body clad in blue.

"We are near the opening now, in the edge of which is our skirmish line, banging away at the enemy [skirmishers], who have taken possession of shallow rifle pits further out in the opening. Something rises in my throat, producing a choking sensation, and I can plainly hear my heart beat. Pallor may not be felt, but I think I must have been very pale.

" 'Great God, captain, look up there!' exclaims one of my lieutenants as we reach the edge of the open ground, halting to again reform amid the whistling bullets from the enemy. I grow faint and weak as I gaze at the sight before us. A long hill, smooth and bare. In front [and] to the right and left, as far as the eye can reach, the crest crowned with a long line of red earthworks, dotted at fearfully short intervals with black-mouthed cannon, while above the red ridge are thousands of bayonets glistening in the sunlight as it breaks through the morning mist.

"All eyes are fixed upon the unwelcome spectacle, and the faces of my veterans blanch as they read the task before them. The suspense is terrible. The men appear paralyzed, for it seems to everyone useless, hopeless slaughter.

"Without orders, firing has begun to our left, and my men are beginning to follow the example. 'Steady, men! Hold your fire!' I yell. 'Don't you see our skirmishers right before you?'

" 'Keep your men well in hand, captain, and hold your fire till we mount the works,' says the colonel in passing, in a voice so cool and collected, and free from excitement, that for the moment I feel that I am, beyond doubt, the worst coward in the regiment. But his manner does me a world of good. . . . At that moment the command, 'Forward!' rings out above the din. Forward we go, helter-skelter! No time for reflection!

"It is death to which we hasten. Flesh and blood cannot accomplish the task assigned us . . . but on we go. As [our] line shows itself in the field, the earth fairly trembles under the explosion of artillery and small arms from the crest of the hill, which disappears from view in the cloud of smoke. Onward we go, stooping and crouching from the tornado. The rush of shells and hiss of bullets is continuous. Right in our faces the shells are bursting. Men are falling in every direction, and those [on their feet] in the scattered line seem dazed; but on, on we go, up the incline, hurrying to our graves.

"All formation is lost in the headlong rush and by the gaps made by those who have fallen. The very earth seems as if it were swept by the rain of missiles. We haven't fired a shot. It were death, seemingly, to pause for the aim. All depends on reaching the works as quickly as possible. Our column seems little more than a scattered group of skirmishers. On we scramble, and we are momentarily expecting the clash of bayonets when the works are reached.

"Now all fear is gone. It is horrible, but it is exhilarating. We are not men now. Animals, beasts of prey, blood-thirsty devils we are. Desperation has routed fear, hope, and mercy. My saber swings high in the air, and the yell of a fox hunter, first at the death, rises to my lips. Onward we go! Will the crest never be reached?

" 'It's no use, captain. There's nobody to our left,' yells old Klutts, my orderly sergeant, in my ear; and the handful of men see it in a moment. True it is; there is no use in going further. My little remaining reason says plainly it is no use.

"The fire has slackened slightly. Doubtless they are getting ready with the bayonet. Nothing remains but to get back as quickly as possible —and that means death for the few survivors.

" 'Back men! Back for your lives!' And the dread retreat commences. The men in the works have heard the shout, and their fire is redoubled. Surely none can escape the storm of lead beating upon us.

"There is a slight ravine in our path [of retreat], a mere wash in the hillside, barely deep enough to hide our bodies. With a common impulse, each one falls despairingly into it, lying prone in its bottom to escape the steady rain of the bullets. The less favored portion of our decimated column, which formed our right, continue the fearful retreat, and we lose sight of them as we flatten ourselves on the ravine's bottom. For some moments not a sound escapes our lips, each one realizing that a few brief minutes will decide whether death or a prison awaits us, for certainly the Federal line will soon advance.

"It was yet some 400 yards to the wood whence we had advanced to the attack, and perhaps 150 paces [behind us] to the enemy's works. Momentarily I expected the shouts of the victorious Federals as their advance began. This meant a prison for us. Little time there is for consideration, yet I cannot make up my mind to risk further retreat. It seems madness, for I well know that our first appearance will be the signal for a hurricane of fire, which has just now greatly diminished.

"The thought of a Northern prison decides me, and in a moment of desperation I cry to the men, 'Get ready! We can't stay here! Be ready at the word to move, one at a time!'

"Either the order was misunderstood or the men lost their heads, for when the man nearest me rose to go, every man followed instantly, and I joined them. In a moment a perfect tornado of fire opened on us. Man after man tumbled headlong as we ran at the top of our speed for the woods. On we flew over the ground, over the fallen bodies of those of our comrades who fell [earlier] as we advanced, down the long hillside, seemingly surrounded by a swarm of bullets. A fearful price we paid in the alternative we had accepted, for more than one-half of those who started on the retreat lay on the frozen hillside to rise no more.

"As we entered the friendly shelter of the woods, [another unit] of our force lying flat on the ground [in the woods], thinking we were the advance of the enemy's skirmishers, opened fire on us, and, before their mistake was discovered, two or three of our little handful fell, wounded at the hands of friends. Out of forty-seven men in the line at daylight, eleven only of my company remained. The others were dead or wounded on the field in our front.

"The Federals did not advance, and the miserable affair was over."

The foregoing episode was only one of a series that occurred during the three days of fighting, with Grant's troops experiencing their own share of bad moments. Federal losses were about 1,500 in killed, wounded, and missing. Confederate losses were not tallied, but one death, in particular, was well noted in Richmond.

As explained in Judith McGuire's diary: "A deep gloom has just been thrown over the city. . . . General John Pegram fell while nobly leading his brigade against the enemy. . . . But two [and a half] weeks before he had been married in St. Paul's Church. . . . Again has St. Paul's, his own beloved church, been opened to receive the soldier and his bride —the one coffined for a hero's grave, the other, pale and trembling . . . in widow's garb."

The Hatcher's Run maneuver gained the Federals some of the desired ground, but numbers of them ended up with no way of sheltering themselves as a cold drizzle began. In the words of Color Sergeant D. G. Crotty of the 3rd Regiment, Michigan Volunteer Infantry: "We lay around here for a few days in great misery, the eyes melted almost out of our heads with the smoke that stays around from the numerous campfires that are built to keep us warm. Oh, what a miserable time, wet to the skin, ragged and dirty, with the scalding water rolling down our cheeks, caused by the smoke. Surely, this is another blunder, caused by someone. We can all see that no good will come of this move, but, on the contrary, it will be the cause of many a brave man being ruined

Typical soldiers of Grant's army

for life from these few days of hardships. It seems to us that it is the delight of some officers to see the poor soldier suffer.

"Oh, who has suffered that the country might be saved? Is it the officer or the private? . . . The poor privates . . . have stood the brunt of every battle and braved the hardships of the campaigns. . . . Oh, yes, but it was the officers that led the men into battle. But how long would the majority of them stay after they did go in? A very short time, as thousands of brave soldiers can testify, who had to fight the battles that saved the Union, and to them the praise is due of every true American citizen.

"After enduring untold miseries for a few days . . . we get the order to move back, and build more quarters. It is dreadfully cold and the suffering is intense. The wet clothing on our backs freeze stiff, and we have to lay out and take the snow and sleet that falls unpiteously on our heads. The people of the North probably think there is no such cold weather in the South, but let them experience one winter's campaign and they will find their mistake. At last we have our quarters built, and hardships are forgotten once more.

"About the 21st of February the good news comes that the hot-bed of treason, Charleston, has fallen before Sherman's triumphal army that marched to the sea [and was now moving northward]. The Army of the Potomac feels jubilant, and are ready, as soon as the weather permits, to end this war, which has lasted long enough. All are tired of soldiering, especially those that have marched with the army from the commencement of the war."

4

Stirrings as Spring Approaches

N ow in its ninth month, the siege of Richmond and Petersburg had included a great many incidents known as "affairs of the pickets," most of which did not make the record. One that occurred on February 26, however, had a noteworthy twist. As recalled by Union Private J. P. Ward: "About six o'clock A.M., our orderly sergeant informed me that I was detailed for picket duty. I put on my equipments, grasped my rifle, and joined the detachment on the parade ground. We passed through the works . . . and, after passing some open ground, reached a strip of heavy pine timber which screened our camp from the view of the rebels. Here we halted to load, after which we moved on. When we emerged from the woods into the clear space beyond, we came in full view of both the Union and Confederate picket lines.

"The picket posts were built of pine logs, breast-high, with dirt banked up in front. There were eight men in the post, with a corporal in charge. With the exception of one man—a tent-mate—I was unacquainted with the men on our post, our regiment having been largely recruited [in the North] during the winter. Everything being quiet, we made ourselves as comfortable as circumstances would permit. A fire was kindled for making coffee, and, lighting their pipes, the boys began conversation.

"The corporal, who was a stout, resolute-looking man, took the opportunity to change his clothing, and I noticed an ugly scar on his breast. Out of curiosity I asked where he got that mark. He answered, 'At Gettysburg, my lad.'

"I soon noticed that the other six men in the post were acquainted with him, and addressed him as Corporal Dave. After lighting his pipe, Corporal Dave told how he got wounded. 'You see,' said he, 'I'm a Texan, and belonged to Hood's famous Texas brigade, which got cut up so at Gettysburg, July 2, 1863. We were on the right of the line and were trying to turn the left flank of the Yankees in order to get possession of a ridge called Round Top. Longstreet was driving the Yankees in the peach orchard, and we were hurrying to take possession of those hills. Colonel Vincent's brigade of Yankees got there a few minutes ahead of us. I tell you, boys, it was the hottest place I was ever in, and I have been in a good many hot places, too. The bullets flew like hail, and pretty soon one hit me where you see the scar. We lost Little Round Top, and I was taken prisoner. I tell you, if we had taken those hills we would have whipped Meade and captured Washington, Baltimore, and Philadelphia; the North would have made peace, the South would have gained its independence, and the fighting would have been over.'

"I ventured to dissent from the corporal's opinion, and the consequence was that we had an angry discussion. I asked how it was that he was serving in the Union army, and he replied that after his wound healed he had escaped from prison and enlisted in the Union army for a big bounty. I began to think that Corporal Dave was a rebel still. After that I found that three others of the men had served in the Southern army. . . . My tent-mate, an honest Irishman, whispered that we were among a lot of secesh [i.e., secessionists], and had better look out.

"I noticed through the day that the corporal and his chums had a good deal of private consultation; but in the evening, when my turn came to stand vidette [out in front], I had almost forgotten my suspicions. It grew dark, and, the wind being from the northwest, I could hear the . . . pickets [in Lee's lines] talking, laughing, and singing an old-fashioned camp-meeting tune.

"Pretty soon I heard the relief coming, and Corporal Dave came out with a squad to relieve the pickets. He told me to go back into the picket post. I noticed that all the ex-rebels were with him, but had no suspicion that anything was wrong.

"When I reached the picket post, there was no one there but my Irish tent-mate. As it was getting chilly, I unstrapped my overcoat from my knapsack, took off my cartridge box; and, leaning my musket against the logs, began to put my coat on. I was standing up, plainly visible . . . by the light of the picket fire. I had got one arm in my overcoat sleeve, and was feeling for the other, when a musket was discharged and a ball struck the logs by my side; and before I had time to change

James Longstreet

my position six more shots were fired in quick succession. Two more balls struck the logs, and the others whizzed by me.

"I got my coat on as quickly as possible, grasped my musket, and fired as near as I could guess in the direction of the enemy, and then dropped under cover. The whole line fired a few rounds, and an officer came to inquire the cause of the disturbance. I told him the circumstances, and he ordered my tent-mate and myself to go with him to the vidette post. On our arrival we found that the corporal and the six men were no longer there.

"A few minutes later we heard the rebel pickets challenge someone, and then came a volley of musketry. When the firing ceased, we heard groans of agony, and we recognized the voice of Corporal Dave.

"We remained on vidette duty until next morning, there being no one left in the post to relieve us, and then returned to camp.

"A few nights afterwards, we learned from a rebel deserter that on that Sunday night in question seven Yankee deserters came into their lines and had been fired on by mistake, one of them dying from his wounds.

"So Corporal Dave [in unison with his friends] fired his last shot at me."

February closed with another attempt to end the war without further bloodshed. On the basis of a prewar friendship, Lee's second-in-command, his "old war horse" James Longstreet, and one of Grant's top subordinates, distinguished-looking Edward O. C. Ord, commander of the Army of the James, arranged a between-the-lines meeting at which they agreed to press for the implementation of a novel plan. Its provisions, according to Longstreet, were "that the work as belligerents should be suspended; that General Grant and General Lee should meet and have a talk; that my wife, who was an old acquaintance and friend of Mrs. Grant in their girlhood days, should go into the Union lines and visit Mrs. Grant with as many Confederate officers as might choose to be with her. Then Mrs. Grant would return the call under escort of Union officers and visit Richmond; that while General Lee and General Grant were arranging for better feeling between the armies, they could be aided by intercourse between the ladies and officers until terms honorable to both sides could be found."

Longstreet succeeded in winning Lee's interest in the idea. Unfortunately, Ord had given Longstreet the impression that Grant's authority embraced political matters as well as military. Lee ventured himself unguardedly when, on March 2, he wrote Grant: "Sincerely desiring to

Edward O. C. Ord

leave nothing untried which may put an end to the calamities of war, I propose to meet you at such convenient time and place as you may designate, with the hope that upon an interchange of views it may be found practicable to submit the subjects of controversy between the belligerents to a convention. . . . In such an event I am authorized to do whatever the result of the proposed interview may render necessary or advisable."

Grant referred the matter to Washington, and he got a speedy response from Lincoln's irascible Secretary of War, Edwin M. Stanton: "The President directs me to say to you that he wishes you to have no conference with General Lee unless it be for the capitulation of General Lee's army, or on some minor and purely military matter. He instructs me to say that you are not to decide, discuss, or confer upon any political question. Such questions the President holds in his own hands, and you will submit them to no military conferences or conventions. Meantime, you are to press to the utmost your military advantages."

Grant wrote Lee: "I have no authority to accede to your proposition. . . ." Grant's response to Stanton contained at least one line that included a shade of pique: "It was *because* I had no right to meet General Lee on the subject proposed by him that I referred the matter for instructions."

Lee's embarrassment over this affair was soon replaced by other concerns. Southerner J. F. J. Caldwell explains: "Two things occurred about this time which had an evident tendency to demoralize our troops. One of them was the passage of a bill, in [the Confederate] Congress, which authorized the raising of Negro troops. The matter was left, in great measure, to General Lee's decision, and General Lee consulted the army. Very few of us had any objection to the measure, but it created considerable despondency by showing us how little hope of success was entertained by the Confederate authorities. The other circumstance was the call made upon us for an expression of our sentiments in regard to the war. We had determined to carry on the contest as long as it should be at all possible, and we desired General Lee, the Congress, and the people of the South to know it; and therefore we did not hesitate to publish resolutions of as warlike a tone as the most ultra-secessionist could demand. But we were obliged to feel that that nation was on the point of submission which was required to be sustained in its position by a half-famished, half-naked army of fifty thousand men. . . .

"Drilling was recommenced now. . . . In the month of March General Lee ordered eight drills a day, twice as great a number as I ever heard of being performed in the army. I believe, however, that we contented ourselves with four. The men called this 'a God's plenty,' and, barring the profanity, I was entirely of their opinion. We needed drill, certainly, for we had grown careless and inaccurate in a great degree. But we needed it chiefly as a discipline. The war had reached that stage where something more than the internal impulse is required to urge one up to his whole duty."

In the Union camps, the troops did their own share of drilling, but their schedule included a good many recreational pursuits. Color Sergeant D. G. Crotty tells of a special occurrence: "St. Patrick's Day is at hand, the day which every Irishman loves. It is going to be celebrated at the headquarters of the Prince of Irishmen, General Thomas Francis Meagher. Everyone is going, myself with the rest. A walk of about four miles brings us to the Irish Brigade. We find everything gotten up in grand style for the occasion. A grandstand is erected, on which can be seen [some of] the leading generals of the army . . . the guests of the idolized Meagher. There is to be an old-fashioned hurdle race, and all, too, where the Johnnies [the Confederates] can witness the sport; for everything is carried on in plain sight of the enemy. The horses start, about ten in number, and all present enjoy the sport. The hurdles are leaped in fine style, and the horses come in amid the wild cheers of the spectators, the boys in blue.

"After the races, a banquet is sat down to, where the day is celebrated in fine style, with all the usual toasts on such occasions. On the grounds, too, are booths erected by the *sharks* of the army [the sutlers, or civilian storekeepers], where the soldier may eat his fill at exorbitant prices. After the horse races, come all kinds of games, such as sack racing, wheelbarrow racing, climbing greased poles, and other games, which all enjoy very much, and then return to their camps, well satisfied with the celebration of St. Patrick's Day in the army."

Another view of Union activities in mid-March is given by Private Theodore Gerrish of the 20th Maine Volunteers: "We made life enjoyable. We told stories, sang songs, went out on picket, foraged what we could, and played many games. . . . The weather was unusually fine, the bands played their most delicious strains of music, and the men were all anxious for the forward movement to be made. Each day we saw new indications of the fearful struggle so soon to open. Slowly and surely the cords of death were drawn around the gallant army of General Lee. . . . Notwithstanding all the joy and mirth in our regiment, there were

Federals in the Petersburg lines

some anxious hours in those days of active preparations. Some had been with the regiment every day since it had been mustered into the service, had suffered in all its fatigue, endured all its hardships, and fought in all its battles, and only six months of their three years of service remained unserved. It is not strange that these soldiers were a little anxious about the future, and wondered if they had been spared through all the past, to fall in the last campaign of the war."

These were especially worrisome days for General Grant. "I felt that the situation of the Confederate army was such that they would try to make an escape at the earliest practicable moment, and I was afraid, every morning, that I would awake from my sleep to hear that Lee had gone, and that nothing was left but a picket line. He had his railroad by the way of Danville south, and I was afraid that he was running off his men and all stores and ordnance except such as it would be necessary to carry with him for his immediate defense. I knew he could move much more lightly and more rapidly than I, and that, if he got the start, he would leave me behind so that we would have the same army to fight again farther south—and the war might be prolonged another year.

"I was led to this fear by the fact that I could not see how it was possible for the Confederates to hold out much longer where they were. There is no doubt that Richmond would have been evacuated much sooner than it was, if it had not been that it was the capital of the so-called Confederacy, and the fact of evacuating the capital would, of course, have had a very demoralizing effect upon the Confederate army. . . .

"I was naturally very impatient for the time to come when I could commence the spring campaign, which I thoroughly believed would close the war. There were two considerations I had to observe, however, and which detained me. One was the fact that the winter had been one of heavy rains, and the roads were impassable for artillery and teams. It was necessary to wait until they had dried sufficiently to enable us to move the wagon trains and artillery necessary to the efficiency of an army operating in the enemy's country. The other consideration was that General Sheridan with the cavalry of the Army of the Potomac was operating on the north side of the James River, having come down from the Shenandoah. It was necessary that I should have his cavalry with me, and I was therefore obliged to wait until he could join me south of the James River. . . .

"On the 5th of March I had heard from Sheridan. He had met [Confederate General Jubal A.] Early between Staunton and Char-

Philip H. Sheridan

lottesville [northwest of Richmond] and defeated him, capturing nearly his entire command. Early and some of his officers escaped by finding refuge in the neighboring houses or in the woods. On the 12th I heard from him again. He had turned east to come to White House [on the Pamunkey River about twenty miles east of Richmond]. . . . I had supplies sent around to White House for him. . . .

"Sheridan had about ten thousand cavalry with him, divided into two divisions. . . . They stopped at Charlottesville and commenced tearing up the railroad back toward Lynchburg. He also sent a division along the James River Canal to destroy locks, culverts, etc. All mills and factories along the lines of march of his troops were destroyed also.

"Sheridan had in this way consumed so much time that his making a march to White House was now somewhat hazardous. He determined therefore to fight his way along the railroad and canal till he was as near to Richmond as it was possible to get, or until attacked. He did this, destroying the canal as far as Goochland, and the railroad to a point as near Richmond as he could get. On the 10th he was at Columbia. Negroes had joined his column to the number of two thousand or more, and they assisted considerably in the work of destroying the railroads and the canal. His cavalry was in as fine a condition as when he started, because he had been able to find plenty of forage. He had captured most of Early's horses and picked up a good many others on the road.

"When he reached Ashland he was assailed by the enemy in force. He resisted their assault with part of his command, moved quickly across the South and North Anna, going north, and reached White House safely on the 19th.

"The time for Sherman to move had to be fixed with reference to the time he could get away from Goldsboro [North Carolina], where he then was. [Sherman had just repelled an inferior army under Confederate General Joseph E. Johnston at the Battle of Bentonville.] Supplies had to be got up to him [from the Atlantic Coast] which would last him through a long march, as there would probably not be much to be obtained in the country through which he would pass. . . .

"Sherman was anxious that I should wait where I was until he could come up, and make a sure thing of it; but I had determined to move as soon as the roads and weather would admit of my doing so. . . . [Sheridan] having arrived at White House . . . I was enabled to make my plans.

"Prompted by my anxiety lest Lee should get away some night before I was aware of it, and, having the lead of me, push into North

Abraham Lincoln *(from a photograph taken March 6, 1865)*

Carolina to join with Johnston in attempting to crush out Sherman, I had, as early as the 1st of the month of March, given instructions to the troops around Petersburg to keep a sharp lookout to see that such a movement should not escape their notice, and to be ready to strike at once if it was undertaken."

An aide to Grant, twenty-seven-year-old Colonel Horace Porter, who admired the general's methods, was impressed by the fact that "every possible precaution was taken . . . to prevent Lee from withdrawing his army. Scouts and spies were more active than ever before; about 30,000 men were kept virtually on the picket line, and all the troops were equipped and supplied, ready to make a forced march at a moment's notice in case Lee should be found moving. It was now ascertained that Sheridan could start from White House on March 25 to join the Army of the Potomac, and on the 24th orders were issued for a general movement of the armies operating against Petersburg and Richmond, to begin on the night of the 28th, for the purpose of marching around Lee's right, breaking up his last remaining railroads, the Danville and the Southside, and giving, if possible, the final blow to the Confederacy.

"On March 20 General Grant had telegraphed the President [in Washington]: 'Can you not visit City Point for a day or two? I would like very much to see you, and I think the rest would do you good.' This invitation was promptly accepted, and on the 24th word came that he was on his way up the James aboard the *River Queen*. About nine o'clock that evening the steamer approached the wharf, and General Grant, with those of us who were with him at the moment, including Robert Lincoln [Abraham Lincoln's eldest son, a captain on Grant's staff], went down to the landing and met the President, Mrs. Lincoln, their youngest son, 'Tad,' and several ladies who had come from Washington with the presidential party. The meeting was very cordial. It lasted but a short time, however, as Mr. Lincoln and his family were evidently fatigued by the trip, and it was thought that they might want to retire at an early hour."

5

Lee Fails at Fort Stedman

Among the staff officers in the Confederate army was thirty-four-year-old Captain John Esten Cooke, who had achieved fame as a novelist before the war, had completed a biography of Stonewall Jackson during respites from active duty in 1863, and was now attentive to the fortunes of Robert E. Lee. Cooke relates: "General Lee became aware, as the end of March drew near, that preparations were being made in the Federal army for some important movement. What that movement would be, there was little reason to doubt. The Federal lines had been extended gradually toward the Southside Railroad; and it was obvious now that General Grant had in view a last and decisive advance in that quarter, which should place him on his opponent's communications and completely intercept his retreat southward.

"The catastrophe which General Lee had plainly foreseen for many months now stared him in the face, and, unless he had recourse to some expedient as desperate as the situation, the end of the struggle must soon come. The sole course left to him was retreat, but this now seemed difficult, if not impossible. General Grant had a powerful force not far from the main roads over which Lee must move; and, unless a diversion of some description were made, it seemed barely possible that the Southern army could extricate itself. This diversion General Lee now proceeded to make. . . .

"He had resolved to throw a column against the Federal center east of Petersburg, with the view to break through there and seize the commanding ground in rear of the line. He would thus be rooted in the middle of General Grant's army, and the Federal left would probably

be recalled, leaving the way open if he designed to retreat. If he designed, however, to fight a last pitched battle which should decide all,
he would be able to do so, in case the Federal works were broken.
. . . The point fixed upon was Fort Stedman, near the south bank of the
Appomattox, where the opposing works were scarcely two hundred
yards from each other."

Selected to make the attack was Lee's 2nd Corps, headed by thirty-
three-year-old Lieutenant General John B. Gordon, one of the army's
most aggressive fighters. A volunteer from Georgia, the cultured and
chivalrous Gordon had begun his career as the leader of a single company, but he had risen rapidly. As a brigade commander at Antietam
in the autumn of 1862 he had remained in action after taking four
serious musket wounds, but had finally collapsed when a fifth ball struck
him in the face. He fell forward and landed with his face in his cap, and
he might have drowned in his own blood except for the fact that, before
he fell, a Yankee ball had provided the cap with a drain hole.

Gordon's support troops for his attack on Fort Stedman were sched-
uled to include elements of the army's 1st Corp under James Longstreet
and its 3rd under the frail but indomitable Ambrose Powell ("A. P.")
Hill, plus a detachment of cavalry. In all, about half the army was
alerted for participation. Gordon's plan, arranged in cooperation with
Lee, called for the move to be made during the predawn hours of
March 25. The plan was a bold one. Fifty axmen were to precede the
attack, their job to cut away the obstructions in front of the enemy's
lines. Three hundred men, divided into three teams, were to follow,
their mission to pretend, under cover of the darkness, to be Union
soldiers and to attempt to slip past Fort Stedman and seek out three
additional forts believed to be behind it. In the meantime, the main
attack would be hitting Fort Stedman and the lines that stretched from
its flanks. Many of the attack's support troops were slated to arrive at
the jumping-off point in due time by train.

Gordon himself tells the story of the Confederate army's last-ditch
venture: "All night my troops were moving and concentrating behind
Colquitt's Salient. For hours Mrs. Gordon sat in her room in Petersburg,
tearing strips of white cloth to tie across the breasts of the leading
detachments, that they might recognize each other in the darkness and
in the hand-to-hand battle expected at the Federal breastworks and
inside the fort.

"The fifty heavy keen-edged axes were placed in the hands of the
fifty brave and stalwart fellows who were to lead the column and hew

Fort Stedman

down Grant's obstructions. The strips of white cloth were tied upon them, and they were ready for the desperate plunge. The chosen 300, in three companies, under . . . three officers [who had temporarily adopted] names of Union officers, were also bedecked with the white cotton Confederate scarfs. . . . I explained to the 300 men the nature of their duties, and told them that, in addition to the joy it would give them to aid in giving victory to the army, I would see to it, if the three forts were captured, that each of them should have a thirty days' furlough and a silver medal. . . .

"The hour for the assault (4 A.M.) arrived. The column of attack was arranged in the following order: the 50 axmen in front, and immediately behind and close to them the selected 300. Next came the different commands of infantry who were to move in compact column close behind the 300, the cavalry being held in reserve until the way for them was cleared. . . .

"All things ready . . . I stood on the top of the breastworks, with no one at my side except a single private soldier with rifle in hand, who was to fire the signal shot for the headlong rush. This night charge on the fort was to be across the intervening space covered with ditches, in one of which stood the watchful Federal pickets. There still remained near my works some of the debris of our obstructions, which had not been completely removed and which I feared might retard the rapid exit of my men; and I ordered it cleared away. The noise made by this removal, though slight, attracted the attention of a Union picket who stood on guard only a few rods from me, and he called out, 'What are you doing there, Johnny? What is that noise? Answer quick or I'll shoot.'

"The pickets of the two armies were so close together at this point that there was an understanding between them, either expressed or implied, that they would not shoot each other down except when necessary. The call of this Union picket filled me with apprehension. I expected him to fire and start the entire picket line to firing, thus giving the alarm to the fort, the capture of which depended largely upon the secrecy of my movement. The quick mother-wit of the private soldier at my side came to my relief. In an instant he replied, 'Never mind, Yank. Lie down and go to sleep. We are just gathering a little corn. You know rations are mighty short over here.' There was a narrow strip of corn which the bullets had not shot away still standing between the lines. The Union picket promptly answered, 'All right, Johnny; go ahead and get your corn. I'll not shoot at you while you are drawing your rations.' . . .

John B. Gordon

"My troops stood in close column, ready for the hazardous rush upon Fort Stedman. While the fraternal dialogue in reference to drawing rations from the cornfield was progressing ... the last of the obstructions in my front were removed, and I ordered the private to fire the signal for the assault. He pointed his rifle upward, with his finger on the trigger, but hesitated. His conscience seemed to get hold of him. He was going into the fearful charge, and he evidently did not feel disposed to go into eternity with the lie on his lips, although it might be a permissible war lie, by which he had thrown the Union picket off his guard. He evidently felt that it was hardly fair to take advantage of the generosity and soldierly sympathy of his foe, who had so magnanimously assured him that he would not be shot while drawing his rations from the little field of corn.

"His hesitation surprised me, and I again ordered, 'Fire your gun, sir.' He at once called to his kindhearted foe and said, 'Hello, Yank! Wake up; we are going to shell the woods. Look out; we are coming.' And with this effort to satisfy his conscience and even up accounts with the Yankee picket, he fired the shot and rushed forward in the darkness.

"As the solitary signal shot rang out in the stillness, my alert pickets, who had crept close to the Union sentinels, sprang like sinewy Ajaxes upon them and prevented the discharge of a single alarm shot. Had these faithful Union sentinels been permitted to fire alarm guns, my dense columns, while rushing upon the fort, would have been torn into fragments by the heavy guns. Simultaneously with the seizing and silencing of the Federal sentinels, my stalwart axmen leaped over our breastworks, closely followed by the selected 300 and the packed column of infantry.

"Although it required but a few minutes to reach the Union works, those minutes were to me like hours of suspense and breathless anxiety; but soon was heard the thud of the heavy axes as my brave fellows slashed down the Federal obstructions. The next moment the infantry sprang upon the Union breastworks and into the fort, overpowering the gunners before their destructive charges could be emptied into the mass of Confederates. They turned this captured artillery upon the flanking lines on each side of the fort, clearing the Union breastworks of their defenders for some distance in both directions.

"Up to this point, the success had exceeded my most sanguine expectations. We had taken Fort Stedman and a long line of breastworks on either side. We had captured nine heavy cannon, eleven mortars, nearly 1,000 prisoners, including General [Napoleon B.] McLaughlen, with the loss of less than half a dozen men. One of these fell upon the works, pierced through the body by a Federal bayonet. . . . I was in the fort myself, and relieved General McLaughlen by assuming command of Fort Stedman.

"From the fort I sent word to General Lee, who was on a hill in the rear, that we were in the works and that the 300 were on their way to the lines in the rear. Soon I received a message from one of these three officers . . . that he had passed the line of Federal infantry without trouble by representing himself as Colonel ——— of the 100th Pennsylvania, but that he could not find his fort. . . . I soon received a similar message from the other two, and so notified General Lee.

"Daylight was coming. . . . We had failed to occupy the three forts in the rear. . . . [It is uncertain whether any such forts existed; the attack plan may have been based on erroneous information.] Our wretched railroad trains had broken down, and the troops who were coming to my aid did not reach me. The full light of the morning revealed the gathering forces of Grant and the great preponderance of his numbers.

"It was impossible for me to make further headway with my isolated corps, and General Lee directed me to withdraw. This was not easily accomplished. Foiled by the failure . . . [to find the forts], deprived of the great bodies of infantry which Lee ordered to my support, I had necessarily stretched out my corps to occupy the entrenchments which we had captured. The other troops were expected to arrive and join in the general advance. The breaking down of the trains and the non-arrival of these heavy supports left me to battle alone with Grant's gathering and overwhelming forces, and at the same time to draw in my own lines [from the right and the left] toward Fort Stedman. A consuming fire on both flanks and front during this withdrawal caused a heavy loss to my command. I myself was wounded, but not seriously, in recrossing the space over which we had charged in the darkness. . . .

"When the retreat to our own works had ended, a report reached me that an entire Confederate regiment had not received the order to withdraw, and was still standing in the Union breastworks, bravely fighting. It was necessary to send them orders or leave them to their fate. I called my staff around me and explained the situation and the extreme danger the officer would encounter in carrying that order. I stated to them that the pain I experienced in sending one of them on so perilous a mission was greater than I could express.

"Every one of them quickly volunteered to go; but Thomas G. Jones of Alabama insisted that, as he was the youngest and had no special responsibilities, it should fall to his lot to incur the danger. I bade him good-by with earnest prayers that God would protect him, and without an apparent tremor he rode away. A portion of the trip was through a literal furnace of fire, but he passed through it, both going and returning, without a scratch."

Some of the troops Jones had gone to summon were not so fortunate. In all, Gordon lost about 4,000 men. A good number of these, however, were unharmed prisoners. Federal losses were about 2,000. Lee's casualties were not his only setback. By the time the affair was over, the Federals had advanced and captured a long expanse of the Confederate picket ditches, which put the Petersburg defenses in extra danger.

Grant's aide, Horace Porter, assumes the narrative: "The President, who was aboard his boat anchored out in the river, soon heard of [Gordon's] attack, and he was kept informed of the events which were taking place by his son Robert, who carried the news to him. . . . Mr. Lincoln . . . sent a telegram to the Secretary of War, winding up with the words, 'Robert just now tells me there was a little rumpus up the line this morning, ending about where it began.' . . .

"General Grant proposed to the President that forenoon that he should accompany him on a trip to the Petersburg front. The invitation was promptly accepted, and several hours were spent in visiting the troops, who cheered the President enthusiastically. He was greatly interested in looking at the prisoners who had been captured that morning. . . . The President carried a map with him, which he took out of his pocket and examined several times. He had the exact location of the troops marked on it, and he exhibited a singularly accurate knowledge of the various positions.

"Upon the return to headquarters at City Point, he sat for a while by the campfire; and, as the smoke curled about his head during certain shiftings of the wind and he brushed it away from time to time by waving his right hand in front of his face, he entertained the general-in-chief and several members of the staff by talking in a most interesting manner about public affairs, and illustrating the subjects mentioned with his incomparable anecdotes. . . . The President [afterward] went aboard his boat to spend the night."

General Lee's failure at Fort Stedman was but little understood by the general populace of Richmond and Petersburg, but its implications were all too clear to the Confederate Government. President Jefferson Davis now approached his wife, Varina, and told her that she and the

Grant's headquarters at City Point

children must prepare to leave Richmond. Varina relates: "He said for the future his headquarters must be in the field, and that our presence would only embarrass and grieve, instead of comforting him. Very averse to flight, and unwilling at all times to leave him, I argued the question with him and pleaded to be permitted to remain, until he said, 'I have confidence in your capacity to take care of our babies, and understand your desire to assist and comfort me, but you can do this in but one way, and that is by going yourself and taking our children to a place of safety.' He was very much affected and said, 'If I live you can come to me when the struggle is ended, but I do not expect to survive the destruction of constitutional liberty.'

"He had a little gold, and, reserving a five-dollar piece for himself, he gave it all to me, as well as all the Confederate money due to him. He desired me not to request any of the citizens of Richmond to take care of my silver plate, of which we possessed a large quantity, for, said he, 'They may be exposed to inconvenience or outrage by their effort to serve us.'

"All women like bric-a-brac, which sentimental people call their 'household goods,' but Mr. Davis called it 'trumpery.' I was not superior to the rest of my sex in this regard. However, everything which could not be readily transported was sent to a dealer for sale. . . . Leaving the house as it was, and taking only our clothing, I made ready with my young sister and my four little children, the eldest only nine years old, to go forth into the unknown. Mr. Burton N. Harrison, the President's private secretary, was to protect and see us safely settled in Charlotte [North Carolina], where we had hired a furnished house. Mr. George A. Trenholm's lovely daughters were also to accompany us to remain with friends there.

"I had bought several barrels of flour, and intended to take them with me, but Mr. Davis said, 'You cannot remove anything in the shape of food from here; the people want it, and you must leave it here.'

". . . The day before our departure, Mr. Davis gave me a pistol and showed me how to load, aim, and fire it. He was very apprehensive of our falling into the hands of the disorganized bands of troops roving about the country, and said, 'You can at least, if reduced to the last extremity, force your assailants to kill you. . . . If you cannot remain undisturbed in our own country, make for the Florida coast and take a ship there for a foreign country.'

"With hearts bowed down by despair, we left Richmond. Mr. Davis almost gave way when our little Jeff begged to remain with him, and

Jefferson Davis

Maggie clung to him convulsively, for it was evident he thought he was looking his last upon us. . . . A special train was not contemplated, for the transportation was now very limited, and as we pulled out from the station and lost sight of Richmond the worn-out engine broke down, and there we sat all night. There were no arrangements possible for sleeping, and at last, after twelve hours' delay, we reached Danville. A hospitable and wealthy citizen of that place invited me to rest with his family, but we gratefully declined and proceeded to Charlotte [where the rented house awaited]."

Varina's flight from Richmond was followed by the exodus of many other citizens who had begun to worry about their security from Grant's army. Kate Burwell Bowyer, with a baby's welfare to consider, decided to take a train westward to Bedford County, Virginia, where her parents resided, the home of her childhood. Kate found the Richmond station in an uproar. "The car in which we *stifled* was packed with double tiers of human beings, as they sat in each other's laps and almost stood on each other's heads, and surrounded by a frenzied mob threatening to impede its course because no longer able to cling about its platforms or upon its sides. The confusion was so dire that the train even seemed to be without its necessary corps of management. No conductor or other employee was seen, and it appeared at last as if by accident that the engine fired up and puffed slowly away.

"We moved laboriously along in the dark, for the whole machinery of the road was now worn out, the very lamps being broken and useless, and after about two hours of this travel with a terrible bump we came to a sudden halt. Nobody knew why. A third hour of this uncertainty next ensued, when a man whom we *never saw* [because of the lack of lamplight] screamed out from the door, 'Train off the track! Passengers must get out!' We obeyed, of course, amidst the wildest scene of pushing, pressing, jostling, rushing, struggling, screaming, cursing, praying —and all this, too, in impenetrable darkness!

"I first found myself thrown out of the car in some mysterious way, my feet plunged in water many inches deep; and I called to my nurse to reach the baby to me. This she, with almost superhuman effort, chanced to do successfully, afterwards herself descending; and if there was ever on this earth a picture of utter forlornness it was ours this night as we stood, ejected from the only shelter at hand, chilled in the water, and surrounded by thick darkness, with literally no idea which way to turn for another step.

"A man now approached with the welcome ray of a lantern, and an

order was heard to put all the women into a car not far off, from which
cattle had just been unloaded. Now, if the Confederate passenger cars
were in the condition I have described—and far, far worse, for I do not
care to go into revolting details—what must those devoted to Confederate *cattle* have been!

"For the moment, any prospect of change was hailed with relief; but
when we came to be rudely dashed from one [man's] hand to another
and crowded into this close [and foul-smelling] boxcar, as the cattle had
lately left it, I implored to be taken out, and found myself happy to be
once more in the deep cut, my feet laved in water and mud. As daylight
dawned, a freight train passed and took us up as far as the junction. Here
we were again dropped, and, after camping by the roadside, a third
chanced along, which brought us on our way to Farmville, where we
hung up in a wrecked car for two successive days and nights.

"The provision for sustenance on the journey had long since given
out, and there being no means on the route for obtaining a fresh supply
I resolved to see whether the country around could afford enough to
keep starvation off from a baby, and, making mine as presentable as the
circumstances would admit, I instructed the nurse to carry her to any
respectable-looking house in view, and there, stating our miserable
case, ask for any morsel to eat which the inmates could spare.

"This experiment of the child, literally begging her bread from door
to door, proved eminently successful. Both servant and child presently
came back, transported with what they had received, and even bringing the little mendicant's mother a slice of delicious apple pie. . . .

"Finally, with many adventures . . . and by a multiplicity of trains,
we were thankful once more to cast anchor in the blessed haven of
home. The trip from Richmond to this point, Bedford County, properly
made in five hours, occupied as many days. . . ."

6

The Hand of Lincoln

Back in the Richmond-Petersburg combat arena, after the fight at Fort Stedman, Grant's troops had begun harassing Lee's in an effort to keep them off balance. It was a difficult time for Confederate General John Gordon. "The shifting scenes and threatening demonstrations on my front, and in front of A. P. Hill on my right, kept me on horseback until my tired limbs and aching joints made a constant appeal for rest. The coming of night brought little or no cessation of the perplexing and fatiguing activities. . . . Troops were marching, heavy guns were roaring, picket lines were driven in and had to be reestablished; and the great mortars from both Union and Confederate works were hurling high in the air their ponderous shells, which crossed each other's paths and, with burning fuses like tails of flying comets, descended in meteoric showers on the opposing entrenchments.

"The breastworks protecting the battle lines were so high and broad that the ordinary cannonballs and shells could not penetrate them and reach the soldiers who stood behind them. In order, therefore, to throw shells into the ranks of the opposing army, these mortars were introduced. They were short, big-mouthed cannon, and were pointed upward but leaning slightly toward the enemy's lines, and their great shells were hurled skyward and then came whirling down, exploding with terrific force among the men who stood or slept behind the breastworks.

"At a point near where the left of A. P. Hill's corps touched the right of mine, a threatened attack brought together for counsel a number of officers from each of these commands. After this conference as to the

A Union mortar

proper disposition of troops for resisting the expected assault, we withdrew into a small log hut standing near, and united in prayer to Al-
mighty God for His guidance. As we assembled, one of our generals was
riding within hailing distance, and General Harry Heth of Hill's corps
stepped to the door of the log cabin and called to him to come in and
unite with us in prayer. The officer did not understand the nature of
General Heth's invitation, and replied, 'No thank you, general; no more
at present; I've just had some.'

"This amusing incident, while it convulsed the small assemblage
with laughter, did not delay many moments the earnest petitions for
deliverance. From the commander in chief to the privates in the ranks,
there was a deep and sincere religious feeling in Lee's army. Whenever
it was convenient or practicable, these hungry but unyielding men
were holding prayer meetings. Their supplications were fervent and
often inspiring, but now and then there were irresistibly amusing
touches.

"At one of these gatherings for prayer was a private who had lost one
leg. Unable to kneel, he sat with bowed head, while one of his comrades,
whom we shall call Brother Jones, led in prayer. Brother Jones was
earnestly praying for more manhood, more strength, and more courage. The brave old one-legged Confederate did not like Brother Jones's
prayer. . . . So he called out from his seat, 'Hold on there, Brother Jones.
Don't you know you are praying all wrong? Why don't you pray for
more provisions? We've got more courage now than we have any use
for!' "

President Lincoln had continued his visit at City Point. On the
morning of March 26, according to Horace Porter, "he wandered into
the tent of the headquarters telegraph operator, where several of us
were sitting. . . . Three tiny kittens were crawling about the tent at the
time. The mother had died, and the little wanderers were expressing
their grief by mewing piteously. Mr. Lincoln picked them up, took
them on his lap, stroked their soft fur, and murmured, 'Poor little
creatures, don't cry; you'll be taken good care of,' and, turning to [Theo-
dore S.] Bowers, said, 'Colonel, I hope you will see that these poor
motherless waifs are given plenty of milk and treated kindly.' Bowers
replied, 'I will see, Mr. President, that they are taken in charge by the
cook of our mess, and are well cared for.'

"Several times during his stay Mr. Lincoln was found fondling these
kittens. . . . It was a curious sight at an army headquarters, upon the eve
of a great military crisis in the nation's history, to see the hand which

had affixed the signature to the Emancipation Proclamation, and had signed the commissions of all the heroic men who served the cause of the Union, from the general in chief to the lowest lieutenant, tenderly caressing three stray kittens. It well illustrated the kindness of the man's disposition, and showed the childlike simplicity which was mingled with the grandeur of his nature.

"General Grant had sent word to Sheridan, whose troops were now crossing the James, to come in person to headquarters, and early on the morning of March 26 he arrived. . . . It was decided that upon this day Mr. Lincoln would review a portion of the Army of the James on the north side of the James River [where the lines were quiet], and Sheridan was invited to join the party from headquarters who were to accompany the President. The boat started from City Point at eleven o'clock.

"At breakfast General Grant [had] said to me, 'I shall accompany the President. . . . I wish you would take Mrs. Lincoln and Mrs. Grant to the reviewing ground in our headquarters ambulance.' I expressed my pleasure at being selected for so pleasant a mission, and arranged to have the ambulance and two good horses put aboard the headquarters boat. . . .

"The President was in a more gloomy mood than usual on the trip up the James. He spoke with much seriousness about the situation, and did not attempt to tell a single anecdote. As the boat passed the point where Sheridan's cavalry was crossing the river on the pontoon bridge, he manifested considerable interest in watching the troopers, and addressed a number of questions to their commander.

"When the boat reached the landing on the north side of the river, I helped the two distinguished ladies who had been intrusted to my care into the ambulance, and started for the reviewing ground, about two miles distant. The horsemen [including Lincoln and Grant] got the start of us and made good time; but as the road was swampy, and part of it corduroyed with the trunks of small trees, without much reference to their relative size or regularity of position, the ambulance could make but slow progress. Some additional springs had been put under it, and cross-seats arranged so as to make it ride more easily than the ordinary army ambulance; but the improved springs only served to toss the occupants higher in the air when the wheels struck a particularly aggravating obstacle.

"Mrs. Lincoln, finding we were losing time, and fearing we would miss part of the review, expressed a wish to move faster, and I reluctantly gave the order to the driver. We were still on a corduroyed

Mary Todd Lincoln

portion of the road, and when the horses trotted the mud flew in all directions, and a sudden jolt lifted the party clear off the seats, jammed the ladies' hats against the top of the wagon, and bumped their heads as well. Mrs. Lincoln now insisted on getting out and walking, but as the mud was nearly hub-deep Mrs. Grant and I persuaded her that we had better stick to the wagon as our only ark of refuge.

"Finally we reached our destination, but it was some minutes after the review had begun. Mrs. Ord, and the wives of several of the officers who had come up from Fort Monroe [at the mouth of the Chesapeake] for the purpose, appeared on horseback as a mounted escort to Mrs. Lincoln and Mrs. Grant. This added a special charm to the scene, and the review passed off with peculiar brilliancy.

"Mrs. Grant enjoyed the day with great zest, but Mrs. Lincoln had suffered so much from the fatigue and annoyances of her overland trip that she was not in a mood to derive much pleasure from the occasion. [As a matter of fact, Mrs. Lincoln, who was emotionally unstable, threw several tantrums, and the episodes embarrassed her attendants.] I made up my mind that ambulances, viewed as vehicles for driving distinguished ladies to military reviews, were not a stupendous success, and that thereafter they had better be confined to their legitimate uses of transporting the wounded and attending funerals.

"Upon the return trip on the boat, the President seemed to recover his spirits. Perhaps the manifestation of strength on the part of the splendid Army of the James which he had witnessed at the review had served to cheer him up. . . . It was nearly dark when the party returned to City Point. After dinner the band was brought down to the steamboat, and a dance was improvised. Several ladies were aboard, and they and the officers danced till midnight. Neither the President nor General Grant joined, even in a square dance, but sat in the after part of the boat conversing."

The pleasures of the evening were marred by outbursts by Mrs. Lincoln, who was still in a fret over her bad day in the field, her complaints including imagined slights to her position as First Lady. When the dance was over, the President was obliged to spend part of the night trying to placate the troubled woman. This sort of thing was nothing new. Mrs. Lincoln's fits of anger had become the talk of Washington. One of the observers of her conduct during the City Point interlude was Lieutenant Commander John S. Barnes, a member of the presidential party, who came to believe that Mrs. Lincoln was largely responsible for the sad look often worn by the President. Barnes wrote later: "She

Julia Dent Grant, the general's wife

was at no time well. The mental strain upon her was great, betrayed by extreme nervousness approaching hysteria, causing misapprehensions, extreme sensitiveness as to slights or want of politeness or consideration. I had the greatest sympathy for her, and for Mr. Lincoln, who I am sure felt deep anxiety for her. His manner towards her was always that of the most affectionate solicitude, so marked, so gentle and unaffected that no one could see them together without being impressed by it."

Returning to narrator Horace Porter: "Sherman, in his correspondence [from North Carolina] had intimated a desire to have a personal conference with his chief before the general movement of all the armies took place; and it was learned on March 27 that he had arrived at Fort Monroe and was on his way up the James. Grant telegraphed to several prominent officers to meet Sherman that evening at headquarters. Late in the afternoon the *Russia*, a captured steamer, arrived with Sherman aboard, and General Grant and two or three of us who were with him at the time started down to the wharf to greet the Western commander.

"Before we reached the foot of the steps, Sherman had jumped ashore and was hurrying forward with long strides to meet his chief. As they approached, Grant cried out, 'How d'you do, Sherman!' 'How are you, Grant!' exclaimed Sherman; and in a moment they stood upon the steps with their hands locked in a cordial grasp, uttering earnest words of familiar greeting. Their encounter was more like that of two schoolboys coming together after a vacation than the meeting of the chief actors in a great war tragedy.

"Sherman walked up with the general in chief to headquarters, where Mrs. Grant extended to the illustrious visitor a cordial greeting. Sherman then seated himself with the others by the campfire, and gave a most graphic description of the stirring events of his march through Georgia. . . . Never were listeners more enthusiastic; never was a speaker more eloquent. The story, told as he alone could tell it, was a grand epic related with Homeric power."

In the evening a number of officers arrived to pay their respects to Sherman, among them General George G. Meade, commander of the Army of the Potomac since Gettysburg, but now, like General Ord of the Army of the James, subordinate to Grant. There were several high-level meetings during Sherman's visit, and the correspondent of the Boston *Journal*, the popular Charles Carleton Coffin, was privileged to witness an unforgettable scene. "I was sitting in the office of General

George G. Meade

Grant's Adjutant-General on the morning of the 28th of March, and saw President Lincoln, with Generals Grant, Sherman, Meade, and Sheridan, coming up the walk. Look at the men whose names are to have a conspicuous place in the annals of America. Lincoln, tall, round-shouldered, loose-jointed, large-featured, deep-eyed, with a smile upon his face. He is dressed in black, and wears a fashionable silk hat. Grant is at Lincoln's right, shorter, stouter, more compact; wears a military hat with a stiff, broad brim, had his hands in his pantaloons' pockets, and is puffing away at a cigar while listening to Sherman. Sherman, tall, with high, commanding forehead, is almost as loosely built as Lincoln; has sandy whiskers, closely cropped, and sharp, twinkling eyes, long arms and legs, shabby coat, slouch hat, his pants tucked into his boots. He is talking hurriedly, gesticulating now to Lincoln, now to Grant, his eyes wandering everywhere. Meade, also tall, with thin, sharp features, a gray beard, and spectacles, is a little stooping in his gait. Sheridan, the shortest of all, quick and energetic in all his movements, with a face bronzed by sun and wind; courteous, affable, a thorough soldier."

That same morning another top-echelon figure appeared at Grant's headquarters. He was Rear Admiral David Dixon Porter, commander of the North Atlantic Blockading Squadron, who had a part of his fleet on the James River. The admiral was the son of Commodore David Porter, daring hero of the War of 1812, and his own record in the present war was notable. When Grant commanded in the western theater, Porter and his fleet played a vital role in the general's capture of Vicksburg, key to control of the Mississippi River. Just recently the admiral had helped the army to take Fort Fisher, on the North Carolina coast. Now, on the morning of March 28, Porter joined Lincoln, Grant, and Sherman in a parley held on the *River Queen*.

Colonel Horace Porter explains that "it was in no sense a council of war, but only an informal interchange of views between the four men who, more than any others, held the destiny of the nation in their hands. . . . General Grant afterward told us the particulars of the interview. It began by his explaining to the President the military situation and prospects, saying that the crisis of the war was now at hand, as he expected to move at once around the enemy's [right] and cut him off from the Carolinas, and that his only apprehension was that Lee might move out before him and evacuate Petersburg and Richmond, but that if he did there would be a hot pursuit.

"Sherman assured the President that in such a contingency his army, by acting on the defensive, could resist both Johnston and Lee till Grant

David D. Porter

could reach him, and that then the enemy would be caught in a vise and have his life promptly crushed out. Mr. Lincoln asked if it would not be possible to end the matter without a pitched battle, with the attendant losses and suffering; but was informed that that was a matter not within the control of our commanders, and must rest necessarily with the enemy. Lincoln spoke about the course which he thought had better be pursued after the war, and expressed an inclination to lean toward a generous policy. . . .

"Sherman related many interesting incidents which occurred in his campaign. Grant talked less than anyone present. The President twice expressed some apprehension about Sherman being away from his army; but Sherman assured him that he had left matters safe. . . .

"That afternoon Sherman took leave of those at headquarters and returned to his command [in North Carolina] in the *Bat*, as that vessel was faster than the one which had brought him up the coast.

"The troops [of Grant] had been in motion the previous night, and the general had decided that headquarters should be moved on the morning of the 29th. The horses were to be put aboard the train which was to take the general and staff to the Petersburg front. About 8:30 Mr. Lincoln [who planned to remain with Admiral Porter's fleet at City Point] came ashore to say good-by. We had the satisfaction of hearing one good story from him before parting. General Grant was telling him about the numerous ingenious and impracticable suggestions that were made to him almost daily as to the best way of destroying the enemy, and said, 'The last plan proposed was to supply our men with bayonets just a foot longer than those of the enemy, and then charge them. When they met, our bayonets would go clear through the enemy, while theirs would not reach far enough to touch our men, and the war would be ended.'

"Mr. Lincoln laughed, and remarked, 'Well, there is a good deal of terror in cold steel. I had a chance to test it once myself. When I was a young man, I was walking along a back street in Louisville one night about twelve o'clock, when a very tough-looking citizen sprang out of an alleyway, reached up to the back of his neck, pulled out a bowie-knife that seemed to my stimulated imagination about three feet long, and planted himself square across my path. For two or three minutes he flourished his weapon in front of my face, appearing to try to see just how near he could come to cutting my nose off without quite doing it. He could see in the moonlight that I was taking a good deal of interest in the proceeding, and finally he yelled out, as he steadied the knife close to my throat, 'Stranger, kin you lend me five dollars on that?' I never reached in my pocket and got out money so fast in all my life. I handed him a bank note and said, 'There's ten, neighbor; now put up your scythe.' "

The laughter occasioned by Lincoln's story was soon replaced by solemnity. General Grant, according to Porter, now "bade an affectionate good-by to Mrs. Grant, kissing her repeatedly as she stood at the front door of his quarters. She bore the parting bravely, although her pale face and sorrowful look told of the sadness that was in her heart. The party, accompanied by the President, then walked down to the railroad station. Mr. Lincoln looked more serious than at any other time since he had visited headquarters. The lines in his face seemed deeper, and the rings under his eyes were of a darker hue. It was plain that the weight of responsibility was oppressing him. Could it have been a premonition that with the end of this last campaign would come the end of his life?

"Five minutes' walk brought the party to the train. There the President gave the general and each member of the staff a cordial shake of the hand, and then stood near the rear end of the car while we mounted [its] platform. As the train was about to start we all raised our hats respectfully. The salute was returned by the President, and he said in a voice broken by an emotion he could ill conceal, 'Good-by, gentlemen. God bless you all! Remember, your success is my success.' The signal was given to start; the train moved off; Grant's last campaign had begun."

7

Grant Prevails at Five Forks

Thanks to the reports of their scouts, the Confederates were aware of what was happening. "The hour of the final struggle," says staff officer John Esten Cooke, "now rapidly drew near.... General Grant was plainly about to make a decisive attack on the Confederate right ... and, if that attack succeeded, Lee was lost. Had not General Lee and his men become accustomed to retain their coolness under almost any circumstances of trial, the prospect now before them must have filled them with despair.... It was no secret in the little body of Southerners that Lee would be able to send [to the right] only a painfully inadequate force, unless his extensive works [protecting Richmond and Petersburg] were left in charge of a mere line of skirmishers. This could not be thought of. The struggle on the right must be a desperate one, and the Southern troops must depend upon hard fighting rather than numbers if they hoped to repulse the attack of the enemy.

"Such was the situation of affairs, and neither the Confederate commander nor his men shrunk in the hour of trial.... General Lee had determined to fight to the last. To attribute this determination to despair and recklessness would be doing injustice to the great soldier. It was still possible that he might be able to repulse the assault upon his right, and, by disabling the Federal force there, open his line of retreat."

Something less than half of Grant's army was poised for action on the Union left, the rest of the troops remaining attentive to affairs in the siege lines. Once he had staggered Lee with a blow on his right flank, Grant proposed to move upon Richmond and Petersburg, his intent both to drive Lee from these places and to capture them, at the same time launching a march toward the Confederate general's line of retreat. In position to make the first southwesterly swing were Andrew A. Humphreys' 2nd Corps, Gouverneur K. Warren's 5th Corps, and Phil Sheridan's Cavalry. Sheridan was in top command. The columns marched by different routes, and it was the fortune of the cavalry and the 5th Corps to experience the heaviest involvement with Lee's countermeasures.

The story of the vital maneuver is told as it was seen by 5th Corps member Theodore Gerrish, the private from Maine: "On the 29th of March, we broke camp and moved in the direction of Dinwiddie Court House. It was a rough country through which we passed, and our advance was necessarily slow. Our regiment was commanded by Colonel Walter G. Morrill. A dense forest covered a large portion of the country, broken here and there by small clearings. There were many ridges of land, broken and ragged with rocks and deep ravines, through which rushed and roared deep streams of water.

"Soon after we broke camp, a detail was made for men to go out as flankers, and I was named as one of them. We penetrated the thick forest, and formed our line some eighty rods from the column of troops, and moved in a parallel line with them. We had not gone far before we came in contact with the enemy's skirmish line, which we were ordered to drive back upon their line of battle. This was an exciting and somewhat dangerous task. We advanced on a double-quick through the woods, across fields and ravines in which wild grape vines, thorn bushes, and a thousand obstacles impeded our way. Our clothes were torn into shreds, and blood flowed freely from our lacerated flesh. The enemy would occasionally make a stand and fight, and the minie-balls would fly back and forth in a lively manner. A number of men on both sides were killed and wounded.

"We followed them for a mile, and halted on the edge of a large field. It was now past noon. Heavy firing was heard on our right, both musketry and artillery. It was but a short distance from us, and we knew that our division had encountered the enemy. For an hour we listened with much anxiety, and then the order came for us to advance. We crossed the field, and found the rebels in the woods, on the other side. The roar of battle on our right inspired us, and we rushed upon them. They gave us a heavy skirmish fire, and then fell back for a half mile, we following them very closely.

"Suddenly there was a sheet of flame in our front. Whiz, crash, bang went a dozen shells above our heads. We had reached the enemy's line of battle, and a heavy infantry fire was also opened upon us. It was of course impossible to advance further. It would be folly to remain where we were, and so we fell rapidly back.

"Many of our men were wounded before we got out of the range of the enemy's guns. One, a brave young fellow from Massachusetts, fell shot through both legs. We would not leave him in the hands of the rebels, and laid him upon a blanket to carry him back. He was much excited, and was determined not to be carried off the field. He called us miserable cowards for falling back from the enemy, and pleaded with us to put him down and, with our little skirmish line, charge upon the rebels' line of battle.

"We were soon relieved, and returned to our command. We found that our brigade had not been engaged, but that General [Joshua Lawrence] Chamberlain, with his brigade had fought a severe battle with the enemy on the Boydton Plank Road, and had carried their position with heavy loss. General Chamberlain had gallantly led his troops in their charge [remaining in action in spite of painful body and arm bruises inflicted by a deflected bullet]. . . . Our brigade was sent to relieve his, and we advanced across the field of battle. Many dead were lying upon the ground. The rebels had evidently fallen back upon a stronger line of works in the rear of those carried by Chamberlain. We advanced cautiously along the narrow road.

"Soon there was a fearful roar in the woods, just in our front, and a score of shells came screaming through the air just above our heads. The enemy had an excellent range of our position. We halted while our officers endeavored to ascertain the strength of the enemy's position, which they soon discovered was very great and could only be carried with great loss of life, and, after dark, we were withdrawn. . . .

"One very sad event . . . occurred while we were lying there under the enemy's fire. A gray-haired soldier came down along the road where our dead men were scattered upon the ground. He was evidently in search of something. At last, with a heartrending groan, he sat down beside a dead body, and wept as if his heart would break. It was a father mourning for his son. They were both members of a Massachusetts regiment, and the son had been killed in the brilliant charge they had so recently made.

"We returned a short distance to the rear, and then marched to a position upon the right of the fortifications from which we had just fallen back, and halted in an open field. Our regiment formed a part of a line drawn up beside some farm buildings. It was now ten o'clock at night. Great masses of black clouds obscured the sky, and the darkness was intense. 'Throw up fortifications,' was the order given, and quickly obeyed. The huge barn and out-buildings, built of hewn logs, were torn down and piled up, and upon these we threw an enormous quantity of earth, and soon had a comparatively strong line of defense.

"We were all very tired, but had a jolly time in building these works. Near the barn there was a deep well partially filled with water, which in the darkness we had not noticed. Two of us were carrying a great stick of timber upon our shoulders, my chum carrying the foremost end, while I was staggering along in the rear. Suddenly, without a word of warning, the forward end of the timber came to the ground. It was so dark that I could not see my companion. I called loudly his name, and, to my surprise, when his voice came back in reply it came from the depths of the earth. I quickly made my way to the scene of disaster, and found him in a well twenty feet deep, and up to his ears in water. An alarm was given, assistance quickly arrived, and we at last succeeded in fishing him out.

"At two o'clock in the morning the line of works was completed. The rain was now pouring down in torrents. We spread our blankets upon the driest spots we could find, and lay down to sleep. Daylight [of March 30] dawned, cold, wet, and cheerless. As the thick, heavy mists gradually cleared away we saw the rebels' advanced line intrenched upon the field in our front, some eighty rods distant. Theirs were light defenses, and evidently covered stronger ones in their rear.

"The rain continued to fall in great quantities, but there was no firing between the hostile lines; and so we sat in the mud and looked at each other until late in the afternoon. At four o'clock we advanced and carried the enemy's works by assault, they falling back to the woods beyond. We then moved to the right flank for a short distance and formed our line to charge upon the rebel works, a skirmish line being thrown out in advance. The rebels opened upon us with artillery, and shells fell all around us. It was evident that the enemy was prepared to receive us. The charge was not made, and we returned to the rebel earthworks we had just captured, and these we made as strong as possible.

"Before dark our skirmishers were driven in by the rebel line of battle, which was advancing to recapture the line of works. A battery was sent out to support our regiment. The guns were placed right in the line of battle, and were heavily charged with grape and canister. On came the rebels with a deafening cheer. It was fun to see them advance. Our infantry and artillery opened upon them, but only for a few moments. Their columns were not heavy enough to withstand our fire, and they were driven back, leaving a number of prisoners in our hands.

"We presented a singular appearance at that time, as we had been lying flat upon our faces in red-colored mud that now covered our uniforms; our hands and faces being black with burning powder, and our clothes torn. We did not much resemble the regiment that had moved out of camp at Hatcher's Run only two days before.

"We remained in those works that cold, damp, frosty night. Our wet blankets were spread upon the muddy ground, and we soon forgot all hardships and dangers in a glorious, restful sleep. In the morning [March 31] we were relieved, and marched a mile or two to the left and stacked our guns in a small field surrounded by the dense forest. The storm had passed away and the sun shone down warm and bright through the broken clouds. Our blankets were spread upon the ground to dry. We kindled fires and cooked our coffee.

"As we were enjoying our dinner, there was a fearful roar in our front, less than a mile away—cannons, musketry, and cheering, all mingling in one terrible roar—and to our dismay we found that the awful tide was rolling toward us. We instantly understood its meaning: the rebels had charged upon our line and were driving it back. An orderly came dashing back to General [Charles] Griffin with orders for him to take his division in, on the double-quick, and fill the gap made in our line by the falling back of the 3rd Division. The bugle notes rang out, 'Fall in! Fall in!' The officers shouted their commands; the weary men sprang into line; we caught our guns from the stacks, and, by the right flank, rushed toward the scene of conflict.

"We soon encountered the broken fragments of the retreating division, closely pursued by the rebels, but reached a crest of land overlooking Gravelly Run. It was a good position. The rebels must descend a hill in our front, cross Gravelly Run, and then climb the hill upon which our line would be formed. Our colonel gave the order, 'By battalion, into line!' and we quickly formed upon the crest of the hill. It was an exciting moment. The rebel line was advancing, in plain view, down the hill on the other side of the stream. Artillery had gone into position and was throwing shells over our heads; the bands played; the cannons roared; our muskets crashed with awful force; the hill itself shivered as if with fear.

"The rebel line came to the stream, but could come no further, and was thrown back. General Chamberlain's brigade, on our right, gallantly advanced and occupied the position from which [Samuel W.] Crawford's division had been driven, and the fortunes of the day were restored. Our wounded men were cared for, the dead were buried, and we were soon preparing for the startling events that were to transpire within the next [twenty-four] hours—events that were destined to be death blows to the Southern Confederacy, and also [would] perpetuate the Union of the Stars and Stripes.

"It is four o'clock in the afternoon of March 31st, 1865, and the Battle of Gravelly Run has been fought and won, but a fearful conflict is raging elsewhere. Away beyond us, far down on our extreme left [toward Dinwiddie Court House], we can hear the roar of battle, the booming of cannon, and the heavy crash of musketry. We have no infantry at that point, and it must be Sheridan and his cavalry coping with the enemy. . . . How intently we listened! The battle tides were receding, and it was evident that Sheridan's force was being borne back. . . .

"General Warren, commanding our corps, became nervous and restless. His mission is to support Sheridan's movement. . . . Soon our lines were formed, and we marched in the direction of the distant battle. The narrow road along which we marched was lined on either hand with a dense growth of pine trees. The sun was sinking from view, and the tall trees cast their lengthening shadows across our pathway. It was to us a time of thrilling interest, as we all understood the situation. Our brigade . . . was marching through that great forest to meet an enemy of whose strength and location we knew nothing.

"The sounds of battle in our front died away. The darkness became so intense that it was not prudent to proceed further, especially as nothing was to be gained by such a course. The pickets were sent out, and we lay down to sleep and rest. At midnight we were aroused with the information that our pickets had discovered the enemy, who was in great force in our immediate front, so near that they could easily listen to the conversation of their pickets, and also of the soldiers behind their breastworks. Silently we fell into line, and, retracing our steps along the way we came for several miles, encamped for the remainder of the night.

"The morning of April 1st was clear, but cold and frosty. We were early on the march, moving to the left of the point from which we had fallen back the previous night. The whole corps had arrived. We were moving in a direction that would bring us to a place known as Five Forks, near which Sheridan had fought the day before. About ten o'-clock in the forenoon we halted in the edge of an oak wood, and there remained until two o'clock in the afternoon."

By this time trouble had developed between Warren and Sheridan. Warren was not moving his columns fast enough to suit the impetuous trooper's plans. Grant himself learned of the situation, and he, too, was concerned. He sent Sheridan authority to relieve Warren if he thought it necessary to the success of this critical operation. Sheridan held off, but he found little he liked in Warren's subsequent conduct.

Private Gerrish continues: "The Southside railroad was of great importance to General Lee, because over that road he brought all the provisions for his army in Richmond and Petersburg. It was the lifeline that connected the Confederacy and its capital. If that line of connection was cut, Richmond must be abandoned. To guard this road, General Lee had sent a large force of troops which had constructed a long line of breastworks running parallel with the road for its defense. [Numbering about 10,000, and commanded by the legendary George Pickett, these troops had sung as they worked, the woods and fields ringing with "Dixie" and "Annie Laurie."]

"The center of this line of defenses was at the point known as Five Forks, so named from the five roads that centered there. Sheridan had advanced upon [Five Forks] on the 31st, but, not being supported by infantry, had been crowded back for several miles. But General Warren had now arrived [with 17,000 men to cooperate with the 10,000 troopers], and Sheridan's plan was to advance with his cavalry in front of the works, and, while thus attracting the enemy's attention, cause the 5th Corps to advance [around their left flank] to their rear and take them by surprise.

"At two o'clock our corps was formed for the advance, in two lines of battle, our regiment being in the second line. We were to advance over a rough, broken country filled with ravines and covered with a thick growth of forest trees. Having marched for some two or three miles, the lines were so changed while we were marching, that we soon found we were in the front line. Our regiment and the 1st Michigan were under the command of Colonel Walter G. Morrill, and in all our previous experience we had never been led by a braver or more skillful commander.

"We climbed a hill, looked down through the trees, and saw the breastworks but a short distance in our front. We had advanced so quietly that the enemy [who, at this point in the long line of defenses, happened to possess a substantial numerical strength] was not aware of our presence. Our lines were reformed, and then with a yell we charged. Before the enemy had time to recover from their surprise, we were upon them, so that they threw down their guns without firing a shot and surrendered. The number of prisoners embarrassed us, and we sent them to the rear as fast as we could. . . .

Sheridan and his generals reconnoitering at Five Forks

"They soon discovered the superiority of their numbers and the mistake they had made in surrendering. A large portion of our men had gone to the rear with prisoners when a rebel officer [who had not surrendered] came dashing down the line, calling upon them to rally. A rebel who had surrendered was standing near Colonel Morrill, and, catching up from the ground a loaded rifle, yelled with an oath, 'We can whip you yet,' and deliberately shot a captain of the 1st Michigan Regiment who stood beside him. At the same moment a private of Company D in our regiment thrust his bayonet through the breast of the treacherous rebel, who fell dead at his feet.

"In a moment's time the battle was raging all along our line. It was hot work, and in many places it was a hand-to-hand fight. Men deliberately pointed their rifles in each other's faces and fired. Clubbed muskets came crushing down in deadly force upon human skulls. Men were bayoneted in cold blood. Feats of individual bravery were performed on that afternoon which, if recorded, would fill a volume. I can only refer to a portion of them.

"On the right of Company H [at the time the Union surprise attack was launched] were four men; one of them was Morrison . . . a man of gigantic strength and remarkable bravery. Another of the four was Gilmore; he was equal to Morrison in bravery, and nearly his match in physical strength. The third was Hickey, a man of Scotch-Irish descent, who had served in the regular army of England, and who had deserted and come to our country, and enlisted in our regiment. He was tall and robust, a perfect mass of bone and muscle. The fourth was younger in years, and more slender in form than his companions.

"When we reached the rebel breastworks [as told before], they threw down their arms and surrendered. They were densely packed in our front, as men gather in a crowd upon a public square. Some ten rods from the breastworks upon which we stood, we saw a rebel flag leaning against a tree. To reach it we would have to pass through this great crowd of men. Morrison saw the flag, and, waving his hat, called, 'Come on, boys, and we will capture the flag!' And, suiting his action to his words, he sprang over among the rebels, and was quickly followed by the three men above described.

"There was evidently no danger, as the rebels were not disposed to fight, and the four men easily made their way through the crowd that opened to receive them, until they had passed over one-half the distance between the breastworks and the flag. At least four hundred rebels were packed between them and their comrades. It was at this moment that the enemy rallied, and these four men found themselves surrounded on every hand, cut off from their comrades, and all hope of escape destroyed. But Morrison cried, 'We will fight our way back to the regiment!' And the others turned to obey his command.

"A rebel officer sprang at Morrison's throat and called upon him to surrender. The brave soldier brought the heavy stock of his rifle down with such crushing force upon the officer's head that he fell dead at his feet. It was now a most desperate fight. They were in such close quarters that neither party could well shoot. On one side it was half a hundred men striking and surging back and forth, thinking only of revenge and victory, on the other, four men, single-handed, pounding their way through all opposition.

"The contest was as unequal as it was desperate. The most fearful blows were given and returned, but the four men, standing side by side, managed to stay upon their feet, slowly advancing as they fought, until bleeding, bruised, and stunned, they sprang from the rebel crowd and reached an open space of ground between their comrades and the rebels. At that moment the baffled enemy poured a deadly volley upon the escaping soldiers. Morrison sprang high in the air and fell with a deathly groan. Gilmore sank upon the ground as if dead [which he was]. Hickey reeled and staggered, while the other received a rifle ball in the left arm. . . . [Both made it back to their comrades, Hickey's wound actually slight.]

"This was the supreme moment of the conflict. The rebels would climb up on one side of the breastworks, and our men on the other side would knock them back. We heard bugles in our front, and out from a piece of woods some eighty rods away came dashing squadrons of [Sheridan's] cavalry. With a cheer our men sprang over the works and upon the rebels, who reeled and staggered before us. Colonel Morrill was in the thickest of the fight; Captain Fernald dashed among the enemy and captured a flag; Bickford, Fogler, and a score of other officers in our regiment led on their men.

"It was becoming too hot for the Johnnies, and they turned to run. It was too late. Sheridan threw his lines around them like a girdle of death, and five thousand prisoners were captured."

(George Pickett himself was nearly taken. His time at the front was actually brief, for at the outset of the action he was miles in the rear attending a "shad bake" with some fellow officers. On the scene as the lines were breaking, the general waved a bloodstained set of battle colors while singing, in company with a regimental glee club, "Rally round the flag, boys; rally once again!" Pickett was soon obliged to abandon his dramatic but tardy heroics and gallop for safety.)

George E. Pickett

Returning to Private Gerrish: "General [Romeyn B.] Ayres, with the 1st division, and General Chamberlain, with a brigade of our division, were fighting on our left, and, when the rebels broke before our advance, their whole line was in our possession, save one position on our right. We all rushed with wild enthusiasm in that direction. Sheridan went dashing past us, wild with the excitement of victory, shouting, as he swung his clenched hand through the air, 'Smash 'em! Smash 'em! We have a record to make before the sun goes down. We must have the Southside road!'

"An open field was in front of the last position the rebels held. General Warren caught the corps flag from the hand of the man who carried it, and dashed across this field, leading on a column of soldiers he had hastily formed for the charge. It was the most gallant deed of the whole day's battle, and the whole rebel line was now in our possession.

"The sun was low in the western sky, but there was no rest. Sheridan, like a madman, dashed here and there, urging on his men. The cavalry followed the retreating foe, capturing prisoners by hundreds, while the infantry pressed on after them, and so we soon reached the desired point. . . . [The Southside railroad was not actually in Union hands, but the Confederate hold on it was decisively broken.]

"Our bugles sounded the recall, and we were to march back to the battlefield and reform our lines. Slowly we retraced our steps, joyous over the great victory won, but sorrowful over the loss of our brave men. The battlefield was reached, and we encamped for the night, but we could not think of rest or sleep. The dead were to be buried. The wounded were to be cared for. I secured a short piece of candle and a small spade, and, with a comrade to assist me, went in search of the bodies of Morrison and Gilmore. It was a lonely search in that hour of midnight, dark and damp. The silence was only broken by the groans of the wounded and the low conversation of the soldiers who were caring for them.

"After a long search in the darkness, carrying the lighted candle in my hand, our quest was rewarded by finding the looked-for bodies. They lay as they had fallen. Morrison was shot through the body, and had evidently lived a few moments. Gilmore had received two balls through his heart, and of course had died instantly. . . . We dug two shallow graves under the shadow of a great oak tree, and buried them side by side. We placed boards at their heads, telling their names, company, and regiment, and there left the remains of two men as brave and fearless as any who ever breathed the air of patriotism and liberty."

A Union bugler

8

The Storming of Petersburg

Neither Warren's outstanding deed of valor, nor the fact that his corps had done so much to secure the victory, saved the commander from Sheridan's axe. In Sheridan's words: "General Warren having sorely disappointed me, both in the moving of his corps and in its management during the battle, I felt that he was not the man to rely upon under such circumstances, and deeming that it was to the best interest of the service, as well as but just to myself, I relieved him, ordering him to report to General Grant." This amounted to ruin for the man who had come to fame as the savior of Little Round Top at Gettysburg in 1863.

(It wasn't until fourteen years after the war that Warren was able to win the convention of a Court of Inquiry to review his conduct at Five Forks, and it took the court nearly three years to complete its work. The findings were at least partly favorable to Warren, but he never saw the published report, dying—after leaving orders that his funeral be strictly civilian—three months before it was issued. As for Phil Sheridan, he never changed his point of view, and he was supported by some of the day's leading military figures, including W. T. Sherman.)

Another Gettysburg hero who declined in stature as a result of Five Forks was Southerner George Pickett. His troops had shown something less than their usual combat efficiency, and the general's late arrival on the field was seen as having much to do with this. Pickett made no mention of his remissness when he wrote his wife about the day: "We yielded to an overwhelming force. . . . Ah, my Sally, the triumphs of might are transient; but the sufferings and crucifixions for the right can never be forgotten. The sorrow and song of my glory-crowned division nears its doxology. May God pity those who wait at home for the soldier who has reported to the Great Commander! God pity them as the days go by and the sad nights follow. The birds were hushed in the woods when I started to write, and now one calls to its mate, 'Cheer up— Cheer up.' Let's listen and obey the birds, my darling. Let's try to cheer up—cheer up."

General Lee, who was on the field of Five Forks and witnessed the shattering of Pickett's forces, was himself anything but cheerful when the battle ended at sundown. "It was the only occasion," says Richmond editor Edward Pollard, "on which the Confederate commander ever exhibited anything like reproof in the field. He remarked that the next time the troops were to be taken into action, he would put himself at the head of them; and, turning to one of his brigadiers, he ordered him, with singular emphasis and severity, to gather and put under guard *all* the stragglers on the field, making a plain reference to the conduct of his officers."

Union Colonel Horace Porter, who was present at Five Forks as an observer for General Grant, tells of the battle's aftermath and the part he played in it: "I had sent frequent bulletins during the day to the general in chief. . . . About half-past seven o'clock I started for general headquarters. The roads in places were corduroyed with captured muskets. Ammunition trains and ambulances were still struggling forward for miles. Teamsters, prisoners, stragglers, and wounded were choking the roadway. The coffee-boilers had kindled their fires. Cheers were resounding on all sides, and everybody was riotous over the victory. A horseman had to pick his way through this jubilant condition of things as best he could, as he did not have the right of way by any means."

Once clear of the battle arena, Porter moved at top speed toward headquarters, now established at the southern end of the Petersburg lines. "As I galloped past a group of men on the Boydton Plank Road, my orderly called out to them the news of the victory. The only response he got was from one of them who raised his open hand to his face, put his thumb to his nose, and yelled, 'No you don't—April Fool!' I then realized that it was the 1st of April.

"I had ridden so rapidly that I reached headquarters at Dabney's Mill before the arrival of the last courier I had dispatched. General Grant was sitting with most of the staff about him before a blazing campfire. He wore his blue cavalry overcoat, and the ever-present cigar was in his mouth. I began shouting the good news as soon as I got in sight, and in a moment all but the imperturbable general in chief were on their feet giving vent to wild demonstrations of joy. For some minutes there was a bewildering state of excitement, grasping of hands, tossing up of hats, and slapping of each other on the back. It meant the beginning of the end—the reaching of the 'last ditch.' It pointed to peace and home. Dignity was thrown to the winds.

"The general, as was expected, asked his usual question, 'How many prisoners have been taken?' This was always his first inquiry when an engagement was reported. No man ever had such a fondness for taking prisoners. I think the gratification arose from the kindness of his heart, a feeling that it was much better to win in this way than by the destruction of human life. I was happy to report that the prisoners this time were estimated at over five thousand; and this was the only part of my recital that seemed to call forth a responsive expression from his usually impassive features.

"After having listened to the description of Sheridan's day's work, the general, with scarcely a word, walked into his tent, and by the light of a flickering candle took up his 'manifold writer,' a small book which retained a copy of the matter written, and, after finishing several dispatches, handed them to an orderly to be sent over the field wires, came out and joined our group at the campfire, and said as coolly as if remarking upon the state of the weather, 'I have ordered an immediate assault along the lines.' This was about 9 o'clock. [The assault was to be focused on Petersburg. Success there would ensure the fall of Richmond by severing its southern connections.]

"General Grant was anxious to have the different commands move against the enemy's lines at once, to prevent Lee from withdrawing troops and sending them against Sheridan. General Meade was all activity and so alive to the situation, and so anxious to carry out the orders of the general in chief, that he sent word that he was going to have the troops make a dash at the works without waiting to form assaulting columns. General Grant, at 9:30 P.M., sent a message saying he did not mean to have the corps attack without assaulting columns, but to let the batteries open at once and to feel out the skirmishers; and if the enemy was found to be leaving, to let the troops attack in their own way. The corps commanders reported that it would be impracticable to make a successful assault till morning, but sent back replies full of enthusiasm. The hour for the general assault was now fixed at four the next morning."

In the words of Union Color Sergeant D. G. Crotty: "About ten

Union and Confederate works southwest of Petersburg

o'clock on the ever-to-be-remembered Saturday night, the 1st of April, 1865, a tremendous fire is opened along the lines. It seems as though bedlam was let loose, and such was the fact, for Fort Hell opened with her neighboring forts and poured the shot and shell into the enemy's lines as quick as Uncle Sam's powder monkeys could load and fire."

Crotty was part of a Petersburg sector whose officers ordered more than simply a probe during the night. Their move was based on impatience rather than on a suspicion that Lee was withdrawing troops. As Crotty tells it: "Our brave pickets advance, supported well by solid lines of infantry, and before the rebel pickets knew there was a Yank around, they were captured ere they could fire a shot. 'Forward!' is heard in suppressed commands by the officers, and the men in an instant are pulling up the abatis in front of the rebel strongholds. The artillery cease firing, and in the dead hour of night the Union army [i.e., that part of it within range of the narrator's perception] advances and captures the outer works of the enemy, with a large number of prisoners. Cheer upon cheer ascends along the lines, and everyone feels jubilant; but there is plenty of work ahead yet to be done, for the enemy have several lines of works in front of Petersburg."

Confederate officer J. F. J. Caldwell was stationed on the extreme right, or in the southwestern sector of the city's defenses. "At several points opposite the left of the brigade," Caldwell relates, "the enemy charged our picket, and at one or two places effected a lodgment. But our troops fought them with commendable resolution, never yielding any great length of the line to them, and sometimes recovering positions from them. We stretched our main line to the right, took a portion of the sharpshooters from the picket and placed them on the extreme right, threw out videttes [i.e., sentinels] at points where the enemy lay nearest us, and thus prepared to hold our position.

"The night was extremely dark and still, so that we could see the flashes of musketry for a great distance, and could hear the roar that rang along the line for miles. . . . However unpleasant our [own] situation, we soon ascertained that there was another point, or several points, where the conflict raged in earnest. Several miles on our left, and rather more than halfway to Petersburg, the volleys of musketry were furiously fast and concentrated. They were not continuous like our [own] slow fire, but they would break out in an instant, with a fierce roar of small arms accompanied by a rapid discharge of artillery, then melt away almost to a complete calm, then reopen with the former violence—so alternating between the two extremes as to give us assurance of no ordinary struggle. Every old soldier recognized the firings as the accompaniments of charges.

"We were not surprised. Hundreds of men in our army had predicted, long ago, that Grant would continue to stretch until he forced us to draw out our line as thin as a skirmish, and then storm some point with massed columns. Men listened to these charges, and, although they said little, seemed to feel that the end was drawing near. So the night passed, in watching, in closing [our ranks] to the right or the left, in listening to the great roll of musketry that swept for miles along the line and was returned to us in horrible echoes from a hundred forests. When day dawned we were exhausted by waking and anxiety, and every pale face appeared to ask, 'What next?' "

The night had been hardly less trying for the citizens of Petersburg. "With light," says an unnamed resident, "came sounds of conflict which grew louder and more frightful. Did they not draw nearer? It sounded so. And soon strange rumors filled the streets. The church bells rang out their first call to prayer, but no one heeded the summons. The clear, sweet tones fell upon the agony of hearts that listened, as bird notes sound to those who mourn the dead. Men gathered in groups around [suburban] corners, and looked, with straining eyes, towards the clouds of battle smoke that hung around the town—stood silently and listened to the dull reports of heavy ordnance and the sharp rattle of musketry, upon which their fate hung trembling.

"Men grew white in the agony of suspense, and women wept. The old town clock struck eight—the breakfast hour—but the scanty meal stood on the board untasted. The houses were deserted, and eager questioners crowded around the men, who now came in [from the suburbs] with haggard faces and wild eyes. 'What is it?' "

While the men were making their sketchy reports to the groups in the streets, the town itself gave rise to an omen of disaster. "A cry of 'Look!' was heard, and, turning, we saw from the warehouses, where, by order of the military authorities, had been stored all the tobacco of the city, columns of black, thick smoke go up above a mass of lurid flames." This act of destruction, performed by the Confederate military so early in the day, robbed the townspeople of hope. "The groups dispersed and sought their homes. Agonizing suspense had become certainty. . . ."

Developments on the battlefield are reported by Southern staff officer John Esten Cooke, who spent a part of that critical Sunday, April 2, at General Lee's headquarters west of Petersburg, a spot overlooking the right flank of the great arc of defenses. "The Federal forces advanced all along the Confederate front [and] made a furious attack. . . . In this attack fell the eminent soldier General A. P. Hill, whose record had been so illustrious, and whose fortune it was to thus terminate his life while the Southern flag still floated."

As early as 10 A.M. General Lee wired the War Department in Richmond: "I see no prospect of doing more than holding our position here till night. I am not certain I can do that. . . . I advise that all preparation be made for leaving Richmond tonight."

Except for a few stubborn forts, Lee's outer lines were soon overrun. Returning to the narrative by John Esten Cooke: "Standing on the lawn in front of his headquarters, General Lee now saw, approaching rapidly, a heavy column of Federal infantry. . . . The spectacle was picturesque and striking. Across the extensive fields, houses set on fire by shell were sending aloft huge clouds of smoke and tongues of flame; at every instant was seen the quick glare of the Federal artillery, firing from every knoll; and in front came on the charging column, moving at a double-quick, with burnished gun barrels and bayonets flashing in the April sunshine.

"General Lee watched with attention, but with perfect composure, this determined advance of the enemy; and, although he must have realized that his army was on the verge of destruction, it was impossible to discern in his features any evidences of emotion. He was in full uniform and had buckled on his dress sword, which he seldom wore—having, on this morning declared, it is said, that if he were compelled to surrender he would do so in full harness. Of his calmness at this trying moment . . . [I am] able to bear . . . personal testimony. Chancing to hear a question [I] addressed to a member of his staff, General Lee turned with great courtesy, raised his gray hat in response to [my] salute, and gave . . . the desired information in a voice entirely measured and composed. It was impossible to regard a calmness so striking without strong sentiments of admiration. . . ."

The troops approaching Lee's position were those of Grant's 6th Corps, and the brigade commanded by Colonel Thomas W. Hyde played a key role in the maneuver. The Union colonel relates: "As we advanced in a handsome line of battle over rolling and open country, our batteries galloped to the front and opened fire in a most spirited manner. But soon a rebel battery opened on our left. . . . Several times, as it was forced to change position by the fire of the 1st Maine, we noticed each time a fine-looking old officer on a gray horse, who seemed to be directing its movements.

"At length the guns went into battery again on a hill near a large house, and their audible presence became more annoying than ever. By common consent the three brigades attempted to charge the hill, but the canister fire was so hot and the division now so small and wearied, the first attack was a failure. While our men were getting in shape to charge again, I sent Lieutenant Nichols with fifty men of the 1st Maine off to the left and around the hill with orders to shoot the battery horses, as we knew we could get on their flank, and they were probably standing hitched to the caissons and would be a fine mark from that side.

"As soon as he had disappeared in a piece of woods, on we started again, this time through a swamp where many sank to the waist, and where shot was splashing the mud and water in every direction. Here I saw two color sergeants of the 1st Maine fall, but the colors were picked up promptly, and everyone struggled over as best he could; but the wounded, as well as the dead, had to stay there for a time. The first five hundred men across made a run for the battery, and, as we went up the hill amid the roar of guns and whir of canister, amid Yankee cheers and rebel yells, I detected the crack of Nichols' rifles and knew the [enemy's] guns could not be got away.

"The din was terrible! Brass Napoleons were never better served, but they were doomed. I saw Sergeant Highill of my brigade, General [James M.] Warner's orderly, and two Vermont colors go between the guns at the same time, so neither brigade could claim the sole honor. Riding through the guns, I could not see the road beyond where the enemy were retreating, for dust, and most of the battery horses lay in their tracks.

"I asked a mortally wounded artillery officer who was propped up against a limber what battery it was. 'Captain Williams' North Carolina, of Poague's Battalion,' said he. 'And who was the officer on the gray horse?' I continued. 'General Robert E. Lee, sir, and he was the last man to leave these guns,' replied he, almost exhausted by the effort.

"What a prize we had missed! This gallant old man, struggling like a Titan against defeat. He . . . had done all one brave man could do to save his fortunes from the wreck. They told us the house had been his headquarters during the Siege of Petersburg."

Southerner John Esten Cooke says that Lee "slowly rode back, accompanied by a number of officers, toward his inner line. He still remained entirely composed, and only said to one of his staff, in his habitual tone, 'This is a bad business, colonel.' . . . He said afterward to another officer, 'It has happened as I told them it would at Richmond. The line has been stretched until it has broken.'

"The Federal column was now pressing along the Cox Road toward Petersburg, and General Lee continued to ride slowly back in the direction of the city. He was probably recognized by officers of the Federal artillery, for his cortege drew their fire. The group was furiously shelled, and one of the shells burst a few feet in rear of him, killing the horse of an officer near him, cutting the bridle-reins of others, and tearing up the ground in his immediate vicinity. This incident seemed to arouse in General Lee his fighting blood. He turned his head over his right shoulder, his cheeks became flushed, and a sudden flash of the eye showed with what reluctance he retired before the fire directed upon him.

"No other course was left him, however, and he continued to ride slowly toward his inner line—a low earthwork in the suburbs of the city —where a small force was drawn up, ardent, hopeful, defiant, and saluting the shell, now bursting above them, with cheers and laughter. It was plain that the fighting spirit of the ragged troops remained unbroken; and the shout of welcome with which they received Lee indicated their unwavering confidence in him, despite the untoward condition of affairs."

Some of Lee's forward troops were still fighting. The last stand of any consequence was made, between noon and 2 P.M., at a set of earthworks known as Fort Gregg. Here about 350 Confederates managed to kill or disable several hundred Federals while themselves sustaining fifty-seven dead and scores wounded. The final moments of the attack are described by a Union participant, Colonel Rufus P. Lincoln: "Not a man flinched, although dead and dying comrades were lying stretched upon the ground. The ditch around the fort was reached at last, and, although the water in it stood waist-deep, the brave fellows hesitated not to jump in and scramble up the bank of the fort, vainly attempting to rush in *en masse* and end the bloody struggle.

"Soon the Stars and Stripes could be seen floating by the side of the Rebel flag. Cheer after cheer rent the air—the Rebels fighting with the desperation of madmen, and shouting to each other, 'Never surrender! Never surrender!' For twenty-seven minutes we hung upon the works, knowing we could not retreat if we wished to. One more rush, and we were inside the fort, and for a minute or two there was a hand-to-hand contest. The works were ours, *and* the garrison—dead and alive."

Again in the words of Southerner John Esten Cooke: "Any further resistance on the part of General Lee seemed now impossible, and nothing appeared to be left him but to surrender his army. This course he does not seem, however, to have contemplated. It was still possible that he might be able to maintain his position on an inner line near the city until night; and, if he could do so, the friendly hours of darkness might enable him to make good his retreat . . . and shape his course toward North Carolina where General Johnston awaited him. If the movements of the Federal forces, however, were so prompt as to defeat his march in that direction, he might still be able to reach Lynchburg [about 100 miles west of Richmond], beyond which point the defiles of the Alleghenies promised him protection against the utmost efforts of his enemy. . . .

"Arrangements were speedily made to hold the inner line, if possible, until night. To General Gordon had been intrusted the important duty of defending the lines east of the city. . . . Except that the Federal army continued firing all along the front, no other active operations took place. To those present on the Confederate side this fact appeared strange. . . . General Lee's numbers for the defense of Petersburg . . . did not amount to much. . . . That, with [a] large force at his disposal, the Federal commander did not at once attack, and so end all on that day, surprised the Confederate troops. . . ."

Explains Grant's aide Horace Porter: "Prominent officers . . . urged the general to make an assault on the inner lines, and capture Petersburg that afternoon; but he was firm in his resolve not to sacrifice the lives necessary to accomplish such a result. He said the city would undoubtedly be evacuated during the night, and he would dispose the troops for a parallel march westward, and try to head off the escaping army."

9

Civilians in Terror

The message that Lee sent to the War Department in Richmond during the morning hours of that fateful Sunday had sparked a series of events that caught the city unaware. "It is a most remarkable circumstance," says Confederate newsman Edward Pollard, "that the people of Richmond had remained in profound ignorance of the fighting which had been taking place for three days in General Lee's lines. There was not a rumor of it in the air. Not a newspaper office in the city had any inkling of what was going on. Indeed, for the past few days there had been visible reassurance in the Confederate capital. There were rumors that Johnston was moving to Lee's lines, and a general idea that the combined force would take the offensive against the enemy.

"But a day before Grant had commenced his heavy movement a curious excitement had taken place in Richmond. The morning train had brought from Petersburg the wonderful rumor that General Lee had made a night attack in which he had crushed the enemy along his whole line. John M. Daniel, the editor of the Richmond *Examiner* [the narrator's superior], died the same day under the delusion that such a victory had been won; and John Mitchel, who wrote his obituary in the morning papers, expressed the regret that the great Virginian had passed away just as a decisive victory was likely to give the turning point to the success of the Southern Confederacy!

"The circumstance shows how little prepared the people of Richmond were on the bright Sabbath morning of the 2nd of April for the news that fell upon them like a thunderclap from clear skies, and smote the ear of the community as a knell of death. . . . One could see the quiet streets stretching away, unmolested by one single sign of war. Across the James the landscape glistened in the sun. Everything which met the eye spoke of peace and made it impossible to picture in imagination the scene which was to ensue. There were but few people in the streets. No vehicles disturbed the quiet of the Sabbath. The sound of the church-going bells rose into the cloudless sky and floated on the blue tide of the beautiful day."

Sallie Putnam takes up: "At St. Paul's Church the usual congregation was in attendance. President Davis occupied his pew. It was again the regular monthly return for the celebration of the sacrament of the Lord's Supper. The services were progressing as usual, no agitation nor disturbance withdrew the thoughts from holy contemplation, when a messenger was observed to make his way up the aisle and to place in the hands of the President a sealed package. Mr. Davis arose, and was noticed to walk rather unsteadily out of the church. An uneasy whisper ran through the congregation, and intuitively they seemed possessed of the dreadful secret in the sealed dispatch—the unhappy condition of General Lee's army and the necessity for evacuating Richmond. . . .

"At the Second Presbyterian Church, Dr. [Moses] Hoge, who had received information of the dire calamity impending over us, told his congregation of our situation and the probability that never again would they meet there for worship; and, in . . . thrilling eloquence . . . bade them farewell.

"The direful tidings spread with the swiftness of electricity. From lip to lip, from men, women, children, and servants, the news was bandied; but many received it at first as only a 'Sunday sensation rumor.' Friend looked into the face of friend to meet only an expression of incredulity."

According to a young woman named Lee Hampton, the news was utterly confounding. "Every heart realized that if this report was true, our cause was lost and our desperate struggles and sacrifices were all in vain. We were living in the country, about four miles from town. That Sunday we had driven into church with our father . . . leaving the rest of the family at home, quiet and unexcited. We waited only long enough to ascertain that our worst fears were realized, and then drove rapidly homeward burdened with the news we had to break to the helpless ones so totally unprepared to hear it. Incredulity, dismay, despair, and dumb endurance each in turn greeted our sad recital. They had not believed it possible that the God of battles would permit our defeat and overthrow, so firmly convinced were they we 'had our quarrel just.' "

This period around noontime found Virginia "Miss Lucy" Dade in the rooms of her boarding house. She had missed church because she was caring for her sister Fannie, who was seriously ill. "The first person I saw at the door was a fellow-lodger, Miss Bowers, who came tottering up the steps, pale and agitated, exclaiming, 'Oh! Have you heard the dreadful news? General Lee's right flank has given way. . . .' Next came Mrs. Porter from St. Paul's Church, crying, 'Oh! Miss Lucy, have you heard that the city is to be evacuated immediately and the Yankees will be here before morning? . . . What can it all mean? And what is to become of us poor defenseless women God only knows!' 'Don't be so desponding, Mrs. Porter,' said I. 'I don't believe they are going to evacuate. . . .' 'Ah, my child, no! The calamity has indeed come upon us at last; I feel that it is true.' Though I spoke hopefully and tried to look as if I did not believe the rumor, a nervous shiver came over me and my limbs were so tremulous and weak that I thought I should fall.

"Asking Mrs. Porter to sit with my sick sister to prevent anyone from breaking the news suddenly to her before I came back, I ran down to the house of a neighbor, Mrs. Wright, to ask for a little brandy to give my sister to enable her to bear the dreadful communication I had to make. On reaching Mrs. Wright's door I found her running from room to room, wringing her hands, tearing her hair, and crying, 'Oh, my poor child! And her father not here to protect us! And they say the black wretches [i.e., black military units that included Southern slaves appropriated and freed by the Union] are in the very front of Grant's army, and will rush into the city before any decent white men are here to restrain them! Oh, what is to become of us?'

"Meanwhile her lovely daughter Lulu, a beautiful girl of sixteen, was clinging to her mother and begging her not to weep so, for she did not believe that all Yankees were as bad as people said they were, and that maybe General Lee would drive them back yet. 'Oh, my child, you don't know what you are talking about, and have little idea what is before us.'

"Finding I could say nothing to comfort her, I helped myself to the brandy, and, hastening home, gave it to my sister, and then broke the news to her as gently as I could.

"My married sister, Mrs. Carter, with her little daughter Daisy, four years old, and an infant of four weeks, was then living a few squares from us, her husband being at the front with General Lee. Thinking we could better bear what was before us when we were all together to comfort and strengthen each other, I brought her and her little ones around to our rooms. There we sat all huddled together in almost breathless suspense. . . .

"Seeing the consternation into which the whole household was thrown by the news that the Yankees were coming, our little mulatto maid, Lettie, while sympathizing with the alarm and distress of her elders, was somewhat perplexed to understand exactly what the threatened evil was. So, anxious to get a little light on the mysterious subject, she crept shyly up to my side and whispered timidly, 'Miss Lucy, what sort o' looking things is Yankees? Does dey have horns? 'Cause if dey does, I seen one on 'em at de show, and he had a tail like a cow.' Her little brain was evidently sadly confusing Yankees and buffaloes."

Sallie Putnam explains that the indications of Richmond's evacuation soon "became obvious to even the most incredulous. Wagons were driven furiously through the streets to the different departments [of the government], where they received as freight the archives . . . and carried them to the Danville Depot, to be there conveyed away by railroad. Thousands of citizens determined to evacuate the city with the government. Vehicles commanded any price. . . . The streets were filled with excited crowds hurrying to the different avenues for transportation, intermingled with porters carrying huge loads, and wagons piled up with incongruous heaps of baggage of all sorts and descriptions.

"The banks were all open, and depositors were busily and anxiously collecting their specie deposits, and directors were as busily engaged in getting off their bullion. Millions of dollars of paper money, both State and Confederate, were carried to the Capitol Square and burned."

"The disorder," adds newsman Pollard, "increased each hour. . . . Pale women and little shoeless children struggled in the crowd. Oaths and blasphemous shouts smote the ear. . . . In the afternoon a special train [was readied to carry] from Richmond President Davis and some of his Cabinet. . . . At the Department all was confusion. There was no system. There was no answer to inquiries. Important officers were invisible. . . .

"Outside, [in addition to] the mass of hurrying fugitives, there were collected here and there mean-visaged crowds, generally around the commissary depots. They had already scented prey. They were of that brutal and riotous element that revenges itself on all communities in a time of great public misfortune."

There were also a few squads of military guards in the streets. Blacks not employed by their masters stood about in small groups, talking quietly, obviously wondering how they would be affected by what was happening. There were no demonstrations of joy.

Returning to Edward Pollard: "The only convocation—the only scene of council—that marked the fall of Richmond took place in a dingy room in a corner of the upper story of the Capitol Building. In this obscure chamber assembled the City Council of Richmond to consult on the emergency and to take measures to secure what of order was possible in the scenes about to ensue. It appeared to represent all that was left of deliberation in the Confederate capital. It was a painful contrast to look in upon this scene; to traverse the now almost silent Capitol House, so often vocal with oratory, and crowded with the busy scene of legislation; to hear the echo of the footstep; and at last to climb to the dismal show of councilmen in the remote room where half a dozen men sat at a rude table, and [fewer] vacant idlers listened to their proceedings. . . .

"Here and there, hurrying up with the latest news from the War Department, was Mayor [Joseph] Mayo, excited, incoherent, chewing tobacco defiantly, but yet full of pluck, having the mettle of the true Virginia gentleman, stern and watchful to the last in fidelity to the city that his ancestors had assisted in founding, and exhibiting, no matter in what comical aspects, a courage that no man ever doubted.

"When it was finally announced by the Mayor that those who had hoped for a despatch from General Lee contrary to what he had telegraphed in the morning had ceased to indulge such an expectation, and that the evacuation of Richmond was a foregone conclusion, it was proposed to maintain order in the city by two regiments of militia; to destroy every drop of liquor in the warehouses and stores; and to establish a patrol through the night."

The afternoon had brought no letup in suspense for Virginia Dade and her group at the lodging house. "Friends and neighbors were running in and out, bringing fresh rumors, some hopeful some despairing. About four o'clock we heard an ominous 'boom, boom, boom' like the sound of artillery nearer than any that we had previously heard. For a moment our hearts almost ceased to beat. We thought the enemy must be very close at hand, and, as the booming continued, various conjectures were made as to what quarter we might look for their approach, some thinking the sound came from one direction, and some from just the opposite one. In order to hear more distinctly, Mrs. Porter and I stepped to the door to listen. Hearing it much more plainly outside, we followed on in the direction whence it seemed to proceed, until we reached a neighboring stable door, when . . . we found that it was nothing but the kicking of a horse against his stall, which certainly sounded enough like the distant firing of a cannon to deceive any but the most practiced ear. . . .

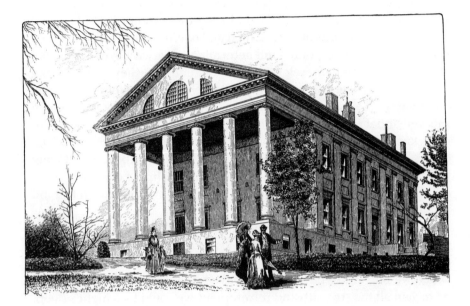

Confederate Capitol

"All through the day the various gentlemen belonging to the house had been running in to get their haversacks, canteens, blankets, etc., with a view to following the retreating army. . . . Just at nightfall two soldier friends whose duties had detained them in the city till that moment, came to bid us good-bye. . . . They asked if they might have the privilege of going into the room 'to say good-bye to Miss Fannie, for we may never see her again.' 'Certainly,' said I, for this was no time to regard empty conventionalities, and I led them to her bedside. . . .

"In their worn suits of gray, armed and equipped with all they could carry . . . , looking desperate and determined, but with eyes moistened at thoughts of the defenseless women and children they were leaving behind them, these two men entered the chamber of illness. . . . It had been many weeks since they had seen my sister, and they were much shocked at her pale and emaciated face. Scarce a word was spoken, but each knew full well the sad forebodings that filled the hearts of the others. One of them dropped on his knee beside the bed, and, taking the little thin white hand in his, he lifted it to his lips and pressed upon it a silent and tearful adieu, and they were gone, to meet us in this life again nevermore.

"Left to ourselves, our first thought was that it would be well to sit up all night to be ready to meet the first warning of approaching danger, but we finally decided that the best preparation for the morrow, which we felt was to be one of those days 'that try men's souls,' would be to gain all the strength and refreshment we could by a night's sleep, if sleep were possible. So, kneeling, we offered our united prayers for Divine protection through the darkness of the night, and the probably still darker scenes awaiting us, supplemented by little Daisy's lisping petition, 'Dod bless dear papa, and bring him home safe to mama and me.' And then we sought our couches, though we all remained in one room for mutual comfort and protection."

Meanwhile, down at Petersburg, according to the unidentified citizen quoted earlier, "dusk came, and with it began the evacuation. Noiselessly from the lines they had so gallantly defended, the Confederates withdrew; and the long, dark columns passed through the streets unattacked, unpursued. We were spared the horror of a fight through the streets, which had been feared. Now began the wild farewells and long embraces with which mothers sent forth their sons to unknown fates, and perchance endless partings."

The army moved northward over the Appomattox River before turning westward. General John Gordon and his command were the last to leave the Petersburg lines. Gordon relates: "After the hour of midnight, when all other troops were safely on the march to the rear, the 2nd Army Corps silently and sadly withdrew from the bloodstained trenches in which Lee's peerless army had exhibited for nine weary months a patience in suffering, a steadfastness under discouraging conditions, and a strength in resistance unexampled in war.

"As the last broken file of that matchless army stepped from the bridge [over the Appomattox] and my pioneer corps lighted the flames that consumed it, there came to me a vivid and depressing realization of the meaning of the appalling tragedy of the last two days. The breaking of Lee's power had shattered the last hope of Southern independence. But another burden—a personal woe—was weighing upon me. I had left behind me in that city of gloom the wife who had followed me during the entire war. She was ill. [She had given birth to a baby while Grant's troops were storming the lines.] But as I rode away from Petersburg during the dismal hours of that night, I found comfort in the hope that some chivalric soldier of the Union army would learn of her presence and guard her home against all intruders."

Confederate staff officer John Esten Cooke says that the retreat was superintended by Lee in person. "He had stationed himself at the mouth of the Hickory Road, and, standing with the bridle of his horse in his hand, gave his orders. His bearing still remained entirely composed, and his voice had lost none of its grave strength of intonation. When the rear was well closed up, Lee mounted his horse, rode on slowly with his men; and, in the midst of the glare and thunder of the exploding magazines at Petersburg, the small remnant of the Army of Northern Virginia . . . went on its way through the darkness. . . ."

Up in the Richmond lines, the final events had developed differently. Top Confederate commander in that arena was the one-legged but animated Lieutenant General Richard S. ("Old Baldhead") Ewell. The Union lines menacing Ewell were manned by a force under Major General Godfrey Weitzel, who was waiting to occupy the city. Newsman Pollard explains that "during the whole day that Grant had been engaged in front of Petersburg, the entire lines [of the Richmond area] were perfectly quiet. . . . Weitzel's command . . . fired no gun during the day, but as darkness came on . . . set all [its] bands of music to work upon national airs. The Confederates vied with the musical entertainment."

A special feature of the Confederate lines of this arena was a set of defenses at Chaffin's and Drewry's Bluffs on the James River below

Richard S. Ewell

Richmond, which, together with a number of warships, had shielded the city against invasion by water. As recounted by Southerner Robert Stiles, a prewar law student who commanded a battalion stationed on the river's left bank: "The orders were, in general, that the men of the fleet and of the James River defenses should leave the river about midnight of the 2nd of April, exploding magazines and ironclads, and join the Army of Northern Virginia in its retreat. Orders such as these were enough to try the mettle even of the best troops in the highest condition, but for my poor little battalion [restricted for a long period to garrison duty, its rations of poor quality] they were overwhelming, well-nigh stupefying. . . .

"The explosions began just as we got across the river. When the magazines at Chaffin's and Drewry's Bluffs went off, the solid earth shuddered convulsively; but as the ironclads—one after another—exploded, it seemed as if the very dome of heaven would be shattered down upon us. Earth and air and the black sky glared in the lurid light. Columns and towers and pinnacles of flame shot upward to an amazing height, from which, on all sides, the ignited shells flew on arcs of fire and burst as if bombarding heaven. I . . . [was certain] that after this I could never more be startled—no, not by the catastrophes of the last great day.

"I walked in rear of the battalion to prevent straggling, and as the successive flashes illumed the darkness the blanched faces and staring eyes turned backward upon me spoke volumes of nervous demoralization. I felt that a hare might shatter the column."

10

Richmond Falls to the Yankees

I n Richmond, the sounds and sights of the cataclysm compounded a consternation already great. The trials of the night had begun when the civil authorities, backed by thin squads of militiamen, moved to destroy the city's supply of alcoholic beverages. "The work," says Pollard, "commenced under the direction of committees of citizens in all the wards. Hundreds of barrels of liquor were rolled into the street, and the heads knocked in. The gutters ran with a liquor freshet, and the fumes filled and impregnated the air. Fine cases of bottled liquors were tossed into the street from third-story windows and wrecked into a thousand pieces. As the work progressed, some straggling soldiers, retreating through the city, managed to get hold of a quantity of the liquor. From that moment, law and order ceased to exist. Many of the stores were pillaged; and the sidewalks were encumbered with broken glass where the thieves had smashed the windows in their reckless haste to lay hands on the plunder within. The air was filled with wild cries of distress or the yells of roving plunderers."

As added by Sallie Putnam: "In the alarm and terror, the guards of the State Penitentiary fled from their posts, and numbers of the lawless and desperate villains incarcerated there, for crimes of every grade and hue, after setting fire to the workshops, made good the opportunity for escape; and, donning garments stolen wherever they could get them, in exchange for their prison livery, roamed over the city like fierce, ferocious beasts. . . .

"While these fearful scenes were being enacted on the streets, indoors there was scarcely less excitement and confusion. Into every house terror penetrated. Ladies were busily engaged in collecting and secreting all the valuables possessed by them, together with cherished correspondence, yet they found time and presence of mind to prepare a few comforts for friends forced to depart with the army or the government. . . .

"[Out of doors] a still more terrible element was destined to appear and add to the horrors of the scene. From some authority—it seems uncertain what—an order had been issued to fire the four principal tobacco warehouses. They were so situated as to jeopardize the entire commercial portion of Richmond. At a late hour of the night, Mayor Mayo had dispatched, by a committee of citizens, a remonstrance against this reckless military order. But in the mad excitement of the moment the protest was unheeded. The torch was applied, and the helpless citizens were left to witness the destruction of their property. . . .

"As the sun rose on Richmond, such a spectacle was presented as can never be forgotten by those who witnessed it. . . . The fire was progressing with fearful rapidity. The roaring, the hissing, and the crackling of the flames were heard above the shouting and confusion of the immense crowd of plunderers who were moving amid the dense smoke like demons, pushing, rioting, and swaying with their burdens to make a passage to the open air. From the lower portion of the city, near the river, dense black clouds of smoke arose as a pall of crape to hide the ravages of the devouring flames, which lifted their red tongues and leaped from building to building as if possessed of demoniac instinct and intent upon wholesale destruction. . . .

"The most remarkable scenes, however, . . . occurred at the commissary depot. Hundreds of Government wagons were loaded with bacon, flour, and whiskey, and driven off in hot haste to join the retreating army. In a dense throng around the depot stood hundreds of men, women, and children, black and white, provided with anything in which they could carry away provisions, awaiting the opening of the doors to rush in and help themselves. . . . About sunrise the doors were thrown open to the populace, and with a rush that seemed almost sufficient to bear off the building itself, they soon swept away all that remained of the Confederate commissariat of Richmond.

"By this time the flames had been applied to or had reached the arsenal, in which several hundred carloads of loaded shells were left. At every moment the most terrific explosions were sending forth their awful reverberations. . . ."

"One shock," says the apartment-dweller, Virginia Dade, "was so violent that we thought the house had been struck, for the window shades were knocked from their fastenings and fell to the floor with a terrible crash, and poor Fannie [the sick sister], with the supernatural strength of terror, sprang from her bed and fell prostrate and fainting many feet from it; and the still-burning fuse from a shell was picked up in the yard."

The last of the Confederate troops east of Richmond and the James River had fallen back, and the earthworks were in possession of Union General Weitzel's forces, who now began their march toward the city in two columns, approaching it from the southeast. In charge of the leading troops on the right was a captain from New England, George A. Bruce, who relates: "It was a refreshing march in the pleasant hours of a delightful morning. The green fields on either side furnished a pleasing contrast to the district about our encampments, pulverized as it was into dust by the constant passage of our innumerable trains. The road was dotted here and there with comfortable farmhouses, which were generally closed, with no evidence of life about them—not even a dog to protest against our pollution of the sacred soil.

"Stragglers [from the Confederate army] in considerable numbers ... were gathered in, some on their way to meet us, while others quietly waited for our approach by the sides of the road. The first one I met saluted me with the financial question, 'What are you paying now when deserters bring in their arms and equipments?'—and then added, as if for the purpose of getting a favorable reply, 'I guess the Confederacy is about played out at last.'

"As the roads [east of the James] on which the divisions were marching gradually converge until they meet about two miles [south of] the capital, when about four miles out ... I ... passed over from the New Market Road to the Osborne Pike. From there I saw that [the other] division was marching rapidly by the flank about a mile and a half in our rear."

General Weitzel and his staff were following the two columns and keeping an eye on their progress. As recalled by one of Weitzel's aides, Thomas Thatcher Graves: "We saw in the distance [units] of our troops, many of them upon the double-quick, aiming to be the first in the city. A white and a colored [unit] were having a regular race, the white troops on the turnpike and the colored in the fields."

Returning to George Bruce: "On a hill just by the line of inner defenses we gained our first sight of Richmond—a sight that none will ever forget. The city was wrapped in a cloud of densest smoke, through which great tongues of flame leaped in madness to the skies. A few houses on the higher hills, a spire here and there half smothered in smoke, and the hospitals to the east were the only buildings that could be seen. Added to the wild tumult of the flames, ten thousand shells bursting every minute in the Confederate arsenals and laboratories were making an uproar such as might arise from the field when the world's artillery joins in battle. But just on the verge of this maelstrom of smoke and fire, cattle were grazing undisturbed on the opposite hillside, and I saw a farmer ploughing in a field while cinders from the burning capital were falling at his feet.

"A little beyond the junction of the New Market Road and the Osborne Pike . . . Joseph Mayo, the Mayor of Richmond, . . . appeared in an open barouche for the purpose of surrendering the city. With him came his brother, who, in a state of extreme excitement and alarm, told me that Richmond was in control of a mob and would soon be totally destroyed by fire which no one was attempting to control. In his opinion everybody would be arrested [by the Federal troops] and their property confiscated. He expressed surprise when I assured him that no one conducting himself properly would be disturbed or deprived of his property."

This interview took place just south of Rocketts Landing, where the James, which flows in from the west, makes its turn southward. Even while Captain Bruce and the mayor's brother were talking, a rearguard detachment of Confederate cavalry was moving northward through Rocketts preparing to swing westward into Richmond and then southward over a James River bridge into Manchester. In the words of a trooper from South Carolina, Major Edward M. Boykin: "Fearing our retreat would be cut off . . . we pushed on rapidly. . . . The peculiar population of that suburb were gathered on the sidewalk; bold, dirty looking women who had evidently not been improved by four years' military association; dirtier, if possible, looking children; and, here and there, skulking, scoundrelly looking men, who, in the general ruin, were sneaking from the holes they had been hiding in. . . .

"One strapping virago stood on the edge of the pavement with her arms akimbo, looking at us with intense scorn as we swept along. I could have touched her with the toe of my boot as I rode by her, closing the rear of the column. She caught my eye. 'Yes,' said she, with all of Tipperary in her brogue, 'afther fighting them for four years ye're running like dawgs!' The woman was either drunk or very much in earnest, for I give her credit for feeling all she said; and her son or husband had to do his own fighting, I will answer for it, wherever he was, or get no kiss or comfort from her. But I could not stop to explain that General Longstreet's particular orders were not to make a fight in the city if it could be avoided, so I left her to the enjoyment of her own notions, unfavorable as they evidently were to us.

"On we went. . . . It was after seven o'clock, the sun having been up for some time. After getting into Main Street [in Richmond] . . . we met the motley crowd thronging the pavement, loaded with every species of plunder. Bareheaded women, their arms filled with every description of goods plundered from warehouses and shops, their hair hanging about their ears, were rushing one way to deposit their plunder and return for more, while a current of the empty-handed surged in a contrary direction towards the scene.

"The roaring and crackling of the burning houses, the trampling and snorting of our horses over the paved streets as we swept along, wild sounds of every description, while the rising sun came dimly through the cloud of smoke that hung like a pall around, made up a scene that beggars description, and which I hope never to see again—the saddest of many of the sad sights of war—a city undergoing pillage at the hands of its own mob, while the standards of an empire were being taken from its capitol, and the tramp of a victorious enemy could be heard at its gates.

"Richmond had collected within its walls the refuse of the war—thieves and deserters, male and female; the vilest of the vile were there; but strict military discipline had kept it down. Now, in one moment, it was all removed—all restraint was taken off—and you may imagine the consequences. There were said to be 5,000 [military] deserters in the city, and you could see the gray jackets here and there sprinkled in the mob that was roaring down the street.

"When we reached somewhere between Twentieth and Twenty-fifth streets—I will not be certain—the flames swept across Main Street so we could not pass. The column turned to the right, and so got into the street above it. On this, Franklin Street, are many private residences. At the windows we could see the sad and tearful faces of . . . Virginia women. . . . And it was a sad thought to every man that was there that day that we seemed . . . to be leaving them to the mercy of the enemy. But their own General Lee was gone before, and we were but as the last wave of the receding tide.

"After getting round the burning square we turned back towards the river. The portion of Mayo's, or, rather, the lesser bridge that crossed the canal, had taken fire from the large flouring mill near it, and was burning, but not the main bridge; so we followed the cross street below the main approach to the bridge, at the foot of which was a bridge across the canal, forcing our horses through the crowd of pillagers gathered at this point, greater than at any other. They had broken into some government stores. A low white man—he seemed a foreigner—was about to strike a woman [in an argument] over a barrel of flour under my horse's nose, when a stout Negro took her part and threatened to throw him into the canal.

"We were the rear regiment at this time. . . . In another moment we moved on, the crowd closed in, and we saw no more. . . . At last we were on the main bridge, along which were scattered faggots. . . . Twenty men . . . were left . . . to burn the bridge, while the rest went slowly up the hill [in Manchester, on the south side of the river]."

It was about this time that Richmond diarist Judith McGuire, appalled by what was happening, began to wonder whether it might yet be possible for her to leave the city by train. "I set off to go to the central depot to see if the cars would go out. As I went from Franklin to Broad Street, and on Broad, the pavements were covered with broken glass. Women, both white and colored, were walking in multitudes from the commissary offices and burning stores with bags of flour, meal, coffee, sugar, rolls of cotton cloth, etc. Colored men were rolling wheelbarrows filled in the same way. I went on and on towards the depot, and, as I proceeded, shouts and screams became louder. The rabble rushed by me in one stream.

"At last I exclaimed, 'Who are those shouting? What is the matter?' I seemed to be answered by a hundred voices, 'The Yankees have come!' I turned to come home, but what was my horror, when I reached Ninth Street, to see a regiment of Yankee cavalry come dashing up, yelling, shouting, hallooing, screaming! All Bedlam let loose could not have vied with them in diabolical roarings. I stood riveted to the spot; I could not move nor speak. Then I saw the iron gates of our time-honored and beautiful Capitol Square, on the walks and greensward of which no hoof had been allowed to tread, thrown open and the cavalry dash in. I could see no more; I must go on with a mighty effort, or faint where I stood."

Union banners were soon flying over the smoke-shrouded capitol, and the first infantry entered the city. Captain George Bruce relates: "From the colored population of Richmond we received such a recep-

Federal troops entering Richmond

tion as could only come from a people who were returning thanks for
the deliverance of their race. There was something peculiarly affecting
in the exhibition of feeling manifested by these unlettered children of
Africa which communicated itself to all. . . . General [Charles] Devens,
by whose side I was riding, [turned] to me, his eyes filled with tears and
voice stifled with emotion, and [said], 'This is a great sight for us to
behold—the deliverance of a race.'

"As soon as the column . . . turned into Main Street all the bands
were brought to the front; and then, with all the regularity of a parade,
colors flying and every musician doing his best at 'Yankee Doodle,'
followed by 'Rally Round the Flag,' with its refrain, 'Down with the
traitor and up with the stars,' and the 'Battle Cry of Freedom,' marched
through various streets to Capitol Square . . . where the brigade was
brought to the front and there stacked their arms. Sweeter music never
reached the human ear than the rattling of those Union muskets as they
dropped upon the pavements of Richmond."

Next, according to Sallie Putnam, "the strains of an old familiar tune
floated upon the air—a tune that, in days gone by, was wont to awaken
a thrill of patriotism. But now only the most bitter and crushing recollections awoke within us, as upon our quickened hearing fell the strains
of 'The Star Spangled Banner.' For us it was a requiem for buried
hopes."

Additional troops soon entered the city. A citizen known only as
"Nathalie" gives this picture: "Stretching from the Exchange Hotel to
the slopes of Church Hill, down the hill, through the valley, up the
ascent to the hotel, was the array, with its unbroken line of blue, fringed
with bright bayonets. Strains of martial music, flushed countenances,
waving swords, betokened the victorious army. As the line turned at the
Exchange Hotel into the upper street, the movement was the signal for
a wild burst of cheers from each regiment. Shouts from a few Negroes
were the only responses. Through throngs of sullen spectators; along
the line of fire; in the midst of the horrors of a conflagration, increased
by the explosion of shells left by the retreating army; through curtains
of smoke; through the vast aerial auditorium convulsed with the commotion of frightful sounds, moved the garish procession of the grand
army, with brave music and bright banners and wild cheers. A regiment
of Negro cavalry swept by the hotel. As they turned the street corner,
they drew their sabers with savage shouts, and the blood mounted even
in my woman's heart with quick throbs of defiance."

11

Of Spreading Flames and Tumult

It was now midmorning, and, according to Union Captain George Bruce, Richmond's Capitol Square "was a scene of indescribable confusion. The inhabitants fleeing from their burning houses—men, women, and children, white and black—had collected there for a place of safety, bringing with them whatever was saved from the flames. . . . As if in anticipation of the destruction of the whole city, the sick and infirm had been hurried from the houses, and, attended by a few friends, were lying on their extemporized beds in the more secluded parts of the yard.

"The wind, increasing with the conflagration, was blowing like a hurricane, hurling cinders and pieces of burning wood with long trails of flame over the houses to distant quarters of the city. The heated air, dim with smoke and filled with the innumerable particles that float from the surface of so great a fire, rendered it almost impossible to breathe. At every gust the crowd turned to escape its fury as men turned to escape the blast of a driving snowstorm. Rising among the trees in the center of the Square, amid this carnival of ruin, stood the great statue of Washington, against which firebrands thumped and rattled, little respecting the majestic form of the Father of His Country.

"The citizens were entirely helpless. . . . The better part of the community were paralyzed at the magnitude of their calamity. There was no one to take charge of the few fire-engines in working order, and the flames at their own wild will leaped on from house to house in triumphant glee. Men living in places of no immediate danger remained at home to protect their own property from being burned from

Richmond citizens during conflagration

cinders that were falling upon every part of the town. Those who were already homeless looked on in utter dismay. . . .

"General Weitzel remained constantly on duty at the State House. General [George F.] Shepley was appointed military governor and General Devens assigned to the command of the city troops. The execution of all orders, and a thousand details in restoring order and providing for the peace and safety of the city fell upon General [Edward H.] Ripley. . . .

"All of these experienced officers at once applied themselves to their important duties. The few fire-engines in order were sought out and placed in the hands of our boys in blue, who worked as earnestly to save the city of Richmond from destruction as if performing a like duty for their native towns. A police was organized, and within an hour every street was under the protection of a Union sentinel. The printing presses were brought into action, and by noon circulars had been prepared and distributed announcing the rules deemed necessary for the temporary government of the inhabitants. Not a soldier was allowed to come within the city limits except those detailed for its special protection. The men seemed to understand that they were called upon to uphold the name of the American soldier in a new sphere of duty, and right nobly did they perform it."

Many of Richmond's male residents were pressed into service against the fire. A sidelight to this measure is given by Union staff officer Thomas Thatcher Graves: "As one of our aides was riding through the streets, engaged in gathering together the ablebodied men . . . he was hailed by a servant in front of a house, toward which the fire seemed to be moving. The servant told him that his mistress wished to speak to him. He dismounted and entered the house, and was met by a lady who stated that her mother was an invalid, confined to her bed, and, as the fire seemed to be approaching, she asked for assistance. The subsequent conversation developed the fact that the invalid [a victim of arthritis] was no other than the wife of General R. E. Lee, and the lady who addressed the aide was her daughter, Miss Lee. An ambulance was furnished . . . and a corporal and two men guarded them until all danger was past."

Obtaining special protection was more difficult for some of the other residents who wanted it. "Only ladies," says Judith McGuire, "were allowed to apply for guards. Of course, this was a very unpleasant duty, but I must undertake it. Mrs. D. agreed to accompany me, and we proceeded to the City Hall—the City Hall which from my childhood I

Mrs. Robert E. Lee

had regarded with respect and reverence as the place where my father had for years held his courts, and in which our lawyers, whose names stand among the highest in the Temple of Fame, for fifty years expounded the Constitution and the laws, which must now be trodden under foot.

"We reached it. After passing through crowds of Negro soldiers there, we found on the steps some of the elderly gentlemen of the city seeking admittance, which was denied them. I stopped to speak to Mr. ———, in whose commission house I was two days ago and saw him surrounded by all the [goods] which usually make up the establishment of such a merchant; it was now a mass of blackened [and still burning] ruins. He had come to ask protection for his residence, but was not allowed to enter.

"We passed the sentinel, and an officer escorted us to the room in which we were to ask our country's foe to allow us to remain undisturbed in our own houses. Mrs. D. leant on me tremblingly; she shrank from the humiliating duty. For my own part, though my heart beat loudly and my blood boiled, I never felt more high-spirited or lofty than at that moment. A large table was surrounded by officials, writing or talking to the ladies, who came on the same mission that brought us. I approached the officer who sat at the head of the table and asked him politely if he was the Provost Marshal. 'I am the Commandant, madam,' was the respectful reply. 'Then to whom am I to apply for protection for our residence?' 'You need none, madam; our troops are perfectly disciplined, and dare not enter your premises.' 'I am sorry to be obliged to undeceive you, sir, but when I left home seven of your soldiers were in the yard of the residence opposite to us, and one has already been into our kitchen.' He looked surprised, and said, 'Then, madam, you are entitled to a guard. Captain, write a protection for the residence on the corner of First and Franklin Streets, and give these ladies a guard.'

"This was quickly done, and as I turned to go out I saw standing near me our old friend, Mrs. ———. Oh! How my heart sank when I looked into her calm, sad face and remembered that she and her venerable and highly esteemed husband must ask leave to remain in peace in their home of many years. The next person who attracted my attention was that sweet young girl, S. W. Having no mother, she of course must go and ask that her father's beautiful mansion may be allowed to stand uninjured. Tears rolled down her cheeks as she pressed my hand in passing. Other friends were there. We did not speak; we could not; we sadly looked at each other and passed on. Mrs. D. and myself came out, accompanied by our guard.

"The fire was progressing rapidly, and the crashing sound of falling timbers was distinctly heard. Dr. Reed's church was blazing. Yankees, citizens, and Negroes were attempting to arrest the flames. The War Department was falling in; burning papers were being wafted about the streets. The Commissary Department, with our desks and papers, was consumed already. Warwick & Barksdale's Mill was sending its flames to the sky. Cary and Main Streets seemed doomed throughout; Bank Street was beginning to burn, and now it had reached Franklin. At any other moment it would have distracted me, but I had ceased to feel anything. . . . Our guard . . . [was] posted. . . ."

Among the Union newsmen who covered the occupation of Richmond was the Boston *Journal*'s Charles Carleton Coffin. "I entered the city in the afternoon. I tried to pass through Main Street, but on both sides the fire was roaring and walls were tumbling. I turned into a side street, rode up to the Capitol and then to the Spottswood Hotel. . . . On the three sides of the hotel the fire had been raging, but was now subdued, and there was a fair prospect that it would be saved. 'Can you accommodate me with a room?' 'I reckon we can, sir, but like enough you will be burnt out before morning. You can have any room you choose. Nobody here.'

"I registered my name on a page which bore the names of a score of Rebel officers who had left in the morning, and took a room on the first floor, from which I could easily spring to the ground in case the hotel should be again endangered by the fire. Throwing up the sash, I looked out upon the scene. There were swaying chimneys, tottering walls, streets impassable from piles of brick, stones, and rubbish. Capitol Square was filled with furniture, beds, clothing, crockery, chairs, tables, looking-glasses. Women were weeping, children crying. Men stood speechless, haggard, woebegone, gazing at the desolation. . . .

"Soldiers from General Devens's command were on the roof of the Capitol, Governor's house, and other buildings, ready to extinguish [encroaching] flames. The Capitol several times caught fire from cinders. 'If it had not been for the soldiers, the whole city would have gone,' said a citizen. The colored soldiers in Capitol Square were dividing their rations with the houseless women and children, giving them hot coffee sweetened with sugar—such as they had not tasted for many months. . . . Women had bags of flour in their arms, baskets of salt and pails of molasses, or sides of bacon. No miser ever gloated over his gold so eagerly as they over their [gifts] of provisions."

Until this time Virginia Dade had remained in her apartment rooms with her sick sister Fannie, her married sister Mrs. Carter (who had been brought to the apartment from her own home the previous day), and a number of children. "We had numerous alarms from the falling of cinders or burning brands upon our house, which did actually take fire three times, and it was with the utmost difficulty extinguished by the little water that women and children would carry up in pails from the hydrant in the yard to the skylight in the roof.

"Little Eddie Mills quite distinguished himself by the heroism with which he kept his place on the roof with the burning coals falling all around him, for we had stationed him there with a broom [and water] to keep wet the blankets spread over the shingle roof; and nobly did this young 'Casabianca' stand to his post . . . for he was, he well knew, the eldest male in a household of twenty-five persons, and, seeming to feel his responsibility, he gallantly refused to be relieved by the various ladies who offered to take his broom from him.

"But there was a spice of the ludicrous, too, even amid these awful scenes. The fire at one time seemed rapidly approaching the block where my sister, Mrs. Carter, lived, and where her storeroom was pretty well filled for war times with provisions which her husband had collected for their sustenance when he should be absent in the field and his delicate wife and little ones have no one to provide for them. . . . We determined to remove [the stores], if possible, to our own apartments, and Mrs. Carter not being able to bear the fatigue, I undertook to transfer them.

"Mustering all the force I could, which consisted of five little children, two whites and three blacks ranging in age from six to ten years, the larger ones being busy toting water to the roof, and encouraging them by the promise of a lump of sugar to each, a rare luxury in those days, off we started on our foraging expedition. The lurid glare of the flames in the burning district, with the masses of smoke-clouds swelling and rolling over our heads . . . and the novel and remarkable aspect of my little squad of foragers as we trudged timidly but resolutely on, presented a scene worthy of a better pen than mine.

"On our route we saw sights to make a toper's heart ache, for in the gutters in several places flowed streams of wines, whiskeys, and brandies, the hoardings of loving mothers and other provident women for the use of the soldier boys who might be brought home sick or wounded. These were now poured out into the streets for fear they might fall into the hands of plunderers. . . . One bottle, however, I rescued for the use of my sick sister. . . .

"On reaching with my little band my sister's deserted house I found the walls already hot to the touch from the close proximity of the fire; and haste was imperative, so, seizing two hams I placed one upon the shoulder of each of my two youngest assistants, then spread a tablecloth upon the floor, into which I threw, pell-mell, tea, coffee, sugar, spices, dried apples, black-eyed peas, infants' clothing, shoes, etc., etc. . . . This I tied together by the four corners and put on the head of number three.

"Dipping into barrels, I filled a pillow case . . . [with] equal parts of cornmeal and flour. This I handed, with a jug of molasses, to number four. Taking a sheet, I filled it with bed and table linen and clothing of all descriptions. This huge bundle I threw on my own back and held it with one hand, while with the other I helped number five to drag along a tin can about three feet high and one in diameter, which contained a few pounds of lard, to which I had added a ham or two, several bars of soap, etc., etc.

"Thus loaded, the procession issued forth. Though fully impressed with the awfulness of the occasion and the solemnity of the fact that I was making a desperate effort to ward off threatening famine, my pack almost rolled off my shoulders in my convulsions of laughter at our ridiculous appearance. . . . I fancied what Colonel ————, Captain ————, and others with whom I had so recently promenaded and flirted, and who had always seemed to imagine that I was not strong enough to bring my own prayer-book home from church, would think could they see me now. But my mirth was soon checked by the thought that they were at that moment going through sterner scenes and harder trials with our vanquished chieftain.

"Fancy my chagrin and distress when, on reaching home and triumphantly opening my bundles to display my dearly won treasures, I found the tea, coffee, sugar, and spices intermingled in sad confusion, while the meal and flour were well shaken up together, and the bars of turpentine soap had slipped down to the very bottom of the lard can!"

At about three o'clock in the afternoon, Judith McGuire, the resident who had been granted a special guard by the Yankees at City Hall, found her security shaken anew. "The guard was drunk and [was] threatening to shoot the servants in the yard. Again I went to the City Hall to procure another. I approached the Commandant and told him why I came. He immediately ordered another guard and a corporal to be sent for the arrest of the drunken man. The flames had decreased, but the business part of the city was in ruins. The second guard was soon posted, and the first carried off by the collar."

By late evening the fire was under control. Confederate journalist Edward Pollard explains that "it had consumed the most important part of Richmond. . . . The pencil of the surveyor could not have more distinctly marked out the business portion of the city. The evening breezes had turned the course of the fire; and, as these still continued, heavy mist-clouds hung upon the horizon or streamed upwards on the varying current of the winds.

"As night came on, there was a painful reaction after the day's terrible excitement. A strange quiet fell upon the blackened city and its scenes of destruction. It was the quiet of a great desolation. Groups of women and children crawled under shelters of broken furniture in the Capitol Square. Hundreds of homeless persons lay down to sleep in the shadows of the ruins of Richmond; and, worn out by excitement, exhausted as by the spasm of a great battle, men watched for the morrow with the dull sense that the work of years had been ruined, and that all they possessed on earth had been swept away."

Pollard goes on to provide some information that he learned second hand: "While Richmond was filled with horror and destruction, and the smoke of its torment ascended to the skies, very different scenes were taking place far away in the cities of the North. It was a strange reverse to the picture we have been contemplating. With those fervors and shows characteristic of the Northern mind, Washington and New York were celebrating the downfall of the Confederate capital. Bells were rung; wild and enthusiastic congratulations ran along the street; and vast crowds collected, whose fantastic exhibitions of joy, not content with huzzas, cheers, and dancing in the streets, broke out into a blasphemous singing of hymns of the church. In New York, twenty thousand persons in the open air sung the doxology.

"There was, of course, an unlimited display of flags; and, as evidence of this characteristic exhibition, it is said that half an hour after the news of the fall of Richmond was known, not a single large flag in the whole city of New York was left unpurchased. These symbols of loyalty not only floated over houses, but were fastened to carts, stages, and wagons.

"The newspapers were mostly occupied with spread-eagles and maps of Richmond. The *World* expressed the opinion that the event of the day 'more fully justified exuberant rejoicing than any previous achievement in the history of the war.' The New York *Herald*—the organ par excellence of Yankee wind—went further, and declared that the taking of Richmond was 'one of the *grandest triumphs that had crowned human efforts for centuries.*' "

News of Richmond's fall reaches the North

Night in the captured city was a time of wonder for Union Captain George Bruce. "The streets were unlighted, silent, and deserted. Above, the stars shone out bright in the bending blue. Hour after hour I walked alone through the streets of that proud but conquered capital, past the luxurious abodes of wealth then knowing the first pangs of hunger, past doors where had proudly entered, and as proudly departed, great military heroes, the tread of whose armies had made the continent to tremble and filled the world with their fame; past homes but yesterday tenanted by the rulers of an empire, now fleeing to escape the threatened punishment of their acts; through narrow lanes and filthy alleys where dwelt the [common people], upon whose humble roofs the calamities of the war had fallen with a double stroke, consigning fathers and sons, with all the savagery of an unpitying fate, to their untimely graves, bringing at last to those desolated hearthstones the horrors of a famine which had blanched the cheek and thinned the blood of wife and child till the coming of [our] hated army was looked upon as their only hope of deliverance—while over all alike, palace, hall, and hut, I could seem to feel the shadow of a great sorrow resting, darker than the shadows of the night. . . .

"From the governor's mansion, which General Devens had taken as his headquarters, one looked over the wide expanse of ruin. The whole valley stretching west of Franklin Street to the river . . . seemed like a lake of liquid flame agitated by a gentle wind. The spectral walls, edged here and there with tufts of flame flickering in the breeze, were all that remained of the great shops and warehouses that once adorned the beautiful city that sits at the headwaters of the James.

"There were many sad hearts, no doubt, about us; and some happy ones, too, for the silken folds of the Union banner were floating once more above Virginia's capital, and Richmond was sleeping securely, if sleep it could, under that protecting power."

12

Lincoln Visits Petersburg

Events at Petersburg on that Monday, April 3, were considerably less dramatic than those at Richmond, but were not without interest or significance. These events, too, began long before dawn. Observers in the Union lines semicircling the city were apprised of the Confederate evacuation by the sight of large fires and the sound of explosions, and at 2:30 A.M. it was learned by scouts that the defenses were empty except for a few pickets. It was Grant's 9th Corps, commanded by General John G. Parke, that was in position to capture Petersburg, and Colonel Ralph Ely's 2nd Brigade, 1st Division, occupied the most advanced encampment.

Ely relates: "I ordered Brevet Major [Clement A.] Lounsberry, assistant adjutant-general, to awaken the command immediately and order the 1st Michigan Sharpshooters and 2nd Michigan to report to him on the picket line for further orders. I instructed the major to form the two regiments as quickly as possible, to throw out scouts and a heavy skirmish line and occupy the main rebel works if possible. I directed that so soon as the balance of the brigade reached the abatis after the occupation of the main works the advance should move rapidly, but cautiously, forward, and plant a color upon some public building in the city.

"At 3:10 A.M., all being in readiness, the advance moved rapidly forward and occupied the main works of the enemy, when the boys gave three hearty cheers, reformed their lines, partially broken by the obstacles they had passed, and pressed forward. The advance pushed forward [toward the city] as rapidly as was possible under the circumstances, as it was necessary to keep scouts well out in front and on the flanks. . . .

"At 4:25 A.M. Major Lounsberry was met in front of the courthouse by three citizens bearing a flag of truce and a communication from the mayor and common council tendering the surrender of the town, and requesting that persons and private property be respected. But the gallant major could listen to no proposition until the 'old flag' was floating from the highest point of the courthouse steeple and proper pickets had been established in the vicinity, and patrols sent out to pick up stragglers, about 500 of whom we captured, many of them with arms; also 7 flags or colors. The major then assured the gentlemen that we came in the name of liberty and in the defense of the right, and that they need have no fear, for all would be well with them so long as they remained at home and conducted themselves properly."

Back in the Union positions outside Petersburg, additional units had been ordered to move in. With them was Charles A. Page, special correspondent of the New York *Tribune.* "As the writer rode through our lines toward the city at daybreak, the troops were all astir; knapsacks were being slung, blankets rolled, and every preparation made for an immediate advance. Portions of our troops had . . . occupied the town two hours before, but the majority were denied the enviable pleasure of breakfasting in the 'Cockade City.' A general fusillade [of blank cannon fire] was sounding along our whole line, and, as if it were impossible to indulge sufficiently in other noisy demonstrations, muskets were emptied of their charges to add to the universal din. Bands were playing 'Hail Columbia,' 'Yankee Doodle,' 'Kingdom Comin','' 'We'll All Drink Stone Blind,' 'Lanigan's Ball,' polkas, waltzes—in fact almost everything of a patriotic or an enlivening character.

"It seemed as if Orpheus himself had gone mad and was trying to render from all his creations of lighter music a grand, triumphant, and heaven-swelling chorus in honor of the occasion. Amid this torrent of mellifluous sounds arose from one of the bands that grand old refrain, 'Praise God from whom all blessings flow; praise Him ye people here below,' indicating that some, at least, believed it but just and proper to blend thanksgiving with the general jubilation. And thus did the noble old Army of the Potomac, and its brethren from above the James [elements of Ord's army] celebrate the victory won by their long years of persevering toil.

"But few evidences were discovered, on entering the town, of great destruction of life on the Rebel side. They had removed their dead and

Union wagon train in Petersburg

wounded. . . . Along the Boydton Road leading to Petersburg I noticed but one poor fellow . . . sacrificed to the devilish ambition of his implacable masters, Davis and Lee. He was dead; but the dark, swarthy countenance almost led one to believe, until he touched his cold and pulseless hand, that life still lingered in his emaciated, half-clad body. He lay in a ditch or gully along the highway, with the water from a pure, perennial spring above trickling musically beneath him; his blanket was neatly rolled and slung across his shoulder; his head was resting upon his arm as if in repose, but the death-glaze upon his eyes told that he slept the sleep which knows no waking. A hideous orifice in the side of the head, surrounded by clotted gore, showed where a fragment of shell had [entered]. . . .

"The city presented the appearance usually noticeable in every Rebel town falling into our possession. Doors were closed and window-blinds shut; but, if I mistake not, I saw many a curious eye intently peering into the street. True, the number of contrabands [black people] of all ages and sizes congregated on street corners was legion, and of ancient and crippled whites not a few; but the fairer sex kept close within doors, disdaining to exhibit their peerless charms to our men in blue. Well, the Union boys took it philosophically enough, seeming to care but little for Confederate calico or linsey, and went marching along as if only intent on the capture or dispersion of Lee's defeated army.

"Stopping at the Jarratt House on Washington Street, we requested breakfast for our party, and were referred by the guard to a colored native, who seemed to be, from his deportment, both proprietor and chief steward of the establishment. After considerable hesitation, and being fully assured that we intended to remunerate him liberally for the entertainment, he set to work and soon produced a repast consisting only of bread of a tenacious tendency and scraps of bacon of a toughness and elasticity which defied the persistent attempts of cuspids and molars to accomplish its necessary mastication.

"Having Confederate notes about us, we decided to test the mercenary African's confidence in Rebel currency, and offered him in payment for our breakfast a handful or two of the article. Viewing it for an instant, he placed his hands in his pockets and, looking at us in astonishment, ejaculated, 'Lord bress ye, massas, I got heaps o' dat ar' stuff, more as a mule can tote. Hasn't ye got any Yankee money?' 'But see here, John,' we replied, 'here is over five hundred dollars for our breakfast; that surely ought to pay you!' 'I know it's a heap o' money, but I don't want it, massas. You alls is welcome to your breakfast if dat's all de money you's got.' We finally astonished his optics with a V of the 'Union persuasion,' and he was appeased.

"Thinking a little genuine Confederate applejack necessary to our temporal well-being, we requested him to produce the article. With a decided shake of the head he informed us that it would be utterly impossible to comply with our request. 'De Rebs took eberyting wid 'em; we's got nuffin.' 'But,' replied we, 'we have greenbacks to pay you for it.' 'Well, now you alls just go in dar,' pointing to an anteroom, said he, his face again brightening, 'and I'll see what I can do.' We did 'go in dar,' and were soon favored with the genuine Virginia stimulant known as applejack or apple whiskey.

"Previous to leaving the Jarratt House, a rather ludicrous incident took place. . . . Happening in the large stable of the hotel, and naturally inquisitive under the circumstances, we were peering into the different apartments contingent. One door, although not locked, seemed to resist our first efforts to open it, and, redoubling our exertions, it finally swung back, revealing to our gaze a genuine grayback [a Confederate soldier], sitting on the floor, his blanket around him, hatless, and with his hair unkempt, projecting in every direction. His blanched face, on seeing several citizens, showed that he was either very ill or excessively frightened; and, on asking him why he was there, he faintly replied that he was very ill. . . .

" 'But why didn't the Johnnies take you with them in an ambulance or place you in a hospital before they evacuated?' one of us inquired. Springing to his feet, his face radiant with joy and relief, he confessed himself a Rebel deserter; stated that he was perfectly well; that he had on the previous night secreted himself there, and that he had been afraid to venture out for fear the Rebel rear-guard had not yet left the town; and that when he saw us he was uncertain whether we were Yankees or Confederates. He stated that he desired to take the oath, and requested us to take him to the house of a friend before delivering him over to the provost marshal, which we did.

"The eastern portion of the town exhibits on every side marks of the solid shot and shell thrown by our guns during last summer. The buildings on Bolingbroke Street, which run nearly east and west, are literally perforated in every part. Chimneys have been razeed [cut off at the top] on every building, windows knocked and splintered to pieces, brick walls crumbled and torn, porches carried away. Ruin and desolation reign supreme.

"Petersburg was undoubtedly before the war one of the very neatest of Virginia towns, and even now is attractive in appearance. Market Street contains, perhaps, the finest residences, while Sycamore can boast of stores and warehouses which would certainly not disgrace a Northern city."

General Grant and his staff rode into Petersburg at about 9 A.M. and set up a temporary headquarters on the piazza of an abandoned house. The general's purpose in tarrying in the city while his army marched westward was to meet there with President Lincoln, who had remained with Admiral David Porter's fleet on the James River. The admiral relates: "Mr. Lincoln received a message from General Grant informing him that a railway car would be ready for him at City Point, that he could come out on the railroad which ran within a few miles of Petersburg, and that he would find horses at the nearest point to take him to the city. In consequence, we prepared to start at the appointed time. The President got into the car of which I was the only other occupant, seated himself, and, as he never lost any time, proceeded to read his newspapers. . . .

"I wore a naval cap which had been copied from those worn by railroad conductors, and a blue flannel short sack with four small navy buttons on it. I might easily have been mistaken for a conductor. I was standing on the front [platform] of the car, having locked the rear door to prevent anyone from intruding upon the President. We expected the locomotive [which was to draw the car] every minute. Three men came up to the car. They were nicely enough dressed—had even white cravats, which would seem to indicate that they were either divines or theological students, but I could tell at a glance that they were neither of these; they had not a clerical look aside from their neckwear, and, to save my life, I could not have placed them. They were impudent enough to be anything.

"One of them spoke. 'Conductor,' he said to me, 'is that the President?' 'Yes,' I answered, 'it is.' 'We want to see him,' said the other. 'Can't do it,' I replied. 'Who will prevent us,' said the first. 'I will; the President won't see anyone.' 'He will see us,' was the retort, 'and see him we must.' 'It cannot be done,' I said; 'the President cannot be intruded upon.' 'We will see for ourselves. . . . Have you any orders to prevent persons from approaching the President?' 'No,' I said, 'none. I do it on my own responsibility.' 'Then, in that case, you have taken a responsibility quite unauthorized, and we will call.'

"With that, two of them came up on the platform. I merely closed the car door and put my hand on the doorknob. 'Will you let us pass?' said one of the white neckties. 'You can pass on over the platform,' I said, 'but nowhere else; you can't pass through this door.' 'Who will stop us?' queried the white ties. 'I will, if possible,' I answered. At that they all laughed. They were well-made fellows, and, being quite [certain] they could master me, they became very insolent.

"All this time the President was apparently reading his newspaper, but in reality looking over the top of it, very much amused at the controversy going on between me and the white ties. . . . The two men on the platform, having expended all their eloquence on me . . . proceeded to extremities. One put his hand on mine to remove it from the knob, and the other took me by the shoulder.

"Quick as thought, both the white ties were sprawling in the mud—one at each side of the car—and they were invited up to try it again, with the information that the next time they ventured upon the car they would get a pistol-ball through them. I had no pistol; I only told them so for effect. They were very angry at their unceremonious removal, but did not care to attack the citadel again. . . . Mr. Lincoln laughed heartily when he saw the two white ties lying in the mud, and wanted to know 'how much I would sell that trick for. . . .' "

By this time the locomotive had arrived, and it was shortly hitched to the car. David Porter continues: "Off we went on our way. But what a careless thing it was to be going about with the President without a guard to protect him! I had never thought of any danger to him at the time. Our people were not given to assassination, and if anyone had told me that the President stood in danger of his life, I would have laughed at him.

"There were no guards to be obtained at City Point; every soldier had gone with the army. I might have brought some Marines, but, confident in my own ability to keep off loafers, I neglected to take any cautionary measures, and I only wonder that the catastrophe which finally took place did not occur while the President was at City Point—there were so many opportunities. . . .

"We arrived at Petersburg Landing, and found [Captain] Robert Lincoln, the President's son, there with horses for the President and his son 'Tad,' but none for me. The escort [sent by Grant] was not a very large one, consisting only of the [captain], a sergeant, and three or four troopers. . . . [Lincoln] was much amused . . . when I got one of the soldiers to dismount and let me have his raw-boned white horse, a hard trotter and a terrible stumbler. How the Government became possessed of such an animal the Lord only knows.

"I won't pretend to describe my adventures on that horse, and the number of times he ran away with me—the only way by which I could keep up with the President, who was splendidly mounted; but we finally reached Petersburg in safety, and were received at headquarters. I had no sooner arrived than I inquired of Lieutenant [William M.] Dunn, one of Grant's staff, if I could buy the horse upon which I had ridden. He said he thought I could, and would see the quartermaster about it; but the President, who heard our conversation, put in a protest.

" 'Why in the name of all that's good do you want that horse, Admiral?' exclaimed the President. 'Just look at him first; his head is as big as a flour barrel!' 'That's the case with all horses' heads,' I said. 'Well, look at his knees; they're sprung. He's fourteen years old if he's a day; his hoofs will cover half an acre. He's spavined, and only has one eye. What do you want with him? You sailors don't know anything about a horse. Get some of these soldier fellows to pick you out a beast, and you will get a good one. Don't you let him buy that horse, Mr. Dunn; get him a good one.' 'But I want it for a particular purpose,' I said; 'I want to buy it and shoot it, so that no one else will ever ride it again.' That pleased the President mightily. . . ."

This light moment took place on the street in front of the piazza headquarters. Now, according to Grant's aide, Horace Porter, "Mr. Lincoln, accompanied by his little son 'Tad' . . . came in through the front gate with long and rapid strides, his face beaming with delight. He seized General Grant's hand as the general stepped forward to greet him, and stood shaking it for some time and pouring out his thanks and congratulations with all the fervor of a heart that seemed overflowing with its fullness of joy. I doubt whether Mr. Lincoln ever experienced a happier moment in his life. The scene was singularly affecting. . . . He then said, 'Do you know, General, I have had a sort of sneaking idea for some days that you intended to do something like this, though I thought some time ago that you would so maneuver as to have Sherman come up and be near enough to cooperate with you.'

" 'Yes,' replied the general, 'I thought at one time that Sherman's army might advance so far as to be in supporting distance of the Eastern armies when the spring campaign against Lee opened, but I have had a feeling that it is better to let Lee's old antagonists give his army the final blow and finish up the job. . . . The Western armies have been very successful in their campaigns, and it is due to the Eastern armies [with a less impressive record] to let them vanquish their old enemy single-handed.'

" 'I see, I see,' said Mr. Lincoln, 'but I never thought of it in that light.

In fact, my anxiety has been so great that I didn't care where the help came from so long as the work was perfectly done. . . .' Mr. Lincoln then began to talk about the civil complications that would follow the destruction of the Confederate armies in the field, and showed plainly the anxiety he felt regarding the great problems in statecraft that would soon be thrust upon him. He intimated very plainly, however, in a rambling talk of nearly half an hour, that thoughts of mercy and magnanimity were uppermost in his heart. . . .

"... After the interview had lasted about an hour and a half, the general said he must ride on to the front . . . and took leave of the President, who shook his hand cordially, and with great warmth of feeling wished him God-speed and every success."

Lincoln and Admiral Porter rode about the city for a time before starting back toward their railroad car. "The streets," says the admiral, "were alive with Negroes who were crazy to see their savior, as they called the President. . . . On the return journey, my horse [cut] all kinds of capers without being able to throw me. The President paid me a high compliment. 'Admiral,' he said, 'you mistook your profession; you ought to have been a circus rider. . . .' Several regiments passed us en route, and they all seemed to recognize the President at once. 'Three cheers for Uncle Abe!' passed along among them, and the cheers were given with a vim which showed the estimation in which he was held by the soldiers. . . . One good-natured fellow sang out, 'We'll get 'em, Abe. . . . You go home and sleep sound tonight. We boys will put you through!' It was not a very courtier-like speech, certainly; it was homely and honest. And so they cheered us all along the road."

Upon his return to City Point, Lincoln found a telegram waiting for him. Sent from Washington by Secretary of War Edwin Stanton, the message had arrived too late to be meaningful. The President was urged to stay out of Petersburg. "Allow me respectfully to ask you to consider whether you ought to expose the nation to the consequence of any disaster to yourself in the pursuit of a treacherous and dangerous enemy like the rebel army. If it was a question concerning yourself only, I should not presume to say a word. Commanding generals are in the line of their duty in running such risks. But is the political head of a nation in the same condition?"

Lincoln wired back: "Thanks for your caution, but I have already been to Petersburg. Stayed with General Grant an hour and a half, and returned here. It is certain now that Richmond is in our hands, and I think I will go there tomorrow. I will take care of myself."

13

The President in Richmond

Lincoln planned to make his journey from City Point to Richmond by water. The section of the James that had to be navigated held not only the blackened remains of the ironclads blown up by the Confederates but also many previously created obstructions, some of them placed by the Confederates so that Admiral Porter's fleet could not come up, and others placed by Porter so that the Confederate fleet could not come down. The obstructions included sunken hulks, piles of stones, and large floating mines, or "torpedoes," these last objects laid by the Confederates at the upper end of the series. During the night of April 3 Porter's sailors began clearing a passage through the hulks and the stones.

The work, says Porter, "was completed by eight o'clock the following morning, and several of the smaller vessels went through, got their boats out, and began sweeping the river for torpedoes. . . . When the channel was reported clear . . . I proceeded up to Richmond in the *Malvern,* with President Lincoln on board the *River Queen* and a heavy feeling of responsibility on my mind, notwithstanding the great care that had been taken to clear the river.

"Every vessel that got through the obstructions wished to be the first one up, and pushed ahead with all steam; but they grounded, one after another, the *Malvern* passing them all until she also took the ground. Not to be delayed, I took the President in my barge, and, [pulled by] a tug . . . with a file of marines on board, we continued on up to the city.

"There was a large bridge across the James about a mile below the landing, and under this a party in a small steamer were caught and held by the current, with no prospect of release without assistance. These people begged me to extricate them from their perilous position, so I ordered the tug to cast off and help them, leaving us in the barge to go on alone [propelled by oar].

"Here we were in a solitary boat, after having set out with a number of vessels flying flags at every masthead, hoping to enter the conquered capital in a manner befitting the rank of the President of the United States, with a further intention of firing a national salute in honor of the happy result. . . . 'Admiral,' [said Lincoln,] 'this brings to my mind a fellow who once came to me to ask for an appointment as minister abroad. Finding he could not get that, he came down to some more modest position. Finally he asked to be made a tidewaiter [a waterfront customs inspector]. When he saw he could not get that, he asked me for an old pair of trousers. . . . It is well to be humble.'

"The tug never caught up with us. She got jammed in the bridge, and remained there that tide. I had never been to Richmond before by that route, and did not know where the landing was; neither did the coxswain, nor any of the barge's crew. We pulled on, hoping to see someone of whom we could inquire. . . . The current was now rushing past us over and among rocks, on one of which we finally stuck. . . . I backed out and pointed for the nearest landing."

Porter and his party stepped ashore under the eye of Union newsman Charles Carleton Coffin, who had been in the city since the previous afternoon. Coffin relates: "Forty or fifty freedmen—sole possessors of themselves for twenty-four hours—were at work on the bank of the [nearby] canal, under the direction of a lieutenant, securing some floating timber. They crowded round the President, forgetting work in their wild joy at beholding the face of the author of the great Emancipation Proclamation.

"As he approached, I said to a colored woman, 'There is the man who made you free.' 'What, massa?' 'That is President Lincoln.' 'Dat President Linkum?' 'Yes.' She gazed at him a moment in amazement, joy, rapture, as if in supernal presence, then clapped her hands, jumped and shouted, 'Glory! Glory! Glory!'

" 'God bless you, Sah!' said one, taking off his cap and bowing very low. 'Hurrah! Hurrah! President Linkum hab come! President Linkum hab come!' rang through the street. The lieutenant found himself without men. What cared those freedmen, fresh from the house of bondage, for floating timber or military commands? Their deliverer had come— he who, next to the Lord Jesus, was their best friend! It was not a hurrah that they gave so much as a wild, jubilant cry of inexpressible joy.

"They pressed round the President, ran ahead, and hovered upon the flanks and rear of the little company. Men, women, and children joined the constantly increasing throng. They came from all the streets, running in breathless haste, shouting and hallooing, and dancing with delight. The men threw up their hats, the women waved their bonnets and handkerchiefs, clapped their hands and shouted, 'Glory to God! Glory! Glory! Glory!'—rendering all the praise to God, who had given them freedom, after long years of weary waiting, and had permitted them thus unexpectedly to meet their great benefactor. . . .

"No carriage was to be had, so the President, leading his son, walked [toward] General Weitzel's headquarters—Jeff Davis's mansion. Six sailors, wearing their round blue caps and short jackets and baggy pants, with navy carbines, formed the guard. Next came the President and Admiral Porter, flanked by the officers accompanying him, and the writer, then six more sailors with carbines—twenty of us in all.

"The walk was long, and the President halted a moment to rest. 'May de good Lord bless you, President Linkum!' said an old Negro, removing his hat and bowing, with tears of joy rolling down his cheeks. The President removed his own hat, and bowed in silence. It was a bow which upset the forms, laws, customs, and ceremonies of centuries of slavery. It was . . . a mortal blow to caste."

"Our progress," says Admiral Porter, "was very slow. We did not move a mile an hour, and the crowd was still increasing. Many poor whites joined the throng, and sent up their shouts with the rest."

The city's aristocracy, according to diarist Judith McGuire, tried to ignore Lincoln's visit. "His reception was anything but complimentary. Our people were in nothing rude or disrespectful. They only kept themselves away from a scene so painful."

Admiral Porter resumes: "We were nearly half an hour getting from abreast of Libby Prison to the edge of the city. The President stopped a moment to look on the horrid bastille where so many Union soldiers had dragged out a dreadful existence. . . . 'We will pull it down,' cried the crowd, seeing where his look fell. 'No,' he said, 'leave it as a monument.' He did not say a monument to what, but he meant, I am sure, to leave it as a monument to the loyalty of our soldiers, who would bear all the horrors of Libby sooner than desert their flag and cause.

"We struggled on, the great crowd preceding us, and an equally dense crowd of blacks following on behind. . . . It was not a model style for the President of the United States to enter the capital of a conquered country, yet there was a moral in it all which had more effect than if he had come surrounded with great armies and heralded by the boom-

Libby Prison

ing of cannon. He came, armed with the majesty of the law, to put his seal to the act which had been established by the bayonets of the Union soldiers—the establishment of peace and good will between the North and the South, and liberty to all mankind who dwell upon our shores.

"We forced our way onward slowly, and, as we reached the edge of the city, the sidewalks were lined on both sides of the streets with black and white alike—all looking with curious eager faces at the man who held their destiny in his hand. . . . It was a warm day, and the streets were dusty, owing to the immense gathering which covered every part of them, kicking up the dirt. The atmosphere was suffocating, but Mr. Lincoln could be plainly seen by every man, woman, and child, towering head and shoulders above that crowd. . . . He carried his hat in his hand, fanning his face, from which the perspiration was pouring. . . .

"We were brought to a halt by the dense jam before we had gone a square into the city, which was still on fire near the Tredegar Works and in the structures thereabout, and the smoke, setting our way, almost choked us. I had not seen a soldier whom I could send to General Weitzel to ask for an escort. . . .

"While we were stopped . . . a white man in his shirt sleeves rushed from the sidewalk toward the President. His looks were so eager that I questioned his friendship, and prepared to receive him on the point of my sword; but when he got within ten feet of us he suddenly stopped short, took off his hat, and cried out, 'Abraham Lincoln, God bless you! You are the poor man's friend!' Then he tried to force his way to the President to shake hands with him. He would not take 'no' for an answer until I had to treat him rather roughly, when he stood off, with his arms folded, and looked intently after us. The last I saw of him he was throwing his hat into the air.

"Just after this a beautiful girl came from the sidewalk with a large bouquet of roses in her hand, and advanced, struggling through the crowd toward the President. The mass of people endeavored to open to let her pass, but she had a hard time in reaching him. Her clothes were very much disarranged in making the journey across the street. I reached out and helped her within the circle of the sailors' bayonets, where, although nearly stifled with the dust, she gracefully presented her bouquet to the President and made a neat little speech, while he held her hand. The beauty and youth of the girl—for she was only about seventeen—made the presentation very touching.

"There was a card on the bouquet with these simple words: 'From Eva to the Liberator of the Slaves.' She remained no longer than to

deliver her present; then two of the sailors were sent to escort her back
to the sidewalk. There was no cheering at this, nor yet was any disappro-
bation shown; but it was evidently a matter of great interest, for the girl
was surrounded and plied with questions. [This girl's origins are a mystery. She may have belonged to the city's Unionist faction, whose sym-
pathies could now be openly expressed.] . . .

"At length I got hold of a cavalryman. He was sitting his horse near
the sidewalk, blocked in by the people, and looking on with the same
expression of interest as the others. . . . 'Go to the general,' I said to the
trooper, 'and tell him to send a military escort here to guard the President and get him through this crowd!' 'Is that Old Abe?' asked the
soldier, his eyes as large as saucers. The sight of the President was as
strange to him as to the inhabitants; but off he went as fast as the crowd
would allow him, and, some twenty minutes later, I heard the clatter
of horses' hoofs over the stones as a troop of cavalry came galloping and
clearing the street, which they did, however, as mildly as if for a parade.

"For the first time since starting from the landing we were able to
walk uninterruptedly. In a short time we reached the mansion of Mr.
Davis, President of the Confederacy, occupied after the evacuation as
the headquarters of Generals Weitzel and Shepley. It was quite a small
affair compared with the White House, and modest in all its appoint-
ments, showing that while President Davis was engaged heart and soul
in endeavoring to effect the division of the States, he was not, at least,
surrounding himself with regal style, but was living in a modest, comfortable way, like any other citizen. Amid all his surroundings the re-
fined taste of his wife was apparent. . . ."

According to General Weitzel's aide, Thomas Thatcher Graves,
President Lincoln "was shown into the reception room, with the remark that the housekeeper had said that that room was President
Davis's office. As he seated himself, he remarked, 'This must have been
President Davis's chair,' and, crossing his legs, he looked far off with a
serious, dreamy expression. At length he asked me if the housekeeper
was in the house. Upon learning that she had left, he jumped up and
said, with a boyish manner, 'Come, let's look at the house!' We went
pretty much over it. I retailed all that the housekeeper had told me, and
he seemed interested in everything."

The news of Lincoln's "violation" of the Davis mansion reached
Judith McGuire, and it set her fuming. "Our President's house! Ah, it
is a bitter pill! I would that dear old house, with all its associations so
sacred to Southerners, so sweet to us as a family, had shared in the

Lincoln leaving the Davis mansion

general conflagration. Then its history would have been unsullied, though sad. Oh, how gladly would I have seen it burn!"

Lincoln and his party were served a meal at the Davis mansion, after which the President conducted an informal reception for a group of Union officers. He also talked with Southerner John Campbell, one of the February peace commissioners, who conceded that the war was over.

It was Union Captain George Bruce, at General Devens's order, who provided the carriage that Lincoln used for a further tour of the city. "It was a light carriage, with three seats and covered with black oilcloth. The President and the General [Devens] took the middle seat, Admiral Porter and Tad the rear one. I am particular in giving these details for the reason that the New York illustrated newspapers represented Mr. Lincoln riding through Richmond in an open barouche, with hat in hand, bowing to the crowds lining the streets through which he passed."

Union newsman Charles Coffin says that the President's carriage was "escorted by a squadron of cavalry [and] followed by thousands of colored people shouting 'Glory to God!' "

Lincoln's itinerary included a stop at the house where Confederate General George Pickett had left his wife, his "Sally of the Sunset Eyes," and their baby. Mrs. Pickett relates: "There was a sharp rap at the door. The servants had all run away. The city was full of Northern troops. . . . With my baby on my arm, I answered the knock, opened the door, and looked up at a tall, gaunt, sad-faced man in ill-fitting clothes, who, with the accent of the North, asked, 'Is this George Pickett's place?' 'Yes, sir,' I answered, 'but he is not here.' 'I know that, ma'am,' he replied, 'but I just wanted to see the place. I am Abraham Lincoln.' 'The President!' I gasped. The stranger shook his head and said, 'No, ma'am; no, ma'am; just Abraham Lincoln; George's old friend.' 'I am George Pickett's wife and this is his baby,' was all I could say. I had never seen Mr. Lincoln but remembered the intense love and reverence with which my Soldier always spoke of him.

"My baby pushed away from me and reached out his hands to Mr. Lincoln, who took him in his arms. As he did so, an expression of rapt, almost divine, tenderness and love lighted up the sad face. . . . My baby opened his mouth wide and insisted upon giving his father's friend a dewy infantile kiss. As Mr. Lincoln gave the little one back to me, shaking his finger at him playfully, he said, 'Tell your father, the rascal, that I forgive him for the sake of that kiss and those bright eyes.'

View of Richmond's ruins—Main Street

"He turned and went down the steps, talking to himself, and passed out of my sight forever. . . . It was through Mr. Lincoln that my Soldier, as a lad of seventeen, received his appointment to West Point. Mr. Lincoln was at that time associated in law practice with George Pickett's uncle, Mr. Andrew Johnson, a distinguished lawyer and scholar who was very anxious that his nephew should follow in his footsteps and study for the law—an ambition which, it is needless to say, my Soldier did not share. He confided his perplexities to Mr. Lincoln, who was very fond of the boy; and the great statesman went at once to work to secure his appointment."

The President's carriage took him on a tour of the burned-out section of the city and to Capitol Square. At the square, according to Captain Bruce, "he stopped immediately in front of Crawford's great statue of Washington, which faces west . . . the right hand . . . pointing in the same direction. After looking at it for a moment, the President quietly said, 'Washington is looking at me and pointing to Jeff Davis.' "

(Washington was pointing in the general direction of the Confederate leader's flight. Davis was captured by a party of Union troops on May 10.)

Lincoln next entered the Capitol building, the late seat of the Confederate Congress. "It was," says Admiral Porter, "in dreadful disorder, betokening a sudden and unexpected flight; members' tables were upset, bales of Confederate scrip were lying about the floor, and many official documents of some value were scattered about. . . . After this inspection I urged the President to go on board the *Malvern.* I began to feel more heavily the responsibility resting upon me through the care of his person. The evening was approaching, and we were in a carriage open on all sides [albeit roofed]. He was glad to go; he was tired out and wanted the quiet of the flagship. . . . I was oppressed with uneasiness until we got on board and stood on deck with the President safe; then there was not a happier man anywhere than myself."

14

Lee Moves Westward

After his evacuation of Richmond and Petersburg during the night of April 2–3, General Lee turned his full attention westward. He ordered the various columns from the two sectors to converge in the vicinity of Amelia Court House, about thirty-five miles away, where a large supply of rations and forage, requisitioned during the final days of the Richmond government, was supposed to be waiting. The route of march ran roughly parallel to the Appomattox River in the direction of its source waters. The bulk of the army was north of the river, but some of the units that had been stationed southwest of Petersburg, on the army's extreme right flank, used south-bank roads.

South Carolina trooper Edward Boykin, last heard from as he crossed the James River from Richmond to Manchester at sunrise on April 3, tells of the first day's march as he saw it while riding with the Richmond army's rear guard: "Moving slowly out of Manchester, we soon got among the host of stragglers who, from a natural fear of the occupation of the towns both of Petersburg and Richmond, were going with the rear of our army. Civilians, in some cases ladies of gentle nurture, without means of conveyance, were sitting on their trunks by the roadside—refugees from Petersburg to Richmond a few days before, now refugees from Richmond into the highway. Indeed, the most were from Petersburg, driven out literally by the artillery fire. . . . Two ladies here got into our regimental ambulance, rode for a few miles, and then took refuge in some farmhouse, I suppose, as they disappeared before the day was over.

"By the roadside . . . were sitting on their bags some hardy, weather-

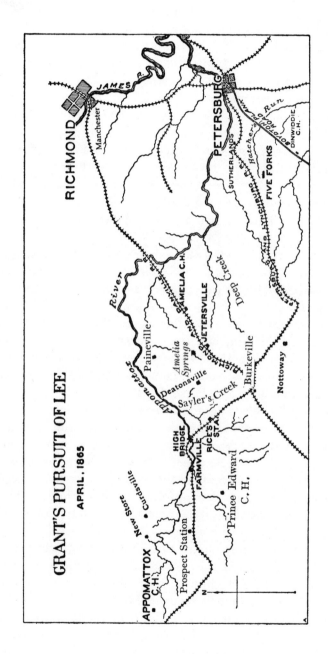

GRANT'S PURSUIT OF LEE

APRIL, 1865

beaten looking men. They were what was left of the crew of the famous *Alabama,* and had just landed from the gunboats that had been blown up on the river. . . . Admiral [Raphael] Semmes was with them. . . . Some of our young men [jested] with the bronzed veterans, but we did not then know the renowned Captain of the great Confederate warship was there in person, or he should certainly have not have [been] . . . left standing in the road and dusted by the . . . cavalry rear-guard. . . . Someone . . . would have been dismounted, and his horse given to the man who had carried our flag so far and fought so well.

" . . . We moved very slowly, giving time for all stragglers, wagons, and worn out artillery horses to close up. Already we began to come upon a piece of artillery mired down, the horse dead beat, the gun left, and the horses double-teamed into the remaining pieces."

Confederate battalion commander Robert Stiles, recently of the James River defenses, says that his unit halted early in the day "at a country crossroad in Chesterfield to allow other bodies of troops to pass, the bulk of my men lying down and falling asleep in a grove; but, seeing others about a well in the yard of a farmhouse over the way, I deemed it best to go there to see that nothing was unnecessarily disturbed. I sat in the porch, where were also sitting an old couple, evidently the joint head of the establishment, and a young woman dressed in black, apparently their daughter, and, as I soon learned, a soldier's widow. My coat was badly torn, and, the young woman kindly offering to mend it, I thanked her and, taking it off, handed it to her.

"While we were chatting, and groups of men sitting on the steps and lying about the yard, the door of the house opened and another young woman appeared. She was almost beautiful, was plainly but neatly dressed, and had her hat on. She had evidently been weeping, and her face was deadly pale. Turning to the old woman as she came out, she said, cutting her words off short, 'Mother, tell him if he passes here [i.e., if he does not quit the army at this point] he is no husband of mine,' and turned again to leave the porch.

"I rose and placed myself directly in front of her, extending my arm to prevent her escape. She drew back with surprise and indignation. The men were alert on the instant, and battle was joined. 'What do you mean, sir?' she cried. 'I mean, madam,' I replied, 'that you are sending your husband word to desert, and that I cannot permit you to do this in the presence of my men.' 'Indeed! And who asked your permission, sir? And pray, sir, is he your husband or mine?' 'He is your husband, madam, but these are my soldiers. They and I belong to the same army with your husband, and I cannot suffer you, or anyone, unchallenged, to send such a demoralizing message in their hearing.'

" 'Army! Do you call this mob of retreating cowards an army? Soldiers! If you are soldiers, why don't you stand and fight the savage wolves that are coming upon us defenseless women and children?' 'We don't stand and fight, madam, because we . . . have to obey orders, but if the enemy should appear on that hill this moment I think you would find that these men *are* soldiers, and willing to die in defense of women and children.'

" 'Quite a fine speech, sir, but rather cheap to utter, since you very well know the Yankees are not here, and won't be, till you've had time to get your precious carcasses out of the way. Besides, sir, this thing is over, and has been for some time. The Government has now actually run off, bag and baggage, the Lord knows where; and there is no longer any Government or any country for my husband to owe allegiance to. He *does* owe allegiance to me and to his starving children, and if he doesn't observe this allegiance now, when I *need* him, he needn't attempt it hereafter, when *he* wants *me.'*

"The woman was quick as a flash and cold as steel. She was getting the better of me. She saw it, I felt it, and, worst of all, the men saw and felt it, too, and had gathered thick and had pressed up close all round the porch. There must have been a hundred or more of them, all eagerly listening, and evidently leaning strongly to the woman's side. This would never do. I tried every avenue of approach to that woman's heart. It was congealed by suffering, or else it was encased in adamant. She had parried every thrust, repelled every advance, and was now standing defiant, with her arms folded across her breast, rather courting further attack.

"I was desperate, and with the nonchalance of pure desperation— no stroke of genius—I asked the soldier-question, 'What command does your husband belong to?' She started a little, and there was a trace of color in her face as she replied, with a slight tone of pride in her voice, 'He belongs to the Stonewall Brigade, sir.' I felt, rather than thought it —but had I really found her heart? We would see. 'When did he join it?' A little deeper flush, a little stronger emphasis of pride. 'He joined it in the spring of '61, sir.' Yes, I was sure of it now. Her eyes had gazed straight into mine; her head inclined and her eyelids drooped a little now, and there was something in her face that was not pain and was not fight.

"So I let myself out a little, and, turning to the men, said, 'Men, if her husband joined the Stonewall Brigade in '61, and has been in the army ever since, I reckon he's a good soldier.' I turned to look at her. It was all over. . . . She had not been addressed this time, yet she answered instantly, with head raised high, face flushing, eyes flashing, 'General Lee hasn't a better in his army!'

"As she uttered these words, she put her hand in her bosom, and, drawing out a folded paper, extended it toward me, saying, 'If you doubt it, look at that.' Before her hand reached mine she drew it back, seeming to have changed her mind, but I caught her wrist and, without much resistance, possessed myself of the paper. It had been much thumbed and was much worn. It was hardly legible, but I made it out. Again I turned to the men. 'Take off your hats, boys, I want you to hear this with uncovered heads.' And then I read an endorsement on application for furlough, in which General Lee himself had signed a recommendation of this woman's husband for a furlough of special length on account of extraordinary gallantry in battle.

"During the reading of this paper the woman was transfigured, glorified. No Madonna of old master was ever more sweetly radiant with all that appeals to what is best and holiest in a man. Her bosom rose and fell with deep, quiet sighs; her eyes rained gentle, happy tears.

"The men felt it all—*all.* They were all gazing upon her, but the dross was clean, purified out of them. There was not, upon any one of their faces an expression that would have brought a blush to the cheek of the purest womanhood on earth. I turned once more to the soldier's wife. 'This little paper is your most precious treasure, isn't it?' 'It is.' 'And the love of him whose manly courage and devotion won this tribute is the best blessing God ever gave you, isn't it?' 'It is.' 'And yet, for the brief ecstasy of one kiss you would disgrace this hero-husband of yours, stain all his noble reputation, and turn this priceless paper to bitterness. For the rear guard would hunt him from his own cottage, in half an hour, as a deserter and a coward.'

"Not a sound could be heard save her hurried breathing. The rest of us held even our breath. Suddenly, with a gasp of recovered consciousness, she snatched the paper from my hand, put it back hurriedly in her bosom, and, turning once more to her mother, said, 'Mother, tell him not to come.' I stepped aside at once. She left the porch, glided down the path to the gate, crossed the road, surmounted the fence with easy grace, climbed the hill; and, as she disappeared in the weedy pathway, I caught up my hat and said, 'Now, men, give her three cheers.'

"Such cheers! Oh, God! Shall I ever again hear a cheer which bears a man's whole soul in it?"

According to Southern trooper Edward Boykin, the first day saw only limited progress toward Amelia Court House. "After marching all day, [we were] only eleven miles from Richmond. . . . The brigade went into camp, or bivouac rather, by squadrons, in a piece of woods, the men picketing their horses immediately behind their campfires. The fires burned brightly, the horses ate the corn the men had brought in their bags and what forage they could get hold of during the day. Our surgeon, Dr. McLaurin, had gotten up his ambulance, and helped out our bread and bacon with a cup of coffee and some not-very-salt James River herring that he had among his stores. And so ended the first day's march."

The story of the same day is narrated as experienced by another South Carolinian, J. F. J. Caldwell, marching with the troops from Petersburg who had remained on the south bank of the Appomattox. "We set out soon after daylight pursuing the general direction of the Appomattox. There was an attempt made to organize the various commands; but it proved, in the main, abortive. According to the inelegant, but to us expressive, phraseology of the army, the Confederacy was considered as 'gone up'; and every man felt it his duty, as well as his privilege, to save himself. I do not mean to say that there was any insubordination whatever; but the whole left of the army [the right had become the left when the army about-faced from east to west] was so crushed by the defeats of the last few days that it straggled along without strength, and almost without thought. So we moved on in disorder, keeping no regular column, no regular pace. When a soldier became weary, he fell out, ate his scanty rations—if, indeed, he had any to eat—rested, rose, and resumed the march when his inclination dictated.

"There were not many words spoken. An indescribable sadness weighed upon us. The men were very gentle towards each other—very liberal in bestowing the little food that remained to them. . . . One soldier divided his last scrap of bacon with me . . . and would have shared his bread, but I refused that. I had lost my pipe. He gave me his, and told me to keep it. . . .

"Fortunately, our march was not impeded by wagons or artillery. The most of the former belonging to the troops south of the Appomattox had crossed that stream near Petersburg and were now following the roads between the Appomattox and the James. A large number of

Confederates cutting down an artillery piece

our guns and caissons had gone the same way, and of those which [had been] with us at Sutherland's Station, not a few had been cut down and abandoned.

"We followed the road towards Amelia Court House. . . . A misfortune befell our brigade commander this day which created some merriment even in our sad circumstances. . . . A bridge was needed across Deep Run, not far from its junction with the Appomattox. General [Samuel] McGowan undertook to construct one; but, while in the midst of his operations, the Confederate cavalry rushed up from the rear declaring themselves pursued by an immense body of the enemy's horse. The infantry believed them, crowded upon the frail structure until it sank, and then plunged across the run as they best could— General McGowan among the rest. The water was deep and swift, so that he had a sharp little swim of it. He spoke of it afterwards with great relish and amusement. Our cavalry had exaggerated the danger, but the mistake was not discovered until too late to [save] the bridge.

"In the afternoon, heavy skirmishing was heard in our rear. The wagon and artillery trains of our wing of the army were collected two or three miles west of Deep Run. . . . About midnight, the trains were moved somewhat off from the river. The troops generally followed them. The depression of spirits and exhaustion of the bodies of our men increased. They fell about and slept heavily, or else wandered like persons in a dream. . . . It all seemed to me like a troubled vision. I was consumed by fever, and when I attempted to walk I staggered like a drunken man."

15

Of Flight and Pursuit

For many a weary Confederate, the dawn of April 4 came too soon. Trooper Edward Boykin and his comrades, however, got some extra rest. "We did not move until nearly nine o'clock . . . as, at our slowest gait, we out-traveled the march we were covering [that from Richmond]. The day was spent in following after the movements of the army. Occasional pieces of artillery left upon the roadside showed that the horses were giving out. After dark we crossed [to the south bank of] the Appomattox, some twenty or twenty-five miles from Richmond, at the [Richmond-Danville] railroad bridge, which was planked over so our horses could cross.

"After crossing the river we went into camp, about a mile beyond, surrounded by most of the infantry of the north bank [who had made their own crossing]. . . . One of the young men attached to our mess, a good-looking young fellow, had his pockets filled with ham and biscuits, near the crossing, by some Good Samaritan he had met; and so our herring, grilled by one of the couriers on the half of a canteen, was helped out by this addition.

"We were suddenly roused in the night by a fire in the dry grass on which we were sleeping. It caught from our campfire and was among our blankets before we knew it. There was a general jumping up and stamping it out. One of the men created quite a sensation by shaking his India rubber, which was on fire. It flew to pieces in a shower of flame. . . .

"We were at this point but a few miles from Amelia Court House, between which and our camp of that night the road from Petersburg joins the road from Richmond, and the two columns respectively met —the two streams [of fugitives] flowed into one—forming what was left of Lee's great Army of Northern Virginia—the men exchanging, in the fresh morning air, kindly greetings with one another. . . ."

The successful merger fostered optimism, but the feeling had a short life. In the confusion marking the last days of the Richmond government, the rations and forage Lee wanted sent to Amelia Court House were not provided. He found only a store of ammunition that he could not carry with him. The general laments: "Nearly twenty-four hours were lost in endeavoring to collect in the [surrounding] country subsistence for men and horses. The delay was fatal, and could not be retrieved. The troops, wearied by continual fighting and marching for several days and nights, obtained neither rest nor refreshment."

Southerner Carlton McCarthy, a private with Colonel Wilfred E. Cutshaw's artillery battalion (now armed with muskets and serving as an infantry unit), says that "the 5th was spent at or near the Court House. . . . When application was made for rations, it was found that the last morsel belonging to the division had been issued . . . and the battalion was . . . thrown on its own resources, to wit: corn on the cob intended for the horses. Two ears were issued to each man. It was parched in the coals [and] mixed with salt. . . . Chewing the corn was hard work. It made the jaws ache and the gums and teeth so sore as to cause almost unendurable pain."

Unknown to McCarthy and the other men of Cutshaw's battalion, Lee ordered the useless store of shells and cartridges to be blown up, and it happened to be lying out of sight in a woods not far from Cutshaw's encampment. "The ammunition," McCarthy explains, "had been piled up ready for destruction. An occasional musket ball passed over near enough and often enough to produce a realizing sense of the proximity of the enemy and solemnize the occasion. Towards evening the muskets were stacked, artillery style of course, the men were lying around, chatting and eating raw bacon, and there was a general quiet, when suddenly the earth shook with a tremendous explosion and an immense column of smoke rushed up into the air to a great height. For a moment there was the greatest consternation. Whole regiments broke and fled in wild confusion. Cutshaw's men stood up, seized their muskets, and stood at attention till it was known that the ammunition had been purposely fired and no enemy was threatening the line. Then what laughter and hilarity prevailed, for a while, among these famishing men!"

On the Union side, morale was soaring. In the words of Alfred A. Woodhull, an assistant surgeon who marched with Ord's Army of the James: "How glorious was that last week! The Rebs may have enjoyed it slenderly; but we were filled with new life. . . . The cruel suspense that . . . had enshrouded us during the final movement to the left was torn aside by Five Forks and the storming of Petersburg. Lee was in retreat, and we were in full cry after him. It was a new and agreeable situation. More than once in former days we had retired from before the Rebels. Now it was a wilder chase than ever, and we were not in front.

" . . . The national forces marched in two main columns. The Army of the Potomac, under Meade, and the ubiquitous Sheridan and his centaurs, were directly on the Rebel trail and right; while Ord, with the Army of the James, marched on their left flank along the Lynchburg Railroad—a moving wall to resist their turning southward. Ord's first objective was Burkeville Junction, to cut off the use of the Danville Railroad . . . which the enemy expected . . . to follow south, possibly hoping to unite with Johnston in the Carolinas [where that general was facing Sherman].

"Grant started with [Ord's] column; and we [of this column] knew that affairs on the northerly line were in the full tide of success, by little waifs [of news] borne to us from time to time. . . . How triumphant we felt! The assault and capture of the Cockade City [had] rekindled all the flame that the ashes of a ten-months' siege had covered but not extinguished. A march through its battered streets and its beautiful outskirts had deepened the sense of victory. The balmy air and invigoration of sun and cheerful fields of the Virginia spring stirred the physical man; and the very beasts of burden, escaped from plodding through the winter's mud, seemed to catch the contagion of the march.

"We were like so many schoolboys on a holiday. Sick of the restraints of the earthworks' narrow limits, of the monotonous routine of camp, of shelling and being shelled . . . we started off with perhaps more than usual glee. . . . We expected one sharp fight; but the spirit of prophecy within us announced that the day of retribution for the wicked Rebels was at hand, that we were surely crushing the rebellion. The mother of states and of presidents [Virginia] had presided over many solemn marches and stately minuets in which we had been unwilling participants during the past four years. We had danced, sometimes, when the desire was not in us; we had frequently paid the piper when it was inconvenient; but now we were instituting a veritable Virginia Reel, into which we entered heart and soul.

A Union scouting mission

"But no form of words can describe our exultation, partly physical from pure animal excitement, but chiefly moral from the consciousness of the speedy triumph of the good cause for which we had fought so desperately and so long."

It was still early in the march when Grant's troops began to realize that the victory was to be gained only by dint of strenuous efforts. Augustus Buell, a mounted artilleryman who moved with the pursuit's northern wing (where the leading infantry unit was Meade's 5th Corps), says that "it was only once in a lifetime—and comparatively few lifetimes at that—when one could see in flesh and blood and nerve and pluck and manhood [the likes of] that immortal old 5th Corps on its way to Appomattox! On its way, keeping step and step with Sheridan's cavalry, to get across the path of Lee's army! During these terrible forced marches of the 5th Corps, General Griffin's wonderful power in dealing with soldiers, and his marvellous tact in cheering men on to incredible exertions, became manifest. [This was Charles Griffin, who had assumed command of the corps after Sheridan relieved Warren.] If that noble man had a fault, it was his apparent incapacity to understand that there was a limit to human endurance.

"In those marches . . . the General would see a dozen or so of stragglers by the side of the road. He would then rein up his horse and call out to them, 'Hello there! What is the matter with you fellows?' 'Clean tuckered out, General; can't march another step.' 'Look here, boys,' the General would reply, 'don't you know that we have got old Lee on the run, and our corps and the cavalry are trying to head him off? If he escapes from us, old Sherman and his bummers will catch him and get all the glory, and we won't have anything to show for our four years' fighting! Try it once more! Get up and pull out and rejoin your commands. Don't flicker this way at the last moment!' Then you would see those old fellows straighten up and pull themselves together and shoulder their muskets . . . and Griffin would ride on to find some other squad of stragglers, and go through the same sermon over again.

"It made no difference how tired or faint or sore an Army of the Potomac man might be, he couldn't endure the thought of letting Lee's army get away, so that those Western fellows would catch him and get the glory of winding the thing up. When I was riding along . . . I used to wish that I could dismount and give up my horse to every one of those poor, exhausted, but brave and determined infantry comrades, who were actually 'falling by the wayside,' but who, when their pride was stirred by the thought that Sherman's army might usurp the fruits of their toils and sufferings of four long years, took a new lease on life and strength, and staggered on once more. . . . No one who did not see them can form the faintest idea of what they did and dared and suffered! And General Griffin was a whole provost guard all by himself."

According to the 5th Corps private Theodore Gerrish, Phil Sheridan was another figure who merited special notice. "This is how he appeared on the field: a short, [slight] man with very short legs, his broad shoulders a little stooping as he sat upon his horse, having a very large head with hair clipped close, a short, thick mustache; his uniform being usually the worse for wear and spotted with mud; wearing a soft felt hat at least two sizes too small, and, for safekeeping, usually pressed down upon . . . the back of his head. He rode a splendid horse, usually went at a round gallop, and rolled and bounced upon the back of his steed much as an old salt does when walking up the aisle of a church after a four years' cruise at sea.

"Some of his surroundings were also of a singular character. At his side usually rode a party of a dozen scouts clad in the neat gray uniform of rebel officers, and ranking from captains to colonels. They were evidently brave, jolly, reckless fellows, and theirs was a most dangerous occupation—one that required skill, tact, and cool, deliberate daring. Entering the rebel lines and making themselves familiar with all their movements, dashing from one brigade to another, they would claim to be on one general's staff, and then on that of another, to suit the situation. They would give orders that purported to come from rebel commanders, to colonels, quartermasters, and officers in charge of wagon trains; and, these being obeyed, would add to the confusion of the rebel army and hastened its destruction. . . .

"Brigadier General———was at the head of a rebel brigade, leading them in their hasty retreat. He was met . . . by a rebel staff officer, as he supposed, who accosted him thus: 'General———commands you to take your men into the open field yonder, and halt there for a short rest.' 'In what direction is the field?' questioned the General. The staff officer pointed his hand and then remarked, 'If you will ride with me a few steps I can show it to you.' The General motioned for his staff to remain, and then followed his guide. They passed around a clump of small trees not over a dozen rods from his staff and escort, when two other men in rebel uniforms made their appearance, seized the General's horse by the reins, and bore him a prisoner to the Union army. As he rode past our regiment, to say that he was a disgusted-looking man would be a mild way of putting it.

"Success made these scouts reckless, and quite a number were captured, and some, I believe, were executed. . . . One of them rode up to a rebel general and gave an order as to the disposition of the General's troops. 'Whose staff are you on, sir?' demanded the General. 'General ————'s,' answered the unabashed scout. 'That is too thin, sir,' replied the other, 'for I am General ————, and do not recognize you as belonging to my staff.' The poor fellow had made a mistake. He was instantly captured. . . .

"Another singular feature in Sheridan's procession was at least twenty captured battle flags, which were borne unfurled as trophies of the campaign. His staff officers and body guard were all as rash and daring as Sheridan himself, and whenever they went dashing past us it would stir the boys up to the wildest enthusiasm. . . . They would cheer as if a pandemonium had broken loose.

"On every hand we could see indications that Lee's army would soon melt away. Prisoners were pouring into our lines. . . . Baggage wagons, artillery, mortars, and baggage of all kinds lined the roads along which the rebels were fleeing."

16

Sheridan Takes the Lead

According to Southern battalion commander Robert Stiles, every Confederate soldier involved in the great retreat found it to be "one of the most trying experiences of his life. Trying enough in the mere fact that the Army of Northern Virginia was flying before its foes, but further trying, incomparably trying, in lack of food and rest and sleep, and because of the audacious pressure of the enemy's cavalry. The combined and continued strain of all this . . . can hardly be conceived and cannot be described. Its two most serious effects were drowsiness and nervousness. . . .

"The somewhat disorganized condition of the troops and the crowded condition of the roads necessitated frequent halts, and whenever these occurred—especially after nightfall—the men would drop in the road, or on the side of it, and sleep until they were roused, and it was manifestly impossible to rouse them all. My two horses were in almost constant use to transport officers and men who had given out. . . . Besides, I preferred to be on foot for the very purpose of moving around among the men and rousing them when we resumed the march. With this view I was a good part of the time at the rear of the battalion; but, notwithstanding my efforts in this respect, individually and through a detail of men selected and organized for the purpose of waking the sleepers, we lost, I am satisfied, every time we resumed the march after a halt at night, men who were not found or who could not be roused.

"The nervousness resulting from this constant strain of starvation, fatigue, and lack of sleep was a dangerous thing, at one time producing very lamentable results. . . . One evening an officer, I think of one of our supply departments, passed and repassed us several times riding a powerful black stallion, all of whose furnishings—girths, reins, etc.— were very heavy, indicating the unmanageable character of the horse. When he rode ahead the last time, about dark, it seems that he imprudently hitched his horse by tying his very stout tie-rein to a heavy fence rail which was part of the road fence. Something frightened the animal and he reared back, pulling the rail out of the fence and dragging it after him full gallop down the road crowded with troops, mowing them down like the scythe of a war chariot.

"Someone, thinking there was a charge of cavalry, fired his musket, and, on the instant, three or four battalions, mine among them, began firing into each other. I was never more alarmed. Muskets were discharged in my very face, and I fully expected to be shot down. But, after the most trying and perilous experience, the commanding officers succeeded in getting control of their men and getting them again into formation. But while we were talking to them, suddenly the panic seized them again, and they rushed in such a wild rout against the heavy road fence that they swept it away, and many of them took to the woods, firing back as they ran.

"A second time the excitement was quieted, and a third time it broke out. By this time, however, I had fully explained to my men that we had just put out fresh flankers on both sides of the road, that we could not have an attack of cavalry without warning from them, and that the safe and soldierly thing to do was to lie down until everything should become calm. I was much pleased that this third time my command did not fire a shot, while the battalions in our front and rear were firing heavily. A field officer and a good many other officers and men were killed and wounded in these alarms. . . ."

During Lee's delay at Amelia Court House, the Union troops under Sheridan and Meade marched around his southern flank to Jetersville, seven miles southwest of the Court House, which placed them squarely across the Confederate general's railroad communications with Danville. It was in that southwesterly direction that Lee had planned to march in his effort to join Johnston. On April 5, while Lee was pondering his options, Phil Sheridan sent a brigade of cavalry, that of Brigadier General Henry E. Davies, Jr., on a reconnaissance northward around the front of the Confederate army. Near Paineville the bluecoats came upon a train of wagons and artillery, which they assaulted.

Among the Southern horsemen mustered to fight the raiders was

Federals attacking wagon train near Paineville

Edward Boykin, who relates: "Off we went at a gallop. We soon reached the point they had first attacked and set fire to the wagons—the canvas covers taking fire very easily. Their plan of operation seemed to be to strike the train, which was several miles long, at a given point, fire as many wagons as their number [of men] admitted of doing at once, then making a circuit and striking it again. . . . We did not suppose the troops actually engaged in the firing exceeded three or four hundred well-mounted men, but had a large body of cavalry moving parallel with them in easy supporting distance. This was a very effectual mode of throwing the march of the wagon train into confusion, independent of the absolute destruction they caused.

"The burning caissons, as we rode by, were anything but pleasant neighbors, and were exploding right and left. . . . We could hear the enemy ahead of us as we pressed our tired horses through the burning wagons and the scattered plunder which filled the road, giving our own wagon-rats and skulkers a fine harvest of plunder. Many of the wagons were untouched, but standing in the road without horses, the teamsters at the first alarm taking them out and making for the woods, coming back and taking their wagons again after the stampede was over, some-times to find them plundered by their own cowardly skulkers that I suppose belong to all armies. I have no doubt Caesar had them in his tenth legion, and Xenophon in his famous ten thousand.

"So far the enemy, in carrying out his plan of attack, had kept in motion; but after passing a large creek that crosses the road and runs on by Amelia Springs they halted at an old field on the side of the road and made a front. As the head of our column crossed the creek a lady was standing in the mud by the roadside with a soldier in a gray jacket. She had been with the ordnance train. The ambulance in which she had been riding was taken, the horses carried off; and as we closed up she was left as we found her. She was from Mississippi, and had left Rich-mond with her friends in the artillery, and was much more mad than scared, and she stood there in the mud—she was young and pretty—and gesticulated as she told her story. . . . There was no time to listen, but, promising to do our best to punish the aggressors, who had taken her up and dropped her so unceremoniously in the mud, which was the amount of the damage, and, advising her to take shelter in a large white house on the hill, we moved on to meet the [Union] party ahead, who, near enough [to] their reserve now for support, had halted to give us a taste of their quality.

"At first they called out [for us] to come on . . . seeing the small party [we had] in advance with the General [Martin W. Gary]; but as [our] regiments rode into the field, which was large enough to make a display of the entire line, they stood but to exchange a scattering fire, and then moved in retreat along a road running parallel to the main road and leading to Amelia Springs. The 7th [the narrator's unit], from position, was the leading regiment, and moved at a gallop in pursuit. The road swept round a point of wood on the left, and an old field on the right grown up with pine. In advance rode five well-mounted men of the regiment as a lookout, led by the adjutant—General Gary immediately behind them—and the head of our column, the 7th Cavalry, next.

"As the advance guard rounded the bend in the road it was swept by the fire of the enemy, who had halted for that purpose, wheeling instantly in retreat as soon as they delivered their fire. Four men out of the five, all except the adjutant, were hit, one of them in the spine: Mills, an approved scout and one of the best and bravest men in the army. Throwing his arms over his head with a yell of agony, wrung from him by intense pain, he pitched backwards off his horse, which was going at full speed. The horse, a thoroughbred mare, kept on with us in the rush. (I will here say that I never saw the young man again—he was just in front of me when he fell—until three or four years after, in a pulpit, as a Presbyterian preacher. He had gotten over his wound without its doing him permanent injury.)

"On we went, picking up some of the rear of the [Union] party who had not moved quick enough. The main body had gotten where there were thick woods on both sides of the road, where they halted to make a stand. But we were upon them before they made their wheel to face to the rear, or, rather, while they were in the act of making it, and so had them at advantage. We were among them with the saber. The work was short and sharp, and we drove them along the road clear of the wood into the open field, where [they had] a strong dismounted reserve.

"Here we caught a fire that dropped two of our leading horses—Captain Caldwell's and Lieutenant Hinson's. Caldwell's horse was killed. . . . Hinson's fell with a broken leg, catching his rider under him and holding him until relieved. A heavy fire swept the woods and road, so we dismounted the brigade as fast as the men came up, extending the dismounted line along the front of the enemy's fire, and moving to the left as he fell back to a stronger position. As we moved in advance, they gave up the position by the house they had first taken, fell back across the field and ravine to the top of the opposite hill, where they halted in force and threw up temporary breastworks made from a rail fence, and from that position repeated the invitation to [attack them]. . . .

"We moved up, occupied the ravine immediately in their front, which was deep enough to shelter [our] mounted [staff] officers, the line officers and the men being dismounted. Here General Gary determined to hold his position until General Fitz Lee [a nephew of Robert E.], who commanded our cavalry, came up, not deeming it advisable to attack the enemy in his present position and numbers. In half an hour's time, General Fitz Lee came up with his division, dismounted his men, formed line, flanked the position, charged it in front, two or three heavy volleys, a shout and a rush. The enemy, finding his position untenable, moved off to the main body, not more than two or three miles from them—moving rapidly, as we found several of their wounded on the roadside, left in the hurry of their retreat.

"We moved on slowly after them—the sun being nearly down—to Amelia Springs, some two miles off, crossed the creek, and . . . were politely requested (everybody knows what a military request is) by General Lee [Fitz] to move down the road until we could see the Yankee pickets, put the brigade into camp, post pickets, and make the best of it—all of which we did."

In spite of the vigorous response to his raid, Union General Henry Davies was able to report that he had captured "five guns, eleven flags, 320 white prisoners, an equal number of colored teamsters, and over 400 animals . . . leaving behind me 200 blazing ammunition and head-quarters wagons, caissons, and ambulances."

At Jetersville that afternoon, Union Generals Sheridan and Meade had discussed ways of dealing with Lee's main body but could not agree on a course of action. Matters were not helped by the fact that Meade was struggling with an illness that restricted him to movement by ambulance only. Sheridan decided to send a courier message to Grant, who was still riding with the pursuit's southern column, Ord's Army of the James, which had spent the day passing through Nottoway Court House on its way to Burkeville. This march of the southern troops, as it centered around Grant, is described by assistant surgeon Alfred Woodhull:

"During a midday rest at Nottoway Court House, a group was gath-ered on the stoop or porch of the deserted tavern, which, except for the dusty undress uniforms, might well have been taken for a simple party of travelers. There was no parade, no display. The main road on which

Fitzhugh Lee

the troops were marching was not in immediate view. A few orderlies held the horses and attended to their wants. Some of the dozen men walked hither and thither, evidently unemployed. One or two were half asleep. One or two more were jotting down, or referring to, notes in little books.

"A sturdy, thoughtful, but cheerful-looking man, who seemed the head of the party, talked occasionally with others, who listened respectfully or replied, as the case might be. His voice, as caught, was low, but clear and gentle. There appeared in his manner, or in that of his companions, nothing to excite remark, certainly nothing to inspire awe; and, above all, there was not the least token of . . . 'fuss and feathers,' no glitter and dash such as the heroes of the books are often invested with. The most timid child would not have hesitated to ask a favor of that cigar-smoking, tawny-bearded, kindly looking man, who was General Grant with his staff. A good share of the brains engaged in antagonizing the Rebellion spent an hour or two on that rusty old tavern porch; but no sign of tinsel was hung out, and no nerve-power was wasted in attitudes.

"The march that day was long; but, about the middle of the afternoon, glad tidings came over from the other line; and the dispatch was read to the troops while in motion. . . . [This was the news of the cavalry raid on the Confederate train.] As the head of each brigade reached a certain point, the dispatch was read; and it moved along with a livelier tread. Each command in turn gave the cheer of thanksgiving; and it was propagated by contagion front and rear. Those ahead renewed it, glad that others were sharing in the joy they just had felt. Those behind took it up, full of faith that there was good cause for the outburst. After a while they seemed only to fear lest there would be no Rebels left for them to capture.

"A few hours later the western sun looked full in the face of the moving column. The road, which there ran by the side of a forest, was filled with troops who swung along with the free, full stride of men whose legs kept time to the quick-step of earnest hearts. . . . The fairly-reflecting steel of the arms shone like a glory over the entire array. . . . As far as the eye could reach, the curving country road was vivid with . . . blue and steel. On the left were green fields, cultivated and refreshing to the sight. On the right the road was bordered by a forest whose trees were full-grown and old.

"Through this forest, and by the side of this magnificent body, Generals Grant and Ord had been riding together; and their well-mounted staffs and escorts formed a large and sprightly cavalcade, winding in and out between the trees, here comparatively free from undergrowth. Their rattling sabers and their greater vivacity, the more-quickly moving horses, and the occasional change of pace or direction, gave more of the notion of mobility than the monotonous tramp, tramp of the infantry. The swiftly falling sun in the clear heavens threw shadows that magnified the originals into an army of giants, while its direct rays glorified all they touched.

"Ord had just fallen back, and Grant was beginning to move ahead at a livelier gait; the mingled staffs had said good-by, and were again gathered into their proper groups; the escorts had closed up in their respective places—when from the right and rear two troopers in the Rebel uniform dashed out of the wood on literally foam-flecked horses. They were only two; but to the outward eye their dusty gray clothes, their long hair and wild aspect, and their general appearance . . . typical of the Southern cavalry, marked them as unquestionably Rebels. But their bold and rapid advance directly up to the column declared them . . . as scouts.

"Inquiring for General Grant, they fairly pushed their horses to a run in their eagerness to overtake him. . . . Grant . . . halted and read their dispatch, [and,] imperturbable as ever, turned to . . . his staff: 'Colonel———and Colonel———, I wish you to go with me.' While a [fresh] horse was being prepared, he spoke a few words to his adjutant general, and, before remounting, wrote a line or two, using a saddled horse as a desk.

"Meanwhile, the ceaseless stream of infantry was rolling by his side; the lower and lower sun cast greater shadows from the huge trees, and still brighter beams from the polished barrels; the great clusters of horsemen again coalesced, full of chat and conjecture; the hard-riding scouts at first loosened and then tightened their horses' girths and their own belts; and then, just as the sun went down, the lieutenant-general and the . . . aides, with an orderly or two and the mysterious strangers [plus a small escort] started off on a long trot directly through the darkening forest, at right angles to our line of march and into a country which, if it held anything, held Rebels. They were going to the [northern] column, for Grant had news from Sheridan."

One of the aides who accompanied Grant was Horace Porter, who questioned the head scout, a man named Campbell, about the trip. "I . . . found that we would have to follow some crossroads through a wooded country and travel nearly twenty miles. It was now dark, but there was enough moonlight to enable us to see the way without difficulty. After riding for nearly two hours, the enemy's campfires were seen in the distance. . . . Knowing that scouts are seldom trustworthy, and are often in the employ of both sides, and feeling that the general's safety was now entirely in the power of a comparatively unknown man, I, for one, began to grow suspicious.

"Just then Campbell fell back several paces and suddenly turned his horse into a piece of woods which we were skirting, and seemed to be acting in a manner that indicated either confusion or treachery. I cocked my pistol and rode close behind him, thinking his feelings would stand that much in the way of precaution anyhow, and determined that if he was caught giving any suspicious signals I would at once arrest him. The scout, however, was thoroughly loyal and one of Sheridan's most trusted men; no thought of treachery had crossed his mind; he was only looking for a shortcut through the woods.

"About half-past ten o'clock we struck Sheridan's pickets. They could hardly be made to understand that the general-in-chief was wandering about at that hour with so small an escort, and so near to the enemy's lines. The cavalry were sleeping on their arms, and as our little party picked its way through their ranks and the troopers woke up and recognized the general in the moonlight, their remarks were highly characteristic of the men. One said, 'Why, there's the old man. Boys, this means business'; and another, 'Great Scott! The old chief's out here himself. The rebs are going to get busted tomorrow, certain'; and a third, 'Uncle Sam [i.e., Grant] has joined the cavalry sure enough. You can bet there'll be lively times here in the morning.'

"Sheridan was awaiting us, feeling sure that the general would come after getting his dispatch. A good supper of beef, cold chicken, and coffee was soon prepared, and it was quickly demonstrated that the night ride had not impaired anyone's appetite.

"When the general-in-chief had learned fully the situation in Sheridan's front, he first sent a message to Ord to watch the roads running south from Burkeville and Farmville, and then went over to Meade's camp nearby. Meade was lying down, and still suffering from illness. His views differed somewhat from General Grant's regarding the movements of the Army of the Potomac for the next day, and the latter changed the dispositions that were being made. . . ."

17

Skirmishes on the Run

During the night of April 5–6, Lee started his army westward through Deatonsville toward Farmville, the latter about twenty-five miles from Amelia Court House. The column was soon strung over a dozen miles. James Longstreet's 1st Army Corps was in the lead (Longstreet had absorbed Hill's 3rd Army Corps into his own upon the latter's death on April 2). In the center of the long column was a modest corps (lately of the defenses southwest of Petersburg) under Richard H. Anderson, followed by Richard Ewell's Reserve Corps from Richmond. Ewell was senior commander of the central forces. He also outranked John Gordon, whose 2nd Army Corps occupied the column's rear-guard position.

Meade's Army of the Potomac and Phil Sheridan's cavalry got moving at dawn, and, under Grant's supervision, the march soon developed so that one part of the combination was pushing Lee from the rear while another was maintaining a course parallel with his southern flank.

Union General Ord's Army of the James was then closing on Burkeville, nearly ten miles south of the Deatonsville arena. It became Ord's mission to throw a small party of infantry and cavalry northwestward across Lee's front in an attempt to destroy High Bridge, an Appomattox crossing along the route to Farmville. Ord's party, commanded by General Theodore Read and Colonel Francis Washburn, had the misfortune to encounter a strong cavalry force, commanded by General Thomas L. Rosser, that was operating in Longstreet's front, its job to protect the bridge.

Ord tells what happened: "The gallant Read drew up his little band of eighty cavalry and 500 infantry, rode along the front of his ranks, inspired them with all his own daring, and began the battle. . . . Charge after charge was made by the handful of cavalry, led by the chivalrous Washburn. . . . But Read fell mortally wounded, then Washburn; and at last not an officer of that cavalry party remained alive or unwounded to lead the men, and not until then did they [and the infantry] surrender."

Read's sacrificial fight with Rosser was not without effect. Longstreet's van, anticipating the arrival of more of Ord's troops, interrupted its march and began entrenching. One of the officers with the van was Lieutenant Colonel William Miller Owen, who gives a vignette that was part of the fight's aftermath: "I was sitting on my horse, watching the men build a rude breastwork of rails and earth, when I heard a familiar voice behind me, inquiring the whereabouts of General Longstreet. I turned to look, and there was Rosser, mounted upon a superb black horse. I had not seen him for months. We shook hands, and I inquired the news. He said, 'Oh! We have captured those people who were going to destroy the bridge; took them all in. But Jim Dearing is mortally wounded. He had a hand-to-hand encounter with the commanding officer of the Federals, General Read, and cut him down from his horse, killing him; but Read's orderly shot Dearing through the body; and then he, too, was shot. It was a gallant fight. This is Read's horse, and this his saber. Both beauties, aren't they? But I must see Longstreet.' Then for the first time I noticed that Rosser was wounded in the arm; but he always made light of such 'scratches.' We hunted up Longstreet, and . . . Rosser . . . made his report. . . ."

While these incidents were occurring in the forefront of Lee's column, weightier events were convulsing its center and rear. The Union troops involved were Sheridan's cavalry, backed by Horatio G. Wright's 6th Corps, who worked against the center from their route paralleling its southern flank, and Andrew A. Humphreys's 2nd Corps, which came up from the rear to harass Gordon. Sheridan and his cavalry spent a good part of the day galloping along the flank of the gray line, making small strikes at every opportunity and looking for a weak spot against which to hurl a major attack with both cavalry and infantry. Humphreys, meanwhile, had resolved to give Gordon no rest.

Humphreys's leading division was that of Brevet Major General Gershom Mott, and Mott's leading brigade was led by Brigadier General P. Regis de Trobriand, a French soldier of fortune whose men found amusement in his broken English and Continental mannerisms,

A cavalry duel

but were inspired by the quality of his leadership. De Trobriand relates: "It was about nine o'clock in the morning when our division caught up with the rear guard of the enemy. . . . General Mott communicated his instructions to me while my regiments were rapidly advancing. Ten minutes after, we were engaged with the enemy. The 20th Indiana, deployed as skirmishers and supported by the 124th New York, had rapidly ascended a hill and begun to drive the rebels, who fell back along the Deatonsville road.

"We advanced firing, with a rapid step, when Mott, wishing to examine for himself the dispositions I had made, came to join me on the skirmish line. 'Everything goes along finely,' he said. 'Push on vigorously and try to reach the wagons, which are a short distance away. If you capture them, it is quite probable you may find a commission of major general.' He had hardly stepped back four paces when the sound of a ball striking against leather made me turn my head. I remarked a hurried movement among the staff officers. Several leaped from their horses; and, in the midst of a group, I saw the general stretched on the ground. A ball had gone through his leg, passing between the two bones below the knee. When he saw me near him, he raised himself on his elbow to say to me, 'You have command of the division. You already know your instructions. I have nothing to add. Carry them out vigorously. Good luck and good-bye.'

"He was carried off on a litter, suffering less from physical pain than from moral disappointment at not being able to assist at the denouement of the drama in which he had played for four years a part as meritorious as distinguished."

De Trobriand's movement, augmented by a second brigade, was continued. One of the men in the added brigade was Color Sergeant D. G. Crotty. "In this fight," he says, "we lose a great many good men in killed and wounded. But we pass over the bodies of a great number of the enemy, who have fought their last battle for the 'lost cause.' We have got the enemy . . . on the run, and we go for them on the double-quick. Our gallant Colonel [John] Pulford is on horseback, and it would seem as though he would be pierced with a bullet every moment. We try to have him dismount, but he knows no fear. . . .

"The enemy . . . have . . . taken up a position near a brick house, where they fight very wickedly, as they are trying to get a large wagon train away from our reach, which is in their rear. The rebels are posted at every window in the house, and keep up a vigorous fire on us. On the crest of a hill beyond they have a very wicked battery, which they

Eng.ᵈ by A H Ritchie.

Andrew A. Humphreys

use right lively. Now we are exposed too much for nothing, and would much rather charge on them than stand their fire. So the order is given to go forward, and inside of two minutes the brick house is ours. The Johnnies who fired at us are pulled out of the windows and taken prisoners. The enemy's battery still holds its position, and pour in shell thick and fast, but we have good shelter now, and wait for the rest of our lines to come up, which they do in a few minutes."

De Trobriand now ordered forward a section of artillery, and watched as "a lively cannonade followed, to such good purpose that soon guns and horses disappeared before them. During the engagement, General Humphreys had come up on the line. We dismounted in order to advance out of the woods by a road running along a slope from which the movements of the enemy could be better discovered. We must have been noticed, for the balls began to whistle about our ears with a persistency which certainly was not due to chance. But, as General Humphreys paid no attention to them, it was not my place to notice them. He asked me as to the exact position of my three brigades, consulted a topographical sketch which he held in his hand, explained to me where the road led to, where we had a good opportunity to strike the rear of the enemy's train, and, above all, the guns of the rear guard, which he was particularly desirous of capturing. Finally, satisfied on all points, 'I think,' said he in a calm voice, 'we had better get further to the rear.' We retraced our steps without accident."

Among the rear-guard Confederates who participated in the subsequent action was Private Carlton McCarthy, who explains that "some men of Cutshaw's artillery battalion, acting as infantry, made a stand for a while on a piece of high ground. They noticed, hanging around in a lonely, distracted way, a tall, lean, shaggy fellow holding, or, rather, leaning on, a long staff, around which hung a faded battle-flag. Thinking him out of his place and skulking, they suggested to him that it would be well for him to join his regiment. He replied that his regiment had all run away, and he was merely waiting a chance to be useful. Just then the enemy's advancing skirmishers poured a hot fire into the group, and the artillerymen began to discuss the propriety of leaving. The colorbearer, remembering their insinuations, saw an opportunity for retaliation.

"Standing, as he was, in the midst of a shower of musket balls, he seemed almost ready to fall asleep. But suddenly his face was illumined with a singularly pleased and childish smile. Quietly walking up close to the group, he said, 'Any of you boys want to *charge?*' The boys

The coolheaded color-bearer

answered, 'Yes.' 'Well,' said the imperturbable, 'I'm the man to carry this here old flag for you. Just follow me.' So saying, he led the squad full into the face of the advancing enemy, and never once seemed to think of stopping until he was urged to retire with the squad. He came back smiling from head to foot, and suffered no more insinuations."

Returning to Union General de Trobriand: "The chase recommences. A new line, hurriedly made and feebly defended, is again carried. . . . A hundred yards further on, the hill is crowned by a slope strengthened by fences and felled trees, behind which appears a well filled line. . . . [Our] line of battle is formed along a covered hedge, under fire from invisible artillery, which is searching us with shell from beyond the crest where the infantry awaits us. In a few minutes, six regiments are ready to charge. . . . At the command, all dash forward at once. The strife is to see who will pass ahead of the others and first plant the colors on the enemy's intrenchments. No one remains behind. The wounded fall; they will be picked up afterward. The first thing was to strike the enemy.

"It was a beautiful sight. The six flags advanced in line as though carried by six human waves, which ascended without halting until they had extinguished and submerged the flaming dyke which was raised in front of them. And, with no other delay than the time required to collect two or three hundred prisoners and reform the ranks, continually following the retreating enemy, we arrived at Deatonsville."

Union General Humphreys now pushed a second division forward to march abreast of de Trobriand's, and, as the Frenchman goes on to say, the work against Gordon proceeded "at a fine rate. Twenty-eight wagons and five guns had already fallen into our hands. At each capture the ardor of the chase increased. The men no longer halted even to load. When an obstacle presented itself, behind which the enemy made a pretense of standing, the skirmishers ran upon them with cheers. The regiments nearest dashed forward, and the position was carried even before the rest of the column knew what was going on."

It was during these operations in the rear of Lee's column that Union General Phil Sheridan's troopers (forefronted by a division under an aggressive young general named George Armstrong Custer) found the weak spot they had been seeking on the southern flank of Lee's center. As explained by Union General Henry Davies, whose brigade of horsemen took part in the show: "At a point near Rice's Station a break was made in the Confederate line, and the cavalry destroyed several hundred wagons and captured sixteen guns and a large number of prisoners. This attack, of itself producing valuable results, was the more important as it interrupted the line of retreat and closed the road to Ewell's corps [the narrator is speaking of Ewell's and Anderson's troops as a unit, with Ewell in command] that was endeavoring to follow that of Longstreet."

Cut off in front, Ewell ordered a train of wagons moving in his rear to take a road to the right, or to the northwest, his purpose to remove the train from the threat of attack. Confederate General Gordon, who had been following these wagons while fighting his rear-guard action, turned off with them, unaware that he was breaking contact with Ewell, from whom he received no orders. Union General Davies sums up: "This separation of Ewell's corps from the troops in his front and rear gave opportunity for the Battle of Sayler's Creek,* which immediately followed."

---

*Almost invariably given as "Sailor's Creek" in Civil War records. Proper spelling has been substituted here and in passages ahead.

18
The Battle of Sayler's Creek

The Battle of Sayler's Creek comprised two engagements fought simultaneously. When Gordon angled off to the right, bypassing Ewell, Humphreys continued on Gordon's trail, and this part of the proceedings was a running fight. To the south, Sheridan's cavalry kept Ewell occupied until Wright's 6th Corps came up, after which Ewell (Anderson's troops with him) was virtually surrounded. Both engagements took place among the environs of the creek, the waters of which originated south of the combat zone and meandered generally northward to the Appomattox. The attack of Sheridan and Wright upon Ewell was the afternoon's main event.

Ewell's dispositions were made on a set of elevations west of the creek. As it happened, the battalion under Robert Stiles occupied a spot that became the scene of some of the battle's bloodiest work. According to Stiles, things began with a desultory fire. "Bullets began to drop in. I was walking about among the men, seeing that everything was in order and talking cheerfully with them, when I heard a ball strike something hard and saw a little commotion around the battalion colors. Going there, I found that the flagstaff had been splintered. . . . Next moment I heard an outcry, 'There, Brookin is killed!' and saw one of the men writhing on the ground. I went to him. He seemed to be partially paralyzed below the waist, but said he was shot through the neck. I saw no blood anywhere. He had on his roll of blankets, and, sure enough, a ball had gone through them and also through his jacket and flannel shirt. But there it was, sticking in the back of his neck, having barely broken the skin. I took it out and said, 'O, you are not a dead man by a good deal. Here' (handing the ball to him) 'take that home and give it to your sweetheart. . . .' Brookin caught at the ball and held it tightly clasped in his hand, smiling faintly, and the men about him laughed.

"Just then I heard a shell whizzing over us, coming from across the creek, and we were hurried into line facing in that direction, that is, to the rear. I inferred of course, that we were surrounded, but could not tell how strong the force was. . . .

". . . In all the discomfort and wretchedness of the retreat, we had been no little amused by the Naval Battalion [from the James River defenses] under that old hero, Admiral [John R.] Tucker. The soldiers called them the 'Aye, Ayes,' because they responded 'aye, aye' to every order. . . . As this battalion, which followed immediately after ours, was getting into position, and seamen's and landsmen's jargon and movements were getting a good deal mixed in the orders and evolutions . . . a young officer [a soldier] of the division staff rode up, saluted Admiral Tucker, and said, 'Admiral, may I possibly be of assistance to you in getting your command into line?' The Admiral replied, 'Young man, I understand how to talk to my people!' And thereupon followed a grand moral combination of 'right flank' and 'left flank,' 'starboard' and 'larboard,' 'aye, aye,' and 'aye, aye,' until the battalion gradually settled down into place.

"By this time a large Federal force had deployed into line on the other slope beyond the creek, which we had left not long since, two or three lines of battle and a heavy park of artillery which rapidly came into battery and opened an accurate and deadly fire, we having no guns with which to reply and thus disturb their aim. My men were lying down and were ordered not to expose themselves. I was walking backward and forward just back of the line, talking to them whenever that was practicable, and keeping my eye upon everything. . . . A good many men had been wounded and several killed, when a twenty-pounder Parrott shell struck immediately in my front, on the line, nearly severing a man in twain, and hurling him bodily over my head, his arms hanging down and his hands almost slapping me in the face as they passed. . . .

"In a few moments the artillery fire ceased and I had time to glance about me and note results a little more carefully. I had seldom seen a fire more accurate, nor one that had been more deadly . . . in so brief a time. The expression of the men's faces indicated clearly enough its effect upon them. They did not appear to be hopelessly demoralized, but they did look blanched and haggard and awe-struck.

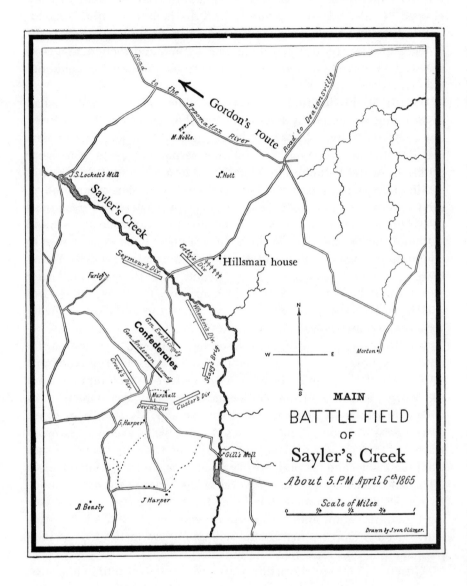

MAIN

BATTLE FIELD

OF

Sayler's Creek

About 5. P.M. April 6th 1865

Scale of Miles

Drawn by J. von Glümer.

"The Federal infantry had crossed the creek and were now coming up the slope in two lines of battle. I stepped in front of my line and passed from end to end, impressing upon my men that no one must fire his musket until I so ordered; that when I said '*ready*' they must all rise, kneeling on the right knee; that when I said '*aim*' they must all aim about the knees of the advancing line; that when I said '*fire*' they must all fire together, and that it was all-important they should follow these directions exactly, and obey, implicitly and instantly, any other instructions or orders I might give.

"The enemy was coming on, and everything was still as the grave. My battalion was formed upon and around a swell of the hill, which threw it further to the front than any other command in the division, so that I was compelled to shape my own course, as I had received no special orders. The Federal officers, knowing, as I suppose, that we were surrounded, and appreciating the fearful havoc their artillery fire had wrought, evidently expected us to surrender, and had their white handkerchiefs in their hands, waving them toward us as if suggesting this course. . . .

"The enemy showed no disposition to break into the charge, but continued to advance in the same deliberate and even hesitating manner, and I allowed them to approach very close . . . before retiring behind my men. I had continued to walk along their front for the very purpose of preventing them from opening fire; but now I stepped through the line, and, stationing myself about the middle of it, called out my orders deliberately, the enemy, I am satisfied, hearing every word. 'Ready!' To my great delight the men rose, all together, like a piece of mechanism, kneeling on their right knees, and their faces set with an expression that meant everything. 'Aim!' The musket barrels fell to an almost perfect horizontal line leveled about the knees of the advancing front line. 'Fire!'

"I have never seen such an effect, physical and moral, produced by the utterance of one word. The enemy seemed to have been totally unprepared for it, and, as the sequel showed, my own men scarcely less so. The earth appeared to have swallowed up the first line of the Federal force in our front. There was a rattling supplement to [our] volley, and the second line wavered and broke. . . . On the instant every man in my battalion sprang to his feet and, without orders, rushed bareheaded and with unloaded muskets down the slope after the retreating Federals. I tried to stop them, but in vain, although I actually got ahead of a good many of them. They simply bore me on with the flood."

Says the Union commander, Horatio Wright: "I was never more astonished. These troops were surrounded—the 1st and 3rd divisions of [my] corps were on either flank, my artillery and a fresh division in their front, and some three divisions of Major General Sheridan's cavalry in their rear. Looking upon them as already our prisoners, I had ordered the artillery to cease firing as a dictate of humanity. My surprise, therefore, was extreme when this force charged upon our front. . . ."

Southerner Robert Stiles resumes: "The standard-bearer was dashing by me, colors in hand, when I managed to catch his roll of blankets and jerk him violently back, demanding what he meant, advancing the battalion colors without orders. As I was speaking, the artillery opened fire again and he was hurled to the earth. . . . I stooped to pick up the flag, when his brother, a lieutenant, a fine officer and a splendid-looking fellow, stepped over the body, saying, 'Those colors belong to me, Major!,' at the same time taking hold of the staff. He was shot through the brain and fell backward. One of the color guard sprang forward, saying, 'Give them to me, Major!' But by the time his hand reached the staff he was down.

"There were at least five men dead and wounded lying close about me, and I did not see why I should continue to make a target of myself. I therefore jammed the color staff down through a thick bush, which supported it in an upright position, and turned my attention to my battalion, which was scattered over the face of the hill firing irregularly at the Federals, who seemed to be reforming to renew the attack. I managed to get my men into some sort of formation and their guns loaded, and then charged the Federal line, driving it back across the creek, and forming my command behind a little ridge, which protected it somewhat.

"I ran back up the hill and had a brief conversation with General Custis Lee [son of Robert E.], commanding the division (our brigade commander having been killed), explaining to him that I had not ordered the advance and that we would be cut off if we remained long where we were, but that I was satisfied I could bring the battalion back through a ravine, which would protect them largely from the fire of the enemy's artillery, and reform them on the old line. . . . He expressed his doubts as to this, but I told him I believed my battalion would follow me anywhere, and with his permission I would try it.

"I ran down the hill again and explained to my men that when I got to the left of the line and shouted to them they were to get up and follow me, on a run and without special formation, through a ravine that

Eng^d by A H Ritchie

Horatio G. Wright

led back to the top of the hill. Just because these simple-hearted fellows knew only enough to trust me, and because the enemy was not so far recovered as to take advantage of our exposure while executing the movement to the rear and reforming, we were back in the original lines in a few moments—that is, all who were left of us.

"It was of no avail. By the time we had well settled into our old position we were attacked simultaneously, front and rear, by over-whelming numbers, and, quicker than I can tell it, the battle degene-rated into a butchery and a confused melee of brutal personal conflicts. I saw numbers of men kill each other with bayonets and the butts of muskets, and even bite each other's throats and ears and noses, rolling on the ground like wild beasts. I saw one of my officers and a Federal officer fighting with swords over the battalion colors, which we had brought back with us, each having his left hand upon the staff. I could not get to them, but my man was a very athletic, powerful seaman, and soon I saw the Federal officer fall.

"I had cautioned my men against wearing [captured] Yankee over-coats, especially in battle, but had not been able to enforce the order perfectly, and almost at my side I saw a young fellow of one of my companies jam the muzzle of his musket against the back of the head of his most intimate friend, clad in a Yankee overcoat, and blow his brains out."

A Union participant on this part of the field, Captain Archibald Hopkins, explains that "clouds of sulphurous smoke obscured every-thing not close at hand, and it was as these opened and shifted that I had glimpses of battle groups and scenes which will always remain in my memory. . . . The battle was now at its height. Blue and Gray mingled in a confused mass, swayed back and forth in the eddying smoke, and fierce cries of 'Down with 'em! Give 'em hell!' and the clashing of crossed bayonets could be heard rising above the sound of the musketry. Intense excitement swallowed up all sense of danger, and every man fought almost with savage fury. . . .

"A corporal who was noted for his quiet promptitude and unvarying good behavior found himself confronted by a rebel officer whose sur-render he demanded. The officer refused, and the corporal fired, shoot-ing him through the body. As he fell, the corporal bent over him and told him that he was sorry he had to shoot him, and that he was a Christian, and, if he wished, he would pray with him. The officer eagerly assented, and the corporal knelt amidst the drifting smoke and flying missiles and the shouts and groans of the combatants, and offered a

Surrender of Ewell's command

fervent prayer for the soul of his dying foeman. When he had finished, they shook hands, and the officer gave the corporal his sword as a memento, and asked him to write to his wife what had befallen him.

"An Irish corporal, whose brother had been killed on the parapet in the assault on Petersburg a few days before, concealed himself in a thicket and killed nine rebels. . . . He said he didn't know as it would help poor Mike any, but somehow he felt 'aisyer about the heart.' "

Other parts of the line were host to similar scenes of slaughter, with the Federals finding another especially stubborn foe in Major General Joseph B. Kershaw's division of Georgians and Mississippians. But it wasn't long before the Confederates everywhere understood the futility of their situation. "I don't think," says Robert Stiles, "I ever suffered more than during the few moments after I saw that nothing could possibly affect or change the result of the battle." As his men began surrendering, Stiles decided to try to escape. "I had always considered it likely I should be killed, but had never anticipated or contemplated capture. . . . Selecting the direction which seemed to be most free from Federal soldiers . . . I started first at a walk and then broke into a run; but in a short distance ran into a fresh Federal force, and it seemed the most natural and easy thing in the world to be simply arrested and taken in. . . . Thus ended my active life as a Confederate soldier, my four years' service under Marse Robert, and I was not sorry to end it thus, in red-hot battle, and to be spared the pain, I will not say humiliation, of Appomattox."

Only about 2,000 of Ewell's men got through the cordon of infantry and cavalry and made their escape. Nearly 6,000 surrendered. Phil Sheridan's dashing subordinate George Custer was able to report: "Lieutenant General Ewell and six other general officers were captured . . . by my command." The Confederate generals in the battle included George Pickett, who got away. He explains: "A squadron of the enemy's cavalry was riding down upon us, two of my staff and myself, when a small squad of my men recognized me and, risking their own lives, rallied to our assistance and suddenly delivered a last volley into the faces of the pursuing horsemen, checking them but for a moment. But in that one moment we, by the speed of our horses, made our escape."

Robert E. Lee had played no part in the fight. He had spent the afternoon up toward the front of his column with James Longstreet. When word of the crisis in his center reached him, Lee detached the division commanded by William ("Little Billy") Mahone from Longstreet's rear and rushed to the scene. It was sunset when the two

Eng⁴ by A.H.Ritchie.

William Mahone

mounted generals topped a rise that gave them a panoramic view of the disaster, dramatized as it was by rows of burning wagons. The 2,000 escapees were streaming toward them, some bareheaded, many without weapons, a column of Federals marching in their wake. In Mahone's words: "At this spectacle General Lee straightened himself in his saddle, and . . . exclaimed, as if talking to himself, 'My God, has the army dissolved?' As quickly as I could control my own voice I replied, 'No, general, here are troops ready to do their duty'; when, in a mellowed voice, he replied, 'Yes, general, there are some true men left. Will you please keep those people [the Federals] back?' As I was placing my division in position to 'keep those people back,' the retiring herd . . . crowded around General Lee while he sat on his horse with a Confederate battle flag in his hand."

Some of the defeated men called for Lee to lead them in a counterattack, but the general was only too glad to see the crisis end with Mahone's deployment, which checked the Federal pursuit. Lee learned with a pang that his son Custis was among those who had fallen into enemy hands.

19

Sayler's Creek Continued

The running fight to the north, that between the relentless Humphreys and the reeling Gordon, had continued with scarcely a lull. Gordon found it regrettable that he had to abandon not only his dead but also his disabled wounded. "There was no longer any room in the crowded ambulances which had escaped capture and still accompanied our trains. We could do nothing for the unfortunate sufferers who were too severely wounded to march, except leave them on the roadside with canteens of water."

The general goes on to give a vignette of Union origin that he learned of later: "A bighearted soldier-boy in blue came across a desperately wounded Confederate shot through legs and body, lying in his bloody bed of leaves, groaning with pain and sighing for relief in death. The generous Federal was so moved by the harrowing spectacle that he stopped at the side of the Confederate and asked, 'What can I do for you, Johnny? I want to help you if I can.' 'Thank you for your sympathy,' the sufferer replied, 'but no one can help me now. It will not be long till death relieves me.'

"The Union soldier bade him good-by and was in the act of leaving when the wounded Southerner called to him, 'Yes, Yank, there is something you might do for me. You might pray for me before you go.' This Union boy had probably never uttered aloud a word of prayer in all his life. But his emotions were deeply stirred, and through his tears he looked around for someone more accustomed to lead in prayer. Discovering some of his comrades passing, he called to them, 'Come here, boys, and come quick. Here is a poor Johnny shot all to pieces, and he's dying. One of you must come and pray for him. He wants me to pray for him, but you know I can't pray worth a damn.' "

The retiring Confederates had to cope with Federals not only in their rear but also on their flanks. As related by Southerner Carlton McCarthy of Cutshaw's battalion: "Some sharp-eyed man discovered three of the enemy's skirmishers in a field away on the left. More for amusement than anything else, it was proposed to fire at them. A group of men gathered on the roadside, a volley was fired, and, to the amazement of the marksmen, for the distance was great, one of the skirmishers fell. One of his comrades started on a run to his assistance, and he, too, was stopped. The third man then scampered away as fast as his legs could carry him. The battalion applauded the good shots and marched on."

It was nearly sundown when Union General Byron R. Pierce's brigade of Regis de Trobriand's division spearheaded the day's final attack. De Trobriand says that "General Pierce, on emerging from a thick wood, found himself in front of an abrupt hill crowned by a slope, behind which the enemy in force opposed a determined resistance. The cause was soon known. On the crest of the hill, which was reached by a winding slope, the road turned sharply to the left, and thus was parallel to our front. The enemy's trains were still defiling there, and it was to save them that the entire rear guard opposed us."

Cutshaw's battalion was among the Confederate units in the fore of the line of battle. "It was amusing," claims Carlton McCarthy (who was in the midst of things but leaves his personal role a mystery), "to see the men hauling out of their pockets a mixture of corn, salt, caps, and cartridges, and, selecting the material needed, loading. . . . The enemy's skirmishers advanced confidently and in rather free and easy style, but suddenly met a volley which drove them to cover. Again they advanced, in better order, and again the improvised infantry [i.e., these troops who had, until recently, been artillerymen] forced them back. Then came their line of battle in overwhelming numbers; but the battalion stubbornly resisted their advance.

"[Our] men, not accustomed to the orderly manner of infantry, dodged about from tree to tree, and with the deliberation of huntsmen picked off here and there a man. When a shot 'told,' the marksman hurrahed, all to himself. There was an evident desire to press forward and drive the advancing foe. Several of the men were so enthusiastic that they had pushed ahead of the line, and several yards in advance they could be seen loading and firing as deliberately as though practicing at a mark.

"Colonel Cutshaw received a wound which . . . shattered his leg. . . . Captain [Asher W.] Garber was struck, and called for the ambulance corps, but on examination found the ball in his pocket. It had lodged against the rowel of a spur which he found the day before and dropped in his pocket.

"At last the enemy appeared in strong force on both flanks, while he pushed hard in front. It was useless to attempt a further stand. The voice of Captain [Lorraine F.] Jones . . . rang out loud and clear, 'Boys, take care of yourselves!' Saying this, he planted himself against a pine, and, as his men rushed by him, emptied every chamber of his revolver at the enemy, and then reluctantly made his way, in company with several privates, down the hill to the creek.

"At the foot of the hill a group of perhaps a dozen men gathered around Lieutenant McRae. He was indignant. He proposed another stand, and his comrades agreed. They stood in the road, facing the gentle slope of the hill from which they had been ordered to retire. The enemy's skirmishers were already on the brow of the hill, dodging about among the trees and shouting to those behind to hurry up. Their favorite expressions were, 'Come along, boys. Here are the damned rebel wagons! Damn 'em; shoot 'em down!'

"In a few moments their line of battle, in beautiful order, stepped out of the woods with colors flying, and for a moment halted. In front of the center of that portion of the line which was visible—probably a full regimental front—marched the colors and color guard. McRae saw his opportunity. He ordered his squad to rise and fire on the colors. His order was promptly obeyed. The color bearer pitched forward and fell, with his colors, heavily to the ground. The guard of two men on either side shared the same fate, or else feigned it.

"Immediately [their] line of battle broke into disorder and came swarming down the hill, firing, yelling, and cursing as they came. An officer [in blue], mounted, rode his horse close to the fence on the roadside, and with the most superb insolence mocked McRae and his squad. . . . McRae, in his rage, swore back at him and . . . called on a man near him to shoot that '———,' calling him a fearfully hard name. But the private's gun was not in working order, and the fellow escaped for a time. Before he reached the woods whither he was going . . . a howitzer let fly at him, and . . . he threw his arms up in the air, and his horse bore him into the woods a corpse.

"A little to the left, where the road crossed the creek, the crack of pistols and the bang of muskets was continuous. The enemy had surrounded the wagons. . . .

Confederate soldier at Sayler's Creek

"In order [for us] to escape from the right of the line it was necessary to follow the road, which was along the foot of the hill, some distance to the left. The enemy, seeing this, were pushing their men rapidly at a right oblique to gain the road and cut off retreat. Consequently those who attempted escape in that direction had to run the gauntlet of a constant fusillade from a mass of troops near enough to select individuals, curse them, and command them to throw down their arms or be shot.

"Most of McRae's squad, in spite of the difficulties surrounding them, gained the creek, plunged in, and began a race for life up the long, open hillside of plowed ground, fired upon at every step by the swarm of men behind, and, before they reached the top, by a battery in close proximity, which poured down a shower of canister. The race to the top of the long hill was exceedingly trying to men already exhausted by continual marching, hunger, thirst, and loss of sleep. They ran, panting for breath, like chased animals, fairly staggering as they went.

"On the top of this long hill there was a skirmish line of [Confederate] cavalry posted, with orders to stop all men with arms in their hands and form a new line; but the view down the hill to the creek and beyond revealed such a host of the enemy, and the men retiring before them were so few, that the order was disregarded and the fleeing band allowed to pass through.

"The men's faces were black with powder. They had bitten cartridges until there was a deep black circle around their mouths. The burnt powder from the ramrods had blackened their hands, and in their efforts to remove the perspiration from their faces they had completed the coloring from the roots of the hair to the chin.

"Here was no place for rest, however, as the enemy's battery behind the creek on the opposite hills, having gotten the range, were pouring in a lively fire."

Darkness was now approaching, and the action wound down. Gordon continued on toward the Appomattox crossing at High Bridge, but his column had been badly hurt. Union corps commander Humphreys explains: "The captures of the corps were 13 flags, 4 guns, and 1,700 prisoners. The enemy's killed and wounded probably exceeded our own [311]. . . . The destruction of the wagon trains must have caused much additional suffering in Lee's army."

Not all of the captured wagons were destroyed. "The boys are tired after their day's work," says Union Color Sergeant D. G. Crotty, "but they must go for the wagons. We find all kinds of rebel clothing and dry goods, from a private's uniform to a major general's. We have plenty of rebel major generals and officers of every grade in our camp, for the boys don the gray uniforms. . . . The enthusiasm of the troops is unbounded, and all feel that the rebellion in Virginia is on its last legs."

Adds Union General Regis de Trobriand: "Among the prisoners we had made in the evening was a young sergeant whose intelligence had been noted by some officers of my staff. I sent for him and conversed some time with him. His replies can be given in a few words. 'General, I can tell you nothing which you do not well know. The Army of Northern Virginia no longer exists. What remains cannot escape you. It must end in that manner, and, since it cannot be otherwise, we do not regret that the day long foreseen has arrived. On the contrary, we are all rejoiced that the war is finished. If we had been consulted, it would have ended many months ago, but the government chose to hold out to the end.

" 'I was taken by the conscription. . . . Of those who volunteered at the beginning of the war, very few now remain. For six or eight months back, our men have deserted by thousands. Those who remain have been held by a sentiment of honor only. They did not wish to disgrace themselves by deserting their flag. They have done their duty to the best of their ability. As to the Southern Confederacy, although they would have liked to have seen it triumph, they lost all hope of it long since.

" 'Personally, I care little for slavery, and it is all the same to me whether the Negroes be free or not. I belong to a family of farmers who sometimes hired black labor, but who owned no slaves. Now, when we employ them, we will pay *them* instead of their masters; that is all the difference. As to politics, I have never taken any part. I know very well that the war was brought on principally for the benefit of the planters; but what could we do? When one is on board of a ship, he must do what he can to keep it afloat. The Confederacy has ruined the South by the war; our hope is now that the Union will raise her out of her ruin by peace.'

"When I had dismissed the prisoner, he halted a few steps away, hesitated an instant, then, turning towards me, said, 'General, your kindness has encouraged me to ask a favor of you. There are a half-dozen of us here who have found nothing to eat since day before yesterday. If you could give us each a cracker . . . we would be very thankful.' We were not very bountifully supplied ourselves; in fact, we were very far from it. But the sergeant did not return to his comrades empty-handed."

Even while de Trobriand and the prisoner were talking, those of Gordon's men who had escaped were completing their march to High Bridge. They did not cross at once, but halted for a rest. "In the darkness," says Carlton McCarthy, "the men commenced calling to each other by name. . . . Brother called brother, comrade called comrade, friend called friend; and there were many happy reunions there that night. Some, alas, of the best and bravest did not answer the cry of anxious friends."

At about midnight, Union General Phil Sheridan, encamped on the Sayler's Creek battlefield (where, incidentally, he had spent the evening sharing his fireside and his rations with Ewell and the other captured generals), sent a dispatch to Grant, then at Burkeville, giving the details of the day's victory. Sheridan explains that "in the same dispatch, I wrote, 'If the thing is pressed, I think that Lee will surrender.' When Mr. Lincoln, at City Point [just before his return to Washington], received this word from General Grant, who was transmitting every item of news to the President, he telegraphed Grant the laconic message, 'Let the thing be pressed.'"

20
High Bridge and Farmville

During the night of April 6–7, while Confederate General Gordon prepared to cross the Appomattox at High Bridge (with Lee having dispatched "Little Billy" Mahone's division and most of the survivors of Ewell's command to cross behind him), Longstreet's troops made their way through the darkness toward the crossings at Farmville, a village on the south bank of the river several miles to the west. By gaining the north bank and burning the bridges, Lee hoped to win a respite from Grant's pursuit.

Preceding Longstreet to Farmville was a detachment of Confederate cavalry, one of whose members was Edward Boykin. "When we got there [we] went through the town to the grove on the other side, and made the best of it. . . . By a big fire we lay down, and slept the sleep of the tired. The nights were cold, so near the mountains, and, with light coverings on the cold ground, the burning down of the fire was a general awakening and building up of the same. At one of these movements we were surprised to find, between Colonel H. and myself, two men, who, attracted by the fire, cold and tired, had crept to its friendly warmth, making a needless apology for their presence. We found one to be a colonel of Pickett's division, the other a lieutenant, and realized fully how complete the destruction of that famous fighting division must have been as an organization, that we should find a regimental commander who did not know where to look for its standard."

Among the organized Confederate regiments on the way to Farmville at this time was that to which J. F. J. Caldwell belonged. "We progressed at a snail's pace—halting, standing in the road a few minutes, closing up a few yards, stopping again for a few minutes, closing up again a few yards, all night long."

At High Bridge, according to Southerner Carlton McCarthy, Gordon's troops got little rest before they were ordered back on their feet. "What strange sensations the men had as they marched slowly across the High Bridge. They knew its great height, but the night was so dark that they could not see the abyss on either side. Arrived on the other side, the worn-out soldiers fell to the ground and slept, more dead than alive. Some [believed they] had slept as they marched across the bridge, and declared that they had no distinct recollection of when they left it, or how long they were upon it." Dawn found Mahone's troops starting across in Gordon's wake, with Gordon already moving along the north bank of the Appomattox toward Farmville.

Grant's pursuit on April 7 was conducted so that elements of Sheridan's cavalry, tailed by Wright and Ord (all of Ord's men were now up from Burkeville), formed the left wing, that which followed Longstreet along the south bank toward Farmville, while Humphreys, still after Gordon, marched on the right toward the High Bridge crossings. Grant's remaining units occupied support positions, Parke's 9th Corps handling the task of covering the Federal railway communications with the rear. At the outset of this day, Phil Sheridan himself rode on the right with Humphreys.

As narrated by Humphreys's division commander, Regis de Trobriand: "In the rapidity of the march, I passed by a crossroad I should have taken, and soon, having some suspicion on the subject, I halted while my aides sought for information. A general, followed by some staff officers and an escort of cavalry, came up by the road near which I had halted. Those around me said, 'It is Sheridan!' which excited my curiosity. I had seen the general once or twice only, but without ever having had an opportunity to exchange a word with him. . . .

"He halted near me, saluting me, calling me by my name as if we had been old acquaintances, and, as soon as I had made known to him my doubt as to which road I ought to take, in a few words he put before me very clearly my line of march. . . . At such an hour we would reach High Bridge. . . . My brigade . . . should take the road that I had passed, and which would bring me out at such a crossroad, where I would meet such and such troops. All this was told so clearly that I could not doubt the perfect accuracy of his information. The general had in his head not only the general character of the movements of the army, but also the details. I left him immediately, in order to repair the delay of some minutes, and at the hour announced we reached High Bridge.

"This is a magnificent viaduct of twenty-one arches, crossing the valley of the Appomattox from one hill to the other. It is designed both for the Lynchburg Railroad and for the inhabitants who wish to cross on foot or in carriage from one side to the other. When we presented ourselves at one end, the enemy . . . was setting fire to the other. [Mahone had completed his crossing.] We had to throw a pontoon bridge across the river. General Humphreys determined to . . . save the viaduct, the second arch of which was already on fire. A strong detachment, armed with axes borrowed from the different regiments, hurried to the fire under the direction of some engineer officers. [While these men worked aloft, their infantry escort skirmished with the enemy's rear guard below.] The upper bridge, on which was the railroad, was saved by the sacrifice of a third span [the senior engineer officer says that four spans were lost], and the lower bridge was open for our trains after some slight repairs. The 2nd division crossed over first."

By this time the trudging Confederates under Longstreet were nearing Farmville, on the south bank to the west. General Lee, in personal charge of Longstreet's wing, saw the possibility of at least a slight rise in his fortunes. There was a good supply of rations at Farmville, brought there by railroad from Lynchburg. At last the men would eat! It was true that the Federals were close behind Longstreet, but Lee believed they could be held off until the rations were distributed, the crossing made, and the bridges burned. Lee was expecting Gordon and Mahone, their columns unpursued, to meet him on the north bank. At first the commander did not know that his jeopardy remained undiminished, that Mahone had failed to destroy the High Bridge crossings and was bringing up the rear of the march from that spot with Humphreys not far behind.

For a time after dawn, before Longstreet's units began arriving in force, Southerner Edward Boykin and his fellow cavalrymen were Farmville's chief military occupants. They continued in their camp amid the trees in the town's northerly environs. "We were waiting for orders by our fire, and filled up the time pressing [i.e., appropriating] horses in the town, from a kind consideration of the feelings of the owners, that they should not fall into the hands of the Yankees, much to the disgust of the said owners, who seemed much to prefer . . . the possible chance of the Yankee to the certainty of the Confederate abstraction. . . .

"One of our young lieutenants had heard of a very fine bay stallion belonging to a gentleman in town, and . . . he went off promptly with a man or two, reached the house, and was met at the door by a young and pretty woman, who, with all the elegant kindness of a Virginia lady, asked him to come in. He felt doubtful, but could not resist; ordering his men to hold on a minute or two while he talked horse with the lady, wishing, in the innocent kindness of his heart, to break it to her gently. After a few minutes' general conversation, he touched on the horse question. 'Oh, yes, sir!' she said, getting up and looking through a window that overlooked the back yard. 'Yes, sir; I am sorry to disappoint you, but as you came in at the front door my husband was saddling the bay, and while you were talking to me I saw him riding out of the back gate. I am so sorry. *Indeed, I am.*' With a hasty good morning our lieutenant rode back to camp. . . . The laugh was with the lady. . . .

"[Finally] a bugle rang out the call for 'boot and saddle.' The bugles of the other regiments took it up. . . . Work was at hand. The rumbling of [Longstreet's] artillery and wagons crossing the bridge [over the Appomattox], with columns of infantry between, could be heard . . . and the cavalry were wanted on the other side of the town [i.e., where Longstreet's van had made its approach, now the scene of the march of his column's central units] . . . to hold the enemy in check and cover the crossing of the river.

"The brigade was soon in the saddle and moving at a swinging trot down the long street that constitutes mainly the town. . . . As the regiment passed a large building on the right, which was shown to be a boarding school for young ladies from the number gathered on the piazza in front, we were greeted by their waving handkerchiefs and moist eyes, while cheer after cheer rose from our men in response to their kindness and sympathy. They did not know, as we did, that their friends and defenders were to pass by, leaving them so soon in the hands most dreaded by them. . . .

"So on through the town . . . and up the hill on the top of which on the right stood a large white building. . . . In the fields around were gathered and gathering large bodies of our cavalry. . . . We took our position among them. As before stated, our column, artillery, and wagon train were pouring in a steady stream across the bridge, and the enemy were pressing up their artillery and already throwing long shots at it from batteries not near enough to do much if any harm, and too much under cover to admit of an effectual attack from us."

Marching with some of the last of Longstreet's troops to approach the town was South Carolinian J. F. J. Caldwell. "The enemy were already pressing upon our rear. . . . Our cavalry now lined the high hills, in order of battle. The skirmishing grew closer and more rapid in our rear. . . . [Alfred M.] Scales' brigade of our division was left behind as rear guard of our column. The rest of the division marched into Farmville.

"Farmville is beautifully situated, occupying a table-ground inclosed by a circumference of lofty hills. The Appomattox flows along the northern and eastern side of the town. Upon the hills on the northern bank of the stream we could see hundreds of wagons quietly lying in park, and, from the numerous columns of smoke that curled among them, it seemed that there were rations being cooked and repose enjoyed after the long-continued labors and perils. . . .

"We entered the town, and proceeded to draw rations of meat. But before the distribution was completed the skirmishing in our rear increased, and we were ordered back [toward the sound]. Cavalry now thronged the streets, and the citizens began . . . hurrying to and fro."

One of the cavalrymen in the streets was Edward Boykin, whose unit had returned from the hill. "The good people of Farmville, in a state of great though natural alarm, were leaving with their goods forthwith. We told them we were going at once; were not to make a fight in the town; to keep quiet in their houses, and it was not probable they would be interfered with."

Returning to Caldwell of the infantry: "We moved just outside of the southeastern limits, but were suddenly ordered to the right about, and carried through the town [toward the Appomattox] almost at the double-quick. Two columns of infantry marched abreast along the streets, and cavalry came pressing among us in confusion.

"When we reached the bridge, we discovered it to be on fire at the other end—the work of excited pioneers placed there for its destruction. At the same moment, the enemy, having driven in our rear guard of cavalry to the town, ran out artillery and opened on the road which led [away] from the opposite end of the bridge. The cavalry . . . rushed forward into the close bridge with us, and the whole mass of men and horses crowded and pushed through in horrible disorder. Fortunately . . . we . . . received no injuries from either flames or horses in the bridge; but, when we passed it, a great danger presented itself in the shells plumping into the middle of the road, and either ricocheting far up the hillsides or bursting and hurling fragments in every direction. [James H.] Lane's brigade moved straight up the ridge, and lost men in doing so. We followed the hollow for some distance before taking the ascent, so that we escaped with an insignificant loss. . . .

"We formed on attaining the crest of the ridge north of the Appomattox. Some Confederate guns now replied to the enemy, but with little effect. The last of our rear guard now quitted Farmville. The enemy's cavalry charged furiously after them down the long, steep hills approaching the southern bank of the Appomattox, firing and hurrahing loudly; but almost all the Confederates escaped across to us. Here the advance of that portion of the Federals ceased [since the bridge accommodations were now gone]; but an attack upon the rear and left flank of the column which had crossed at the High Bridge now became audible."

Lee reacted to these ominous sounds from the northeast with a flash of anger toward Mahone. Then, as he always did in a crisis, the general made a calm assessment of his options. The railroad cars holding rations that, for lack of time, had not been included in the distribution were sent toward Appomattox Station, some twenty miles to the west, on the Confederate line of retreat (where Lee expected to find additional rations from Lynchburg). About 100 supply wagons were burned, their horses now too weak from fatigue and hunger to pull them at the required pace.

Lee led a part of Longstreet's corps on the double-quick toward Mahone, meeting him in the countryside a few miles north of Farmville, a region that became the scene of several hours of confused skirmishing. Fortunately for Lee, Union General Humphreys's corps spent the day unsupported except for a division of cavalry from Grant's southern wing, the unit fording the Appomattox at Farmville.

Southerner J. F. J. Caldwell was on the field. "The enemy seemed to be ubiquitous. We were instructed to be prepared to fight on either flank. On our right flank, firing was pretty steadily kept up. In our front . . . a regular battle was going on. Mahone's division was engaged and a portion of [Charles W.] Field's. We formed a line, first on the right of our line of march, fronting south, then one fronting southwest, and, finally, one fronting almost directly west. The firing increased in rapidity and extent until three sides were at once set upon by the enemy. I saw [cannon] balls cross, each directly from the front and directly from the rear."

At least partly responsible for the ubiquity of the fighting was the Union cavalry division that came upon Lee's rear from Farmville. Confederate Colonel William Miller Owen, commanding a battalion of

Lee's artillery, played a major role in the climactic work against the Union raid. "In the afternoon, while our column was moving through an old field . . . bullets began to whistle around our ears, and presently a brigade . . . of our cavalry appeared on our flank, crying, ' They are coming! They are coming!' I was marching at my post in rear of the column of guns, and . . . gave the order at the top of my voice, "Tention! Fire to the left, in battery!' With great promptitude the guns were wheeled into position, ready for action, just as the Federal cavalry came charging to the crest of the high ground.

"With shell cut for close range, and canister, our twelve guns were let loose, and such a scattering I never saw before. A brigade of our infantry, about 200 men, came marching from the road to our assistance, and [Lieutenant Colonel D. G.] McIntosh and I, now all excitement, drew our sabers and placed ourselves in front to lead them to the charge, when General [James A.] Walker, whose troops they were, and whom I had not observed, cried, 'Gentlemen, I'll lead my men myself!' —and we subsided. [Lieutenant J. H.] Chamberlayne, with one gun, then accompanied the charge; and when our troops rejoined the column of march, they had with them, as a prisoner of war, General [J. Irvin] Gregg, U.S. Cavalry. The general was quite chagrined, and said he had thought he would have had an easy time of it destroying our moving trains, and had not expected to run into the jaws of a whole park of artillery. It was fortunate that we were there just in the nick of time, for had Gregg obtained possession of the road, he stood a good chance of cutting off General Lee and staff and capturing them."

As Owen and his artillery battalion limbered up and began moving on, the column was joined by two mounted infantry officers who reported that they had seen the whole show and wanted to offer their congratulations. "Inviting me into the bushes, [they] produced a canteen of 'medical supplies,' from which I took a hearty pull."

The road saved from Gregg—that on which Lee was organizing his retreat toward Appomattox Station—was also threatened by Humphreys. Some of his troops charged toward it, driving before them a crowd of Confederates they had stampeded. Southerner Carlton McCarthy relates: "The troops hurrying back were panic-stricken. . . . General Gordon ordered General Walker to form his division and drive the enemy back from the road. The division advanced gallantly, and conspicuous in the charge was Cutshaw's battalion. When the line was formed, the battalion occupied rising ground on the right. The line was visible for a considerable distance. In rear of the battalion there was a group of unarmed men. . . . In the distribution of muskets at Amelia Court House the supply fell short of the demand, and this squad had made the trip so far unarmed. Some, too, had been compelled to ground their arms at Sayler's Creek.

"A few yards to the left and rear of the battalion, in the road, was General Lee, surrounded by a number of officers, gazing eagerly about him. An occasional musket ball whistled over, but there was no enemy in sight. In the midst of this quiet a general officer, at the left and rear of the battalion, fell from his horse, severely wounded. . . . After a short while the enemy appeared, and the stampeded troops came rushing by. Cutshaw's battalion stood firmly and quietly, as if on parade, awaiting orders. General officers galloped about, begging the fleeing men to halt, but in vain. Several of the fugitives, as they passed the battalion, were collared by the disarmed squad, relieved of their muskets and ammunition, and with a kick allowed to proceed to the rear.

"There was now between the group [of Confederate officers] in the road and the enemy only the battalion of improvised infantry [Cutshaw's troops, it will be recalled, had been artillerymen until the retreat began]. There they stood, on the crest of the hill, in sharp relief. Not a man moved from his place. Did they know the Great Commander was watching them? Someone said, 'Forward!' The cry passed from lip to lip, and, with cheers, the battalion moved rapidly to meet the enemy, while the field was full of the stampeded troops making to the rear.

"A courier came out with orders to stop the advance, but they heeded him not. Again he came, but on they went. Following the line was the unarmed squad, unable to do more than swell the volume of the wild shouts of their comrades. Following them, also, was the commissary department, consisting of two men, with a piece of bacon swung on a pole between them, yelling and hurrahing. As the line advanced, the bluejackets . . . [retreated] through the broom-straw like hares, followed by a shower of balls.

"Finally an officer . . . rode out to the front of [our] battalion, ordered a halt, and in the name of General Lee thanked the men for their gallant conduct and complimented them in handsome style. His words were greeted with loud cheers, and the battalion marched back to the road carrying several prisoners and having retaken two pieces of artillery which had been abandoned to the enemy.

"After the enemy was driven back out of reach of our trains and column of march, and the troops were in line of battle, General Lee in person rode up in rear of the division, and, addressing himself directly to the men in ranks . . . used language to this effect: 'That is right, men. That is all I want you to do. Just keep *those people* back awhile. I do not wish you to expose yourselves to unnecessary danger.' "

In the end, "those people" desisted, at least temporarily. Union General Regis de Trobriand explains: "From the extent and solidity of the enemy's line, it became evident that we had before us all that remained of Lee's army. . . . We had to do with too strong a force. All the remainder of [our] army was some distance away, on the [south] side of the Appomattox. The cavalry and the 5th Corps were on the road [southwestward] via Prince Edward Court House. The 6th Corps and the 24th [of Ord's command] were still at Farmville, where the bridge was not [yet] rebuilt. . . . We were thus compelled to put off the renewal of the attack. . . ."

21

Letters Across the Lines

Four top Union generals—Grant, Wright, Ord, and Ord's second-in-command, John Gibbon—had converged on Farmville from the southeast soon after Lee and Longstreet fled the town over the Appomattox. Even as the sounds of the day's fighting rolled down from the north, Farmville became a temporary center of Union operations. As related by Alfred Woodhull, the assistant surgeon traveling with Ord: "[The] inhabitants, if not overjoyed to see us, at least were not openly hostile. Lee had been foiled in his effort to escape southward, and was exerting all his energy to gain Lynchburg. We, still in pursuit, were correspondingly elated; and it was a matter of small moment who fell in love with us en route. . . .

"A church was occupied . . . by the staff of General Ord, the general himself resting, by invitation, in the house of a citizen. . . . Diagonally opposite to the church, which was on a corner, was a young ladies' seminary. . . . The surly shutters remained impervious to the levelled field-glasses, although a sanguine few fancied they saw signs of vitality, if not of hostility, through an occasional crevice.

"Strangely enough, we were invited to tea by a gentleman who . . . made no profession of Union sentiments, but seemed actuated by pure, abstract hospitality. It may be that he looked upon it as a gentle species of bribery in the interest of his property against possible destruction. . . .

"But Farmville is preeminently remembered by a comical incident. . . . Falling into conversation with the wife of a civil functionary . . . she finally said something to this effect: 'I don't see what you Yankees want to come down here and take away all our Negroes for. . . . What do you suppose we are going to do without our servants?'

" 'Indeed, I hope you will not lose all your servants.' 'Yes, we will. I know we will. . . . And what do you suppose I will do then? . . .'

" 'I can't imagine you to be so unfortunate as not to be able to get any servants whatever.' 'We won't! I know we won't! . . . And I? Do you suppose I will work? Indeed I won't. . . . I've always had servants. . . . Do you think I'll do what I've always had servants to do? Do you think I will cook? I shall do nothing of the sort. . . .'

" 'As I've said before, madam, I sincerely hope you will be able to obtain servants, if your own should leave; and I can scarcely conceive that you should not. But suppose it should happen so that your own servants should all go, and that you could get no assistance whatever. . . . If you could get literally no one to help you, I presume you would really be obliged to make your own bed and to cook your own food.'

" 'Indeed I won't! . . . I have always had servants. . . . Do you think I will work? Indeed I shall do nothing of the kind!' 'But just imagine the case, madam. If you have no one, and can't possibly get anyone, the question becomes very simple. It is either to do it one's self or to go without; and we know the consequences of going without. I am sure I hope you may not be so compelled; but, since that would be the only alternative, I am afraid you might have to do your own cooking.'

" 'Indeed I won't! I've always had servants, and I won't work. And I don't see what you Yankees want to come down here for, and take our servants away.'

"To that style of argument, what could a man reply?"

General Grant had established his Farmville headquarters on the broad piazza of a brick hotel. "That evening," says staff officer Horace Porter, "Wright's corps was ordered to cross the river and move rapidly to the support of our troops there [Humphreys's corps]. Notwithstanding their long march that day, the men sprang to their feet with a spirit that made everyone marvel at their pluck, and came swinging through the main street of the village with a step that seemed as elastic as on the first day of their toilsome tramp. It was now dark, but they spied the general-in-chief watching them with evident pride from the piazza of the hotel as they marched past. Then was witnessed one of the most inspiring scenes of the campaign.

"Bonfires were lighted on the sides of the street; the men seized straw and pine knots, and improvised torches; cheers arose from their throats, already hoarse with shouts of victory; bands played, banners waved, and muskets were swung in the air. A regiment now broke forth with the song of 'John Brown's Body,' and soon a whole division was shouting the swelling chorus of that popular air, which had risen to the dignity of a national anthem. The night march had become a grand review, with Grant as the reviewing officer.

"Ord and Gibbon had visited the general at the hotel, and he had spoken with them, as well as with Wright, about sending some communication to Lee that might pave the way to the stopping of further bloodshed. [A] Dr. Smith . . . a native of Virginia and a relative of General Ewell, now one of our prisoners, had told General Grant the night before that Ewell had said in conversation that their cause was lost when they crossed the James River [during their retreat from the Rapidan the preceding spring], and he considered that it was the duty of the authorities to negotiate for peace then, while they still had a right to claim concessions, adding that now they were not in condition to claim anything. He said that for every man killed after this somebody would be responsible, and it would be little better than murder. He could not tell what General Lee would do, but he hoped that he would at once surrender his army.

"This statement, together with the news that had been received from Sheridan, saying that he had heard that General Lee's train of provisions, which had come by rail, were at Appomattox, and that he expected to capture them before Lee could reach them, induced the general to write the following communication: ' . . . General R. E. Lee. . . . The results of the last week must convince you of the hopelessness of further resistance. . . . I feel that it is so, and regard it as my duty to shift from myself the responsibility of any further effusion of blood by asking of you the surrender of that portion of the Confederate States army known as the Army of Northern Virginia. . . .

"This he intrusted to General Seth Williams, adjutant-general, with directions to take it to Humphreys's front, as his corps was close up to the enemy's rear guard, and see that it reached Lee."

Williams had trouble getting his flag of truce through the lines. His party was fired upon, and one of his orderlies was hit. Finally, by the light of an early moon, Confederate Colonel Herman H. Perry came forward on foot to consult with Williams. The colonel was a tall, good-looking man with a proud bearing, but his threadbare uniform and old slouch hat were no match for Williams's finery. As Perry tells it: "After I had introduced myself, he felt in his side pocket for documents, as I thought, but the document was a very nice-looking silver flask. . . . He remarked that he hoped I would not think it was unsoldierly if he offered me some very fine brandy. I will own up . . . that I wanted that drink awfully. . . . But I raised myself about an inch higher, if possible, bowed, and refused politely, trying to produce the ridiculous appearance of having feasted on champagne and pound-cake not ten minutes before, and I had not the slightest use for as plebeian a drink as 'fine brandy.'

"He was a true gentleman, begged pardon, and placed the flask in his pocket again without touching the contents in my presence. If he had taken a drink, and my Confederate olfactories had obtained a whiff of the odor of it, it is possible that I should have 'caved.' The truth is, I had not eaten two ounces in two days, and I had my coattail then full of corn, waiting to parch it as soon as an opportunity might present itself. I did not leave it behind me, because I had nobody I could trust it with. As an excuse which I felt I ought to make for refusing his proffered courtesy, I rather haughtily said that I had been sent forward only to receive any communication that was offered, and could not properly accept or offer any courtesies. In fact, if I had offered what I could, it would have taken my corn."

Perry carried Grant's message back to Lee, who had stopped for the evening at a cottage amid his lines. Longstreet, who was with Lee, relates: "I was sitting at his side when the note was delivered. He read it and handed it to me without referring to its contents. After reading it, I gave it back, saying, 'Not yet.' General Lee wrote in reply: ' . . . General—I have received your note of this day. Though not entertaining the opinion you express on the hopelessness of further resistance on the part of the Army of Northern Virginia, I reciprocate your desire to avoid useless effusion of blood, and therefore, before considering your proposition, ask the terms you will offer on condition of its surrender.'

"I was not [then] informed of the contents of the return note, but thought, from the orders of the night, it did not mean surrender. General Lee ordered my command from forward- to rear-guard, and his cavalry in rear of the march . . . [which was resumed] at twelve."

The route embraced obscure country roads, rough fields, and soggy marshes. "And so the retreat rolls on," says Southerner William Miller Owen. "We are passing abandoned cannon and wrecked and overturned wagons and their now useless contents. . . . Horses and mules dead or dying in the mud. . . . Our march is lighted by the fires of burning wagons. . . . The constant marching and fighting without sleep or food are rapidly thinning the ranks of this grand old army. Men who

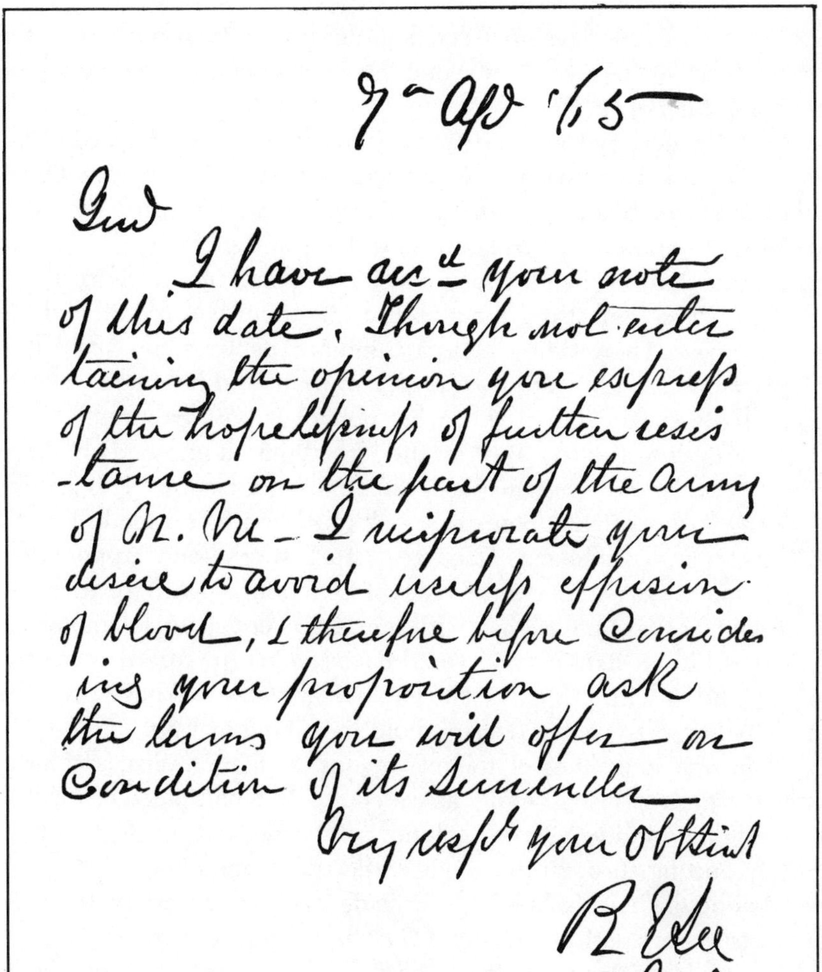

7ᵃ Apl '65—

Genl

I have acᵈ your note of this date. Though not entertaining the opinion you express of the hopelessness of further resistance on the part of the army of N. Va.— I reciprocate your desire to avoid useless effusion of blood—, I therefore before Considering your proposition ask the terms you will offer on Condition of its Surrender—

Very respᵗ your Ob Serᵗ

R E Lee
Genl

Lt Genl U. S. Grant
Commdg Armies of the U. States

Facsimile of one of Lee's letters to Grant

have stood by their flags since the beginning of the war now fall out of ranks . . . simply because it is beyond their power of physical endurance to go any farther."

Adds Carlton McCarthy: "So many muskets were dropped on the road that Cutshaw's unarmed squad armed itself with abandoned muskets, ammunition, and equipments. There was a halt during the night in a piece of stunted woods. The land was low and sobby [sic]. . . . There was a little flour on hand, which had been picked up on the road. An oil-cloth was spread, the flour placed on it, water was found, and the dough mixed. Then some clean partition-boards were knocked out of a limber chest, and dough was spread on them and held near the fire till partially cooked. Then with what delight it was devoured!"

According to Edward Boykin, the forced march imposed almost as great a strain on Lee's cavalry as it did on his foot troops. "This . . . was . . . the hardest night upon us. . . . A push was being made for the mountains at Lynchburg. Had we gotten there—and Appomattox Court House was within twenty miles of Lynchburg—with the men and material General Lee still had with him, Lee's last struggle among the mountains of his native state would have made a picture to swell the soldier's heart with pride. . . . The end, we know, would have been the same. A few more noble hearts would have bled in vain. . . .

"Through long lines of toiling wagons, artillery trains, and tired men, we pushed on as rapidly as we could. At a bad piece of road, at a creek or a muddy hill, the column sometimes got cut in two by a portion getting through the wagons, the train then closing. . . .

"At one of these halts for the brigade to close up and for the regiments to report position, General Gary [the brigade commander] had halted at a large fire made from the rails of some good farmer's fence . . . and round it we all gathered, for the night was cold. The subject of conversation with the brigade staff . . . was that Captain M., the inspector, not being well, had, early in the night, halted at a farmhouse and gone to bed, just to see how it would feel, putting his horse in the farmer's stable; and, when he roused himself to the necessities of his position and sought to ride with the rest, he found his horse was gone. . . .

"I remembered, when I listened to the drowsy talk about the captain's loss, that a couple of enterprising young fellows had reported some horses at a farmhouse and gotten permission to go after them. They had not long [before] returned with their prizes. . . . The horses stood just on the edge of light thrown by the fire against the darkness that rose like a wall behind it. . . . One of the orderlies, looking with sleepy eyes from the log on which he was sitting . . . expressed himself to the effect that he thought that [a] long-legged bay looked about the hindquarters a good deal like the captain's missing charger. And so it proved. While the captain . . . [was] pressing the luxurious blanket of the Virginia farmer, his horse, in camp parlance, was 'lifted' by our enterprising youth. . . .

"Again in the saddle, tramping through mud holes, splashing in ruts, we worked our way amid the long line of wagons, troops and artillery, until daylight [of April 8] came to our relief. About eight o'clock we came upon our own wagon train—the first, and, by the way, the only time we encountered it on our route—comfortably camped in a fine grove. . . . The headquarter wagons of our regiment were parked near a fine fire, and our servants—never expecting to see us again, I suppose —were cooking on a large scale from our private stores for a half dozen notorious wagon rats [presumably, men who had made a career of finding light employment among the wagons in order to avoid front-line duty]. . . .

"Of course, as we rode up our boys declared they expected us and were getting [our] breakfast ready, which statement was sustained by . . . the wagon rats; but the longing look they cast at a big pot of rice steaming by the fire as they drew off indicated a deeper interest than I think it possible for them to have gotten up on anyone's account but their own.

"We had a most comfortable breakfast and a rest of an hour. . . . Bad as the night had been, the day was a beautiful one. The sun was shining bright."

It was during these early morning hours that Union General Grant, still headquartered at the hotel in Farmville, wrote a reply to Lee's request, received during the night, for an explanation of the terms available if he agreed to surrender. "Peace being my great desire, there is but one condition I would insist upon—namely, that the men and officers surrendered shall be disqualified for taking up arms against the Government of the United States until properly exchanged [for Federals in Confederate hands]. I will meet you, or will designate officers to meet any officers you may name for the same purpose, at any point agreeable to you, for the purpose of arranging definitely the terms upon which the surrender of the Army of Northern Virginia will be received."

Grant's aide, Horace Porter, explains that "the last sentence shows great delicacy of feeling on the part of General Grant, who wished to spare General Lee the mortification of personally conducting the surrender. The consideration displayed has a parallel in the terms accorded by Washington to Cornwallis at Yorktown. Cornwallis took advantage of the privilege . . . but Lee [was to rise] superior to the British general, and in a manly way . . . surrender in person.

"There turned up [at Grant's headquarters] at this time a rather hungry-looking gentleman in gray, wearing the uniform of a colonel, who proclaimed himself the proprietor of the hotel. He gave us to understand that his regiment had crumbled to pieces . . . and he thought he might as well stop off at home and look after his property. It is safe to say that his hotel had never before had so many guests in it, nor at such reduced rates. . . .

"General Grant had been marching most of the way with the columns which were pushing along south of Lee's line of retreat; but, expecting that a reply to his last letter would soon be received, and wanting to keep within easy communication of Lee, he decided to march this day with the portion of the Army of the Potomac that was pressing Lee's rear guard. . . . He . . . crossed to the north side of the Appomattox, conferred in person with Meade, and rode with his columns."

Regis de Trobriand says that Humphreys's corps headed the pursuit, "picking up all that was left behind by the Confederate army. This remnant was breaking up more and more, leaving its stragglers in the woods, in the fields, and along the roadside. . . . The wagons were left in the ruts; the cannon abandoned in the thickets or buried in holes, hurriedly dug, that the Negroes hastened to point out to us. . . . We pushed forward 'on a hot trail' like hounds who are coming upon their quarry. As for men, we captured them everywhere.

"Our advance had been so rapid in the 2nd Corps that the trains had not been able to join us. We were without rations. Fortunately, we had a few cattle left, and some provisions in the country around. To secure them, one regiment from each brigade was detailed for foraging. Lee's soldiers were also searching the country for provisions, but in isolated groups. Wherever they met our detachments, they surrendered with eagerness rather than repugnance. They had had enough of the war, and henceforth were less rebels than the Virginia sheep, which [animals] it became necessary to pursue à outrance [i.e., to the utmost], and even to shoot when they refused to surrender."

22

Lee's March Interrupted

The Federals in Lee's rear, as has been shown, achieved nothing of special result on April 8, but it was different with the column that was paralleling his southern flank. Dawn found Phil Sheridan's horsemen, with the infantry preparing to follow, hurrying toward Appomattox Station, their object to get there ahead of Lee's van. Sheridan explains that one of his scouts had informed him "that there were four trains of cars at the depot loaded with supplies for Lee's army. These had been sent from Lynchburg. . . . Custer, having the advance, moved rapidly, and, on nearing the station, detailed two regiments to make a detour southward to strike the railroad some distance beyond and break the track [leading back toward Lynchburg]. These regiments set off at a gallop, and in short order broke up the railroad enough to prevent the escape of the trains, Custer meanwhile taking possession of the station, but none too soon, for almost at the moment he did so the advance guard of Lee's army appeared, bent on securing the trains. Without halting to look after the cars further, Custer attacked this advance guard and had a spirited fight. . . ."

Says Custer himself: "The enemy succeeded in repulsing nearly all our attacks until nearly 9 o'clock at night, when, by a general advance along my line, he was forced from his position and compelled to abandon to our hands twenty-four pieces of artillery, all his trains, several battle flags, and a large number of prisoners. Our loss was slight."

By this time additional units of Union cavalry were on the scene, and Phil Sheridan was in personal command: "I . . . forced the enemy back on the Appomattox road to the vicinity of the Court House; and, that

the Confederates might have no rest, gave orders to continue the skirmishing throughout the night. Meanwhile the captured trains had been
taken charge of by locomotive engineers, soldiers of the command, who
were delighted evidently to get back at their old calling. They amused
themselves by running the trains to and fro, creating much confusion,
and keeping up such an unearthly screeching with the whistles that I
was on the point of ordering the cars burned. They finally wearied of
their fun, however. . . . I made my headquarters at a little frame house
just south of the station."

The Union bivouac fires that glowed west of the Court House, their
makers knew, were precisely where they ought to be to spread discour-
agement among Lee's assembling units. In the words of Union General
Henry Davies, of Sheridan's command: "For the second time during the
pursuit General Sheridan had overtaken the retreating army, and, placing the force at his disposal directly in the front, stood as a bar to further
progress. During the night he felt assured that his position could be
held, but knew that after daylight his force would be insufficient to
withstand the desperate assault he must expect from an enemy whose
last and only hope remained in forcing a passage to the west. Everything depended upon the arrival of additional troops in time to resist
the attack that would surely be made the following morning, and courier after courier was sent back to urge greater speed upon the commanders of the infantry, still far in the rear.

"On the morning of the 8th the 24th Corps had marched from
Farmville and the 5th from Prince Edward Court House, and, uniting
at Prospect Station, had diligently followed the roads taken by the
cavalry. Though for the past ten days they had fought hard, marched
far, and fared poorly, the victories of those days and the knowledge that
the adversary who for four long years had held them at bay, and at
whose hands they had sustained toil, trial, suffering, and sometimes
defeat, was now flying before them, inspired their courage and gave an
endurance that no other source could have supplied."

Alfred Woodhull, the assistant surgeon with the 24th Corps (Ord's
unit), says that the troops persisted manfully. "Towards nightfall, however, they naturally began to droop, for an all day's march is no light
thing. Then, riding along the ranks, Ord addressed them in pithy little
sentences, 'Legs will win this battle, men,' 'It rests with us to head them
off,' 'This march will save all others,' 'Whichever army marches best
wins,' 'The campaign is in your legs, men,' 'Good marching will carry
it,' 'They can't escape, if you will keep up to it,' 'One good, steady

Village of Appomattox Court House

march, and the campaign is ended.' And, strenuously impressing upon the troops that, by getting ahead of them they would corral the Rebels, that the termination of certainly the campaign, perhaps the war, was virtually vested in the endurance of their legs—in other words, by conjoined appeals to their good sense and manly pride—their flagging strength was stimulated. . . ."

Marching behind Ord's troops, those of Griffin's 5th Corps were equally tested. "The sun sunk from view," relates Private Theodore Gerrish, "but there were no indications of halting. Our regiment chanced that day to be marching in the rear of our whole division, a position which . . . is the hardest in the whole line. Just at dark we entered a forest, through which was a single road, narrow and crooked. The road was filled with artillery, cavalry, infantry, baggage wagons, all pushing for the front. The night was dark, and in this blockade our regiment became separated from the division, and was left far in the rear. At ten o'clock the situation had become much worse, so that it was every man for himself.

"The artillery, each gun and caisson drawn by six horses, crashed and thundered along the narrow road, and, by the right of superior strength, claimed the right of way. We marched on as best we could, tired, hungry, and mad. If the artillery horses came too near, we would hammer them over their heads with our guns. This, of course, would enrage their riders, and, in the midst of all the uproar, there was a fierce warfare of words and oaths and threats. We were descending a hill when a gun came crashing down upon us. It was almost a case of life or death. One of our boys brought the heavy stock of his rifle down upon the head of one of the leading horses, and the animal staggered and fell. The sergeant who had command of the gun rode up to a lieutenant commanding a company and ordered the man's arrest. The officer chanced to have a rifle in his hands that he was carrying for one of his men, and with a half-muttered exclamation he dealt the sergeant's horse such a blow that horse and rider went down together, and we rushed on our way."

General Grant was still with Humphreys and Wright, who were pushing Lee from the rear. While the columns continued their march, the Union commander and his staff stopped for the night at Curdsville. According to Horace Porter: "General Grant had been suffering all the afternoon from a severe headache, the result of fatigue, anxiety, scant fare, and loss of sleep; and by night he grew much worse. He was induced to bathe his feet in hot water and mustard, and apply mustard-plasters to his wrists and the back of his neck; but these remedies afforded little relief.

"The dwelling we occupied was a double house. The general threw himself upon a sofa in the sitting-room on the left side of the hall, while the staff officers bunked on the floor of the room opposite, to catch what sleep they could. About midnight we were aroused by Colonel Charles A. Whittier of Humphreys's staff, who brought the expected letter from Lee. [Brigadier General John A.] Rawlins took it and stepped across the hall to the door of General Grant's room. He hesitated to knock, not wishing to awake the commander if he were asleep, and opened the door softly and listened a moment to ascertain whether he could judge by any sound how the chief was resting. Soon the general's voice was heard saying, 'Come in; I am awake. I am suffering too much to get any sleep.' I had in the meantime brought a lighted candle, and now stepped into the room with it. The general, who had taken off only his coat and boots, sat up on the sofa and read the communication."

Lee had written: "To be frank, I do not think the emergency has arisen to call for the surrender of this army; but as the restoration of peace should be the sole object of all, I desired to know whether your proposals would lead to that end. I cannot, therefore, meet you with a view to surrender the Army of Northern Virginia; but as far as your proposal may affect the Confederate States forces under my command, and tend to the restoration of peace, I shall be pleased to meet you . . . between the picket lines of the two armies."

Grant was disappointed. He could not agree to such a meeting, since his authority did not go beyond the discussion of surrender terms. He said to Rawlins and Porter: "It looks as if Lee still means to fight. I will reply in the morning." Then the general lay down again on the sofa, and the two aides, hoping he would be able to get some sleep, left him alone in the darkness.

General Lee, meanwhile, had approached to within a few miles of Appomattox Court House and had learned of the loss of his supplies and of the threat posed by the raiders. His situation, he saw, was now very nearly hopeless. There were enemy troops in his front, in his rear, and on his southern flank. Only the north remained open, and there was no escape route in that direction.

"Then," says Southern corps commander John Gordon, "came the last sad Confederate council of war. . . . It was called by Lee to meet . . . in the woods at his headquarters and by a low-burning bivouac fire. There was no tent there, no chairs, and no camp stools. On blankets spread upon the ground or on saddles at the roots of the trees, we sat around the great commander. A painter's brush might transfer to canvas the physical features of that scene, but no tongue or pen will ever be able to describe the unutterable anguish of Lee's commanders as they looked into the clouded face of their beloved leader and sought to draw from it some ray of hope.

"There were present at this final council the general-in-chief, the commander of his artillery, General [William N.] Pendleton, General Fitzhugh Lee, who . . . commanded the cavalry, and General Longstreet and myself, commanding all that was left of his immortal infantry. These fragments of each arm of the service still represented the consecration and courage that had made Lee's army, at the meridian of its power, almost invincible. . . .

"It would be as impossible to give the words that were spoken, or the suggestions that were made, as it would to photograph the thoughts and emotions of that soldier group gathered at Lee's last bivouac. The letters of General Grant asking surrender, and the replies thereto, evoked a discussion as to the fate of the Southern people and the condition in which the failure of our cause would leave them. There was also some discussion as to the possibility of forcing a passage through Grant's lines and saving a small portion of the army and continuing a desultory [guerrilla] warfare until the government at Washington should grow weary and grant to our people peace and the safeguards of local self-government.

"If all that was said and felt at that meeting could be given it would make a volume of measureless pathos. In no hour of the great war did General Lee's masterful characteristics appear to me so conspicuous as they did in that last council. We knew by our own aching hearts that his was breaking. Yet he commanded himself, and stood calmly facing and discussing the long-dreaded inevitable.

"It was finally determined that with Fitz Lee's cavalry, my infantry, and [the] artillery under Colonel Thomas H. Carter, we should attempt at daylight the next morning to cut through Grant's lines. Longstreet was to follow in support of the movement. The utmost that could be hoped for was that we might reach the mountains of Virginia and Tennessee with a remnant of the army, and ultimately join General Johnston.

"As we rode away from the meeting I directed a staff officer to return to General Lee and ask him if he had any specific directions as to where I should halt and camp for the night. He said, 'Yes; tell General

Gordon that I should be glad for him to halt just beyond the Tennessee line.' That line was about two hundred miles away, and Grant's battle lines and breastworks [those of Sheridan's cavalry] were in our immediate front, ready to check any movement in that direction. But General Lee knew that I would interpret his facetious message exactly as he intended it. His purpose was to let me infer that there was little hope of our escape and that it did not matter where I camped for the night; but if we should succeed in cutting our way out, he expected me to press toward the goal in the mountains."

During the remainder of the night the troops of Lee and Sheridan faced each other in uneasy bivouac, with occasional sheets of gunfire marking the local conflicts initiated by Sheridan's pickets. Struggling along on the last leg of their march from the southeast were the troops of Ord and Griffin, their attempts to rest interrupted by the urging of Sheridan's couriers. Some distance in Lee's rear, the columns of Humphreys and Wright had encamped for the night, their fires strung out for miles, some of them visible to Lee's rear guard. East of Humphreys and Wright, at Curdsville, Grant continued to nurse his headache.

Horace Porter relates: "About four o'clock on the morning of April 9 I rose and crossed the hall to ascertain how the general was feeling. I found his room empty, and upon going out of the front door saw him pacing up and down in the yard, holding both hands to his head. Upon inquiring how he felt, he replied that he had had very little sleep, and was still suffering the most excruciating pain. I said, 'Well, there is one consolation in all this, general; I never knew you to be ill that you did not receive some good news before the day passed. I have become a little superstitious regarding these coincidences, and I should not be surprised if some good fortune were to overtake you before night.' He smiled and replied, 'The best thing that could happen to me today would be to get rid of the pain I am suffering.

"We were soon joined by some others of the staff, and the general was induced to walk over to Meade's headquarters with us and get some coffee, in the hope that it would do him good. He seemed to feel a little better then. . . ."

Grant, not yet fully aware of Lee's present predicament, now wrote him a note refusing his request for a meeting to discuss the end of the war in general. "The terms upon which peace can be had are well understood." A courier was dispatched through the Union lines toward Lee's rear. Much was to happen before the note was received.

Horace Porter continues: "General Grant kept steadily in mind the fact that he was simply a soldier, and . . . could not negotiate a treaty of peace. . . . It was proposed to the general to ride during the day in a covered ambulance which was at hand, instead of on horseback, so as to avoid the intense heat of the sun; but his soldierly instincts rebelled against such a proposition, and he soon after mounted 'Cincinnati' and started from Curdsville toward New Store. From this point he went by way of a crossroad to the south side of the Appomattox, with the intention to moving around to Sheridan's front."

23

Last Throes of a Proud Army

At Appomattox Court House, the clear, cool dawn of April 9, which happened to be Palm Sunday, was aromatic with spring. Out of harmony with its setting, the combination of military forces was staging for the campaign's finale. Sheridan's dismounted troopers were improving their breastworks in Lee's front; the infantry of Ord and Griffin, after a march of thirty miles, had begun arriving from the southeast, assuring Sheridan of the support he needed; Humphreys and Wright, at Meade's direction, were massing in Lee's rear; and Gordon and Fitz Lee were about to undertake their forlorn hope. The Confederate army now numbered less than 30,000 men, the majority of whom were of little use. Only about 8,000 had retained the strength and spirit to keep their weapons.

In Gordon's words: "The audacious movement of our troops was begun. . . . The dashing cavalry leader, Fitzhugh Lee, swept around the Union left flank, while the infantry and artillery attacked the front. I take especial pride in recording the fact that this last charge of the war was made by the footsore and starving men of my command with a spirit worthy the best days of Lee's army. The Union breastworks were carried. Two pieces of artillery were captured. The Federals [Sheridan's troopers] were driven from all that portion of the field, and the brave boys in tattered gray cheered as their battle flags waved in triumph on that last morning.

"The Confederate battle lines were still advancing when I discovered a heavy column of Union infantry coming from the right and upon my rear. I gathered around me my sharpshooters, who were now held for such emergencies, and directed Colonel Thomas H. Carter of the artillery to turn all his guns upon the advancing column. It was held at bay by his shrapnel, grape, and canister.

"While the Confederate infantry and cavalry were thus fighting at the front, and the artillery was checking the development of Federal forces around my right and rear, Longstreet was [threatened] by other portions of the Federal army. He . . . could not join, as contemplated, in the effort to break the cordon of men and metal around us.

"At this critical juncture a column of Union cavalry appeared on the hills to my left, headed for the broad space between Longstreet's command and mine. In a few minutes that body of Federal cavalry would not only have seized the trains but cut off all communication between the two wings of Lee's army and rendered its capture inevitable. I therefore detached a brigade to double-quick and intercept this Federal force."

Among the Federal units still approaching the scene from the southeast at this time was the brigade to which Private Theodore Gerrish belonged. "Heavy firing was heard in our front, not over half a mile distant. Orders were given to double-quick. We dashed through a thick belt of woods, and met cavalrymen riding back, badly broken up and demoralized. They told us they had been fighting all night and holding the rebels in check until we should arrive, and this explained why we had marched all night. We passed through the woods and came out into a field some forty rods in width. For a fourth of a mile in our front there was flat and level ground, and then a ridge of land on whose crest there was a house, barn, and numerous outbuildings. The field on either side, up to this hill, was bordered with a forest, while beyond there was—we knew not what.

"In that field we halted. A group of Union generals were sitting upon their horses near us—Sheridan, Griffin, Chamberlain, and others. Sheridan was evidently much excited, and was talking rapidly, and adding emphasis to his words by bringing his clenched right hand down on the open palm of his left. It was evident to all that some enterprise of importance was on foot."

On the Confederate side, General Gordon had just received a dispatch from Robert E. Lee. "It was borne," says Gordon, "by Colonel Charles S. Venable of his staff. . . . The commander wished me to report at once as to the conditions on my portion of the field, what progress I was making, and what encouragement I could give. I said, 'Tell General Lee that my command has been fought to a frazzle, and unless

Longstreet can unite in the movement, or prevent these forces from coming upon my rear, I cannot long go forward.' "

Colonel Venable takes up the narrative: "When I bore the message back to General Lee, he said, 'Then there is nothing left me but to go and see General Grant, and I would rather die a thousand deaths.' Convulsed with passionate grief, many were the wild words which we spoke as we stood around him. Said one, 'Oh, general, what will history say of the surrender of this army in the field?' He replied, 'Yes, I know they will say hard things of us. They will not understand how we were overwhelmed by numbers. But that is not the question, colonel. The question is: Is it right to surrender this army? If it is right, then I will take all the responsibility.' "

Lee sent word for Longstreet to ride to meet him, and Longstreet found the commander "dressed in a suit of new uniform, sword and sash, a handsomely embroidered belt, boots, and a pair of gold spurs. At first approach his compact figure appeared as a man in the flush of vigor of forty summers, but as I drew near, the handsome apparel and brave bearing failed to conceal his profound depression. He stood near the embers of some burned rails, received me with graceful salutation, and spoke at once of affairs in front and the loss of his subsistence stores. He remarked that the advanced columns stood against a very formidable force which he could not break through, while General Meade was at my rear, ready to call for all the work that the rear guard could do, and, closing with the expression that it was not possible for him to get along [i.e., to do anything of a promising nature], requested my view. I asked if the bloody sacrifice of his army could in any way help the cause in other quarters. He thought not. Then, I said, your situation speaks for itself.

"He called up General Mahone, and made to him a similar statement of affairs. . . . General Mahone was chilled [because he had been] standing in wait without fire. He pushed up the embers and said to the general he did not want him to think he was scared, he was only chilled. General Mahone . . . asked several questions. My attention was called to messages from the troops for a time, so that I failed to hear all of the conversation, but I heard enough of it to know that General Mahone thought it time to see General Grant. Appeal was made to me to affirm that judgment, and it was promptly approved."

Lee rode to the picket line in the rear of his army, for he believed that Grant was still traveling with Meade, Humphreys, and Wright. Grant, of course, was not to be found, but Lee was given the note the

Federal general had written early that morning before he left Curdsville. Lee sent his reply by a courier who sought Grant to the south.
At this time there was no action in the Confederate rear, and Lee
sought to end hostilities in his front as well, sending word to Gordon to
seek a truce with his adversaries.

Gordon relates: "My troops were still fighting, furiously fighting, in
nearly every direction when the final note from General Lee reached
me. . . . I called Colonel Green Peyton of my staff, and directed him to
take a flag of truce . . . to General Ord, who commanded, as I supposed,
the Union infantry in my front. I ordered him to say to the Union
commander this, and nothing more: 'General Gordon has received a
notice from General Lee of a flag of truce, stopping the battle.' Colonel
Peyton soon informed me that we had no flag of truce. I said, 'Well, take
your handkerchief and tie that on a stick, and go.' He felt in his pockets
and said, 'General, I have no handkerchief.' 'Then tear your shirt, sir,
and tie that to a stick.' He looked at his shirt, and then at mine, and said,
'General, I have on a flannel shirt, and I see you have. I don't believe
there is a white shirt in the army.' 'Get something, sir,' I ordered. 'Get
something and go!' "

The final moments of the fighting are described as they were experienced by Union Private Gerrish: "Our brigade was quickly formed
in two lines of battle to make a charge. Our regiment was in the front
line, and General Sheridan formed a cavalry skirmish line in our front.
The enemy's lines of battle were evidently over beyond the hill in our
front, as some of their batteries opened upon us, and threw shot and
shell very carelessly around. The skirmishers advanced at a round gallop, Sheridan leading them on. When they reached the crest of the hill
and entered the forest on our right, we advanced rapidly across the
plain and climbed the hill. Just before we reached its top a shell exploded in the barn, and in a moment it was in flames. In the confusion,
hens and chickens ran from the barn in every direction.

"By this time the enemy was pouring a very heavy artillery fire
upon us, but it always requires something more than shot or shells to
prevent hungry soldiers from chasing chickens, and so after the fowls
we ran. Shells were crashing, officers were shouting for the men to
keep in the ranks, the boys were screaming and laughing as they ran
after the chickens, the flames roared and swept through the air, and
the hens squalled in their most pathetic manner as they were overtaken and captured. Altogether it was a most remarkable medley.
When the poultry excitement subsided and we all got back into the

rapidly advancing line and looked out in our front, our mirth quickly subsided.

"It was a desperate situation—one in which the most careless and indifferent would be brought to his senses. For three-fourths of a mile an open field lay before us. A few rods of this distance was descending ground, then a level plain, and beyond that a ridge of land. At the foot of that ridge was the enemy's skirmish line. We could distinctly see the little rifle pits in which they were entrenched. Beyond their skirmish line, and higher on the side of the hill, was their line of battle, behind breastworks, and back of this was their artillery, all in plain view. Their infantry had not opened fire on us, but their artillery was firing rapidly and with good execution. We saw all this plainly, although advancing at a rapid rate. We well understood what our mission was—to assault their position and silence their batteries.

"We thought of our comrades who had fallen out in the night, and who were then quietly sleeping back in the woods, and were angry with ourselves to think . . . we had been foolish enough to keep up, and, by doing so, get in such a scrape. But it was then too late to fall out, and all we could do was to pull our hats down over our eyes as far as possible, keep up with the line, and endeavor to appear brave. We did not fear the artillery very much, for they fired over our heads, but dreaded the moment when the infantry should open on us. We descended the hill and advanced across the plain, and were not far from their skirmish line.

"Not many words were spoken, but every mind was busy. Like a flash we thought of all the past three years, so many dangers passed through; and here, after all these hardships and narrow escapes, just as the war was about to close, our regiment reduced to a hundred men, was hurled into this desperate position, where nearly all must be slaughtered. It did seem hard, but not a man in that little band flinched, and as coolly as we had ever marched upon the parade ground, we marched up to what we supposed was the gates of death.

"We saw a white object flutter in an orchard up in the rear of their line of battle. 'A signal for their infantry to open fire,' growled the boys as they saw it. Then we expected to see their line of battle mantled in fire and smoke as they poured volleys of death upon us. But a moment passed, and not a gun had been fired. We looked again. We saw the object we had supposed to be a signal flag, but it had changed its position. It was advancing . . . down to their line of battle. It continued to advance, and passed [through] their battle line. Three men [on

The flag of truce

horseback] accompanied it. What could it mean? It was a white flag! We could not believe our eyes. At a brisk gallop the officers rode to within twenty rods of our line, then turned down to our right where Sheridan had disappeared. . . ."

Returning to the Confederate side and General Gordon: "[Colonel Peyton] did not find Ord, but he found Sheridan, and returned to me accompanied by an officer [of Sheridan's command] of strikingly picturesque appearance. This Union officer was slender and graceful, and a superb rider. He wore his hair very long, falling almost to his shoulders. Guided by my staff officer, he galloped to where I was sitting on my horse, and, with faultless grace and courtesy, saluted me with his saber and said, 'I am General Custer, and bear a message to you from General Sheridan. The general desires me to present to you his compliments and to demand the immediate and unconditional surrender of all the troops under your command.'

"I replied, 'You will please, general, return my compliments to General Sheridan and say to him that I shall not surrender my command.' 'He directs me to say to you, general, if there is any hesitation about your surrender, that he has you surrounded and can annihilate your command in an hour.'

"To this I answered that I was probably as well aware of my situation as was General Sheridan; that I had nothing to add to my message informing him of the contents of the note from General Lee; that if General Sheridan decided to continue the fighting in the face of the flag of truce, the responsibility for the bloodshed would be his and not mine.

"In a short time thereafter a white flag was seen approaching. Under it was Philip Sheridan, accompanied by a mounted escort almost as large as one of Fitz Lee's regiments. Sheridan was mounted on an enormous horse, a very handsome animal. He rode in front of the escort, and an orderly carrying the flag rode beside him. Around me at the time were my faithful sharpshooters, and as General Sheridan and his escort came within easy range of the rifles, a half-witted fellow raised his gun as if to fire. I ordered him to lower his gun, and explained that he must not fire on a flag of truce. He did not obey my order cheerfully, but held his rifle in position to be quickly thrown to his shoulder. In fact, he was again in the act of raising his gun to fire at Sheridan when I caught the gun and said to him, with emphasis, that he must not shoot men under flag of truce. He at once protested, 'Well, general, let him stay on his own side.'

"I did not tell General Sheridan of his narrow escape. Had he known the facts—that this weak-minded but strong-hearted Confederate private was one of the deadliest of marksmen—he probably would have realized that I had saved his life.

"Meantime, another member of my staff, Major R. W. Hunter of Virginia, had ridden off with General Custer, who asked to be guided to Longstreet's position.

"As General Sheridan, with the flag of truce, came nearer, I rode out to meet him. Between General Sheridan and myself occurred another controversy very similar to the one I had had previously with General Custer. . . . But upon my exhibiting to him the note from Lee, he at once proposed that the firing cease and that our respective lines be withdrawn to certain positions while we waited further intelligence from the commanders of the two armies."

By this time General Custer was approaching Longstreet's headquarters. Among the Confederate soldiers who were watching was William Miller Owen. "A Federal cavalry officer was observed coming down the road towards our forces. He wore his hair very long, and it was of a light or reddish color. In his hand he carried a white handkerchief, which he constantly waved up and down. He . . . was directed to General Longstreet upon the hill. Upon approaching the general he dismounted and said, 'General Longstreet, in the name of General Sheridan and myself I demand the surrender of this army. I am General Custer.' General Longstreet replied, 'I am not in command of this army. General Lee is, and he [is arranging] to meet General Grant in regard to a surrender.'

" 'Well,' said Custer, 'no matter about General Grant; we demand the surrender be made to us. If you do not do so we will renew hostilities, and any blood shed will be upon your head!'

" 'Oh, well!' said Longstreet, 'if you do that I will do my best to meet you.' Then, turning to his staff, he said, 'Colonel Manning, please order General Johnson to move his division to the front, to the right of General Gordon. Colonel Latrobe, please order General Pickett forward to General Gordon's left. Do it at once!'

"Custer listened with surprise depicted upon his countenance. He had not thought so many of our troops were at hand with Longstreet. He, cooling off immediately, said, 'General, probably we had better wait until we hear from Grant and Lee. I will speak to General Sheridan about it. Don't move your troops yet.' And he mounted and withdrew in a much more quiet style than in his approach.

"As he passed out of hearing, Longstreet said quietly, with that peculiar chuckle of his, 'Ha, ha. That young man has never learned to play the game of Brag!'

"The divisions of Johnson and Pickett were only a myth, and had no existence whatever after . . . Five Forks [and Sayler's Creek].

"Shortly after this little event, General Lee . . . rode through our lines towards Appomattox Court House. . . ."

Word had begun to spread through both armies that Lee was about to surrender. Relief and elation swelled in Union breasts, and only a few of the more resolute Confederates, such as William Miller Owen, found the situation unacceptable. "We had been thinking it might come to that, sooner or later, but when the shock came it was terrible. And was this to be the end of all our marching and fighting for the past four years? I could not keep back the tears that came to my eyes." For the most part, the men on both sides began trading their feelings of contention for stirrings of good will. The pickets fraternized. "Were it not for the restraints of discipline," claims Union surgeon Alfred Woodhull, "the armies themselves, to all appearance, would have coalesced."

24

The Surrender

It was nearly noon when Lee's courier found Grant, who was still some distance south of Appomattox Court House, and handed him the Confederate general's dispatch, which stated: "I received your note of this morning on the picket line whither I had come to meet you and ascertain definitely what terms were embraced in your proposal of yesterday with reference to the surrender of this army. I now request an interview in accordance with the offer contained in your letter of yesterday for that purpose."

Grant explains: "When the officer reached me I was still suffering with the sick headache; but the instant I saw the contents of the note I was cured." The courier was sent galloping back to Lee with Grant's assurance that he would be available for a meeting as soon as he reached the field.

One of the officers riding with Grant was Horace Porter, who relates: "About one o'clock the little village of Appomattox Court House, with its half-dozen houses, came in sight, and soon we were entering its single street. It is situated on rising ground, and beyond it the country slopes down into a broad valley. The enemy was seen, with his columns and wagon trains, covering the low ground. Our cavalry, the 5th Corps, and part of Ord's command were occupying the high ground to the south and west of the enemy, heading him off completely. We saw a group of [Union] officers who had dismounted and were standing at the edge of the town, and at their head we soon recognized the features of Sheridan. No one could look at Sheridan at such a moment without a sentiment of undisguised admiration. In this campaign, as in others, he had shown himself possessed of military traits of the highest order. . . .

"Ord and others were standing in the group . . . and as our party came up General Grant greeted the officers and said, 'How are you, Sheridan?' 'First-rate, thank you; how are you?' cried Sheridan, with a voice and look which seemed to indicate that, on his part, he was having things all his own way. 'Is Lee over there?' asked Grant, pointing up the road, having heard a rumor that Lee was in that vicinity. 'Yes, he is in that brick house, waiting to surrender to you,' answered Sheridan. 'Well, then, we'll go over,' said Grant. . . .

"The building stood a little distance back from the street, with a yard in front, and to the left on entering was a gate for carriages, and a roadway running to a stable in rear. We entered the grounds by this gate, and dismounted. In the yard were seen a fine, large gray horse, which proved to be General Lee's favorite animal, called 'Traveler,' and a good-looking, dark-colored mare belonging to Colonel Marshall [Charles Marshall, an aide to Lee]. An orderly in gray was in charge of them, and had taken off their bridles to let them crop the grass."

The house belonged to a man named Wilmer McLean, whose residency had not been a long one. Horace Porter explains: "It is a singular historical coincidence that McLean's former home was upon a Virginia farm near the battleground of the First Bull Run [fought in 1861], and his house was used for a time as the headquarters of General [Pierre G. T.] Beauregard. When it was found that this fight was so popular that it was given an encore, and a second battle of Bull Run was fought the next year on the same ground, Mr. McLean became convinced that the place was altogether lacking in repose, and to avoid the active theater of war he removed to the quiet village of Appomattox, only to find himself again surrounded by contending armies. Thus the first and last scenes of the war drama in Virginia were enacted upon his property."

General Grant assumes the narrative: "I had known General Lee in the old army [of the United States], and had served with him in the Mexican War; but did not suppose, owing to the difference in our age and rank, that he would remember me; while I would more naturally remember him distinctly because he was the chief of staff of General [Winfield] Scott. . . . When I left camp that morning I had not expected so soon the result that was then taking place, and consequently was in rough garb. I was without a sword, as I usually was when on horseback on the field, and wore a soldier's blouse for a coat, with the shoulder straps of my rank to indicate to the army who I was.

The McLean house

"When I went into the house, I found General Lee. We greeted each other, and after shaking hands took our seats. I had my staff with me, a good portion of whom were in the room during the whole of the interview. What General Lee's feelings were I do not know. As he was a man of much dignity, with an impassible face, it was impossible to say whether he felt inwardly glad that the end had finally come, or felt sad over the result and was too manly to show it. . . . My own feelings, which had been quite jubilant on the receipt of his letter, were sad and depressed. I felt like anything rather than rejoicing at the downfall of a foe who had fought so long and valiantly, and had suffered so much for a cause—though that cause was, I believe, one of the worst for which a people ever fought, and one for which there was the least excuse. I do not question, however, the sincerity of the great mass of those who were opposed to us. . . .

"In my rough traveling suit . . . I must have contrasted very strangely with a man so handsomely dressed, six feet high, and of faultless form. . . . We soon fell into a conversation about old army times. He remarked that he remembered me . . . in the old army, and I told him . . . I remembered him perfectly. . . . Our conversation grew so pleasant that I almost forgot the object of our meeting. After the conversation had run on in this style for some time, General Lee . . . asked . . . the terms I proposed to give his army. I said I meant merely that his army should lay down their arms, not to take them up again during the continuance of the war unless duly and properly exchanged. . . .

"Then we gradually fell off again into conversation about matters foreign to the subject which had brought us together. This continued for some little time, when General Lee again interrupted the course of the conversation by suggesting that the terms I proposed to give his army ought to be written out. I . . . commenced writing out the following terms: '. . . The officers to give their individual paroles not to take up arms against the Government of the United States until properly exchanged, and each company or regimental commander sign a like parole for the men of their commands. The arms, artillery, and public property to be parked and stacked, and turned over to the officer appointed by me to receive them. This will not embrace the side arms of the officers, nor their private horses or baggage. This done, each officer and man will be allowed to return to their homes, not to be disturbed by United States authority so long as they observe their paroles and the laws in force where they may reside.'

". . . As I wrote . . . not one word passed between General Lee and

Grant and Lee discussing surrender terms

myself. . . . When he read over that part of the terms about side arms, horses, and private property of the officers, he remarked . . . that this would have a happy effect upon his army. Then, after a little further conversation, General Lee remarked to me . . . that their army was organized a little differently from the army of the United States—still maintaining by implication that we were two countries; that in their army the cavalrymen and artillerists [i.e., the men in the ranks] owned their own horses; and he asked if he was to understand that the men who so owned their horses were to be permitted to retain them. I told him that, as the terms were written, they would not, that only the officers were permitted to take their private property. . . .

"I then said to him that I thought this would be about the last battle of the war—I sincerely hoped so; and I said further I took it that most of the men in the ranks were small farmers. The whole country had been so raided by the two armies that it was doubtful whether they would be able to put in a crop to carry themselves and their families through the next winter without the aid of the horses they were then riding. The United States did not want them, and I would, therefore, instruct the officers I left behind to receive the paroles of his troops to let every man of the Confederate army who claimed to own a horse or mule take the animal to his home.

"Lee remarked again that this would have a happy effect. He then . . . wrote out [a letter of acceptance]. . . . While duplicates of the two letters were being made, the Union generals present were severally presented to General Lee. . . . After all was completed, and before taking his leave, [Lee] remarked that his army was in a very bad condition for want of food, and that they were without forage; that his men had been living for some days on parched corn exclusively, and that he would have to ask me for rations and forage. . . . I authorized him to send his own commissary and quartermaster to Appomattox Station . . . where he could have, out of the trains we had stopped [those from Lynchburg, intended for Lee], all the provisions wanted. As for forage, we had ourselves depended almost entirely upon the country for that.

"Generals Gibbon, Griffin, and [Wesley] Merritt were designated by me to carry into effect the paroling of Lee's troops before they should start for their homes—General Lee leaving Generals Longstreet, Gordon, and Pendleton for them to confer with in order to facilitate this work. Lee and I then separated as cordially as we had met. . . ."

Confederate officer William Miller Owen tells of Lee's return to his army: "Whole lines of men rushed down to the roadside and crowded

Lee departing McLean house after the surrender

around him to shake his hand. All tried to show him the veneration and esteem in which they held him. Filled with emotion, he essayed to speak, but could only say, 'Men, we have fought through the war together. I have done the best I could for you. My heart is too full to say more.' We all knew the pathos of those simple words, of that slight tremble in his voice, and it was no shame on our manhood 'that something upon the soldier's cheek washed off the stains of powder'; that our tears answered to those in the eyes of our grand old chieftain; and that we could only grasp the hand of 'Uncle Robert' and pray *'God help you, General!'* "

An example of the manner in which the news of the surrender was received among the various Federal units at Appomattox is given by General Regis de Trobriand: "All at once a tempest of hurrahs shook the air along the front of our line. General Meade is coming at a gallop from Appomattox Court House. He has raised his cap and uttered a few words: LEE HAS SURRENDERED! . . . Mad hurrahs fill the air like the rolling of thunder, in the fields, in the woods, along the roads, and are prolonged in echo. . . .

"General Meade leaves the road and passes through my division. The men swarm out to meet him, surrounding his horse. Hurrah for General Meade! Again, Hurrah! And on all sides, Hurrah! The enthusiasm gains the officers of his staff, who cry out like all the rest, waving their hats. Caps fly in the air; the colors are waved in salute . . . [becoming] glorious rags in the breeze; all the musicians fill the air with the joyous notes of 'Yankee Doodle' and the sonorous strains of 'Hail, Columbia.'

". . . All the hopes of four years at last realized; all the fears dissipated, all perils disappeared; all the privations, all the sufferings, all the misery ended; the intoxication of triumph; the joy at the near return to the domestic hearth—for all this, one single burst of enthusiasm did not suffice. So the hurrahs and cries of joy were prolonged. . . ."

Adds Union Private Theodore Gerrish: "Now large numbers of the rebel soldiers came over to us. We were glad to see them. They had fought bravely, and were as glad as we that the war was over. They told us of the fearful condition General Lee's army was in, and we only wondered that they endured the hardships so long as they did. We received them kindly, and exchanged pocket knives and sundry trinkets, that each could have something to carry home as a reminiscence of the great event."

A Union staff officer, Colonel George A. Forsyth, says this of General

Spreading the tidings of victory

Grant: "On his way to his field headquarters on this eventful Sunday evening, [he] dismounted, sat quietly down by the roadside, and wrote a short and simple dispatch ['General Lee surrendered the Army of Northern Virginia this afternoon on terms proposed by myself. . . .'], which a galloping aide bore at full speed to the nearest telegraph station. On its reception in the nation's capital, this dispatch was flashed over the wires to every hamlet in the country, causing every steeple in the North to rock to its foundation [as its bells rung wildly], and sending one tall, gaunt, sad-eyed, weary-hearted man in Washington to his knees, thanking God that he had lived to see the beginning of the end, and that he had at last been vouchsafed that he had led his people aright."

The narrative is taken up by a correspondent of the New York *Times*, William Swinton, who became the Army of the Potomac's chief historian: "As the armies were enemies no longer, there was no need of martial array that night, nor fear of surprise, nor call to arms. . . . Hostile devisement gave place to mutual helpfulness, and the victors shared their rations with the famished vanquished. In that supreme moment these men knew and respected each other. If the one army drank the joy of victory and the other the bitter draught of defeat, it was a joy moderated by the recollection of the cost at which it had been purchased, and a defeat mollified by the consciousness of many triumphs. . . . If at length the Army of Northern Virginia fell before the massive power of the North, yet what vitality had it shown! How terrible had been the struggle! How many hundreds of thousands of brave men had fallen before that result could be achieved!"

(As it happened, the killed and wounded in the Appomattox Campaign, March 29 to April 9, were moderate. Horace Porter lists Grant's losses at 1,316 killed and 7,750 wounded, and Lee's at 1,200 killed and 6,000 wounded.)

William Swinton continues: "And this is the glory of the Army of the Potomac, that it brought to the ground the adversary which had ever been the head and front of the revolt, and that in crushing it, it quelled the rebellion. For so decisive upon the issue of the war was the surrender of that army that the capitulation of all the other Confederate armies [most notably, that of Johnston, who had been standing against Sherman] followed as a corollary therefrom, and the structure of the Confederacy, losing its keystone, fell with a resounding crash.

"Three days after the surrender, the Confederates marched by divisions to a designated spot in the neighborhood of Appomattox Court

Federals sharing their rations with Confederates

The formal surrender. Confederates are shown stacking their muskets and furling their flags.

House, and there the troops stacked their arms and deposited their accoutrements. . . . Paroles were then distributed to the men, and the Army of Northern Virginia passed out of existence."

According to Southerner Carlton McCarthy: "Comrades wept as they gazed upon each other and with choking voices said farewell! And so—they parted. Little groups of two or three or four, without food, without money, but with 'the satisfaction that proceeds from the consciousness of duty faithfully performed,' were soon plodding their way homeward."

Adds Richmond editor Edward Pollard: "A few days after the surrender, General Lee rode into the city . . . he had so long defended, and passed through its blackened streets a paroled prisoner of war. He entered the city with no display, accompanied by five members of his staff, took the shortest route to his house, and appeared anxious to avoid all kind of public demonstration. He had so often passed through those streets the object of all eyes, attended by the admiration of the populace. Though he came back now a fallen commander, though his arrival was unexpected, he found in quickly gathered crowds evidence that the people still loved him; evidence that the [occupying] enemy respected him.

"The first cheers that had been heard from citizens since the scarred and blackened city cringed under the flag of the enemy now ran along the streets, and brave and noble-minded men in Federal uniform raised their caps as the former commander-in-chief of the Southern Confederacy passed before their eyes, with hair white as snow, and care-worn face, but with touching and unspeakable dignity. To the doors of his house he was followed by a large crowd who cheered him as heartily as if he had ridden into Richmond at the head of a victorious army.

"It was no word that he spoke, for he did not open his lips. It was no gesture, no sign of emotion, for he rode on without other recognition of the crowd than occasionally to raise his hat. It was his presence and its signification that moved the people of Richmond to a demonstration in which men forgot their own sorrow, disregarded the presence of a hostile army, and gave way to the glory and gratitude of the past. The occasion was that of the last token of visible public respect to the memory of the Southern Confederacy, made in the face of the enemy, who neither interrupted the demonstration nor gainsaid the tribute it implied."

Northern newsman William Swinton tells what happened to Grant's troops after Appomattox: "[They] retraced their steps to Richmond,

The grand review in Washington

whence they were soon afterwards transferred to Washington. Here uniting with their illustrious sister-army [that of Sherman], they passed in review before the President [this was Andrew Johnson, for Lincoln had died by an assassin's bullet six days after Appomattox] and his cabinet, and the representatives of foreign powers and an immense concourse of citizens, who with great rejoicings welcomed home the men whose valor had won the peace. . . . When the pageant was ended, the troops were mustered out of service, and the men, doffing the Union blue, were quietly reabsorbed into the body of society.

"Thus the Army of the Potomac—that mighty creation of the patriotism of a free people, which for four years had waged a struggle unparalleled in its continuous intensity—ceased to be, closing its career . . . by the happy reestablishment of the Union for which it had fought."

Epilogue

Writing nearly twenty years after Appomattox, an aging Union general, Theodore B. Gates of New York, ventured this nutshell summation: "With the close of the war, the dawn of a new and better era burst upon our country. We emerged from the conflict triumphant not only, but we had shown vitality and resources that amazed the world while they surprised ourselves. The blot upon our escutcheon had been expunged, and we stood before the world in the sublime majesty of a nation *free* in *fact,* as well as in theory. True, we yet bear the marks and scars of the gigantic struggle through which we have passed; but with a people reunited and animated by that indomitable spirit which hitherto has enabled them to accomplish so much, they will march on, in the course of empire, until our continent shall be covered with towns and cities, and peace and good will shall dwell in all our borders."

Quotation Sources

Battles and Leaders of the Civil War, vol. 4. Robert Underwood Johnson and Clarence Clough Buel (eds.). New York: Century Co., 1888.

[Boykin, E. M.]. *The Falling Flag.* New York: E. J. Hale & Son, 1874.

Bruce, George A. *The Capture and Occupation of Richmond.* Publisher and date of publication not given.

Buell, Augustus. *The Cannoneer: Recollections of Service in the Army of the Potomac.* Washington, D.C.: The National Tribune, 1890.

Caldwell, J. F. J. *The History of a Brigade of South Carolinians.* Philadelphia: King & Baird, Printers, 1866. Facsimile edition by Morningside Bookshop, Dayton, Ohio, 1974.

Coffin, Charles Carleton. *The Boys of '61.* Boston: Estes & Lauriat, 1884.

Cooke, John Esten. *Robert E. Lee.* New York: D. Appleton & Co., 1871.

Crotty, D. G. *Four Years Campaigning in the Army of the Potomac.* Grand Rapids, Mich.: Dygert Bros. & Co., 1874.

Davies, Henry E. *General Sheridan.* New York: D. Appleton & Co., 1895.

Davis, Varina Howell. *Jefferson Davis: A Memoir by His Wife.* New York: Belford Company Publishers, 1890.

DeLeon, T. C. *Four Years in Rebel Capitals.* Mobile, Ala.: Gossip Printing Co., 1890.

Gates, Theodore B. *The War of the Rebellion.* New York: P. F. McBreen, Printer, 1884.

Gerrish, Theodore. *Army Life: A Private's Reminiscences of the Civil War.* Portland, Me.: Hoyt, Fogg & Donham, 1882.

Gordon, John B. *Reminiscences of the Civil War.* New York: Charles Scribner's Sons, 1904.

Grant, U. S. *Personal Memoirs.* New York: Charles L. Webster & Co., 1894.

Hale, Edward E. (ed.). *Stories of War Told by Soldiers.* Boston: Roberts Brothers, 1879.

Humphreys, Andrew A. *The Virginia Campaign of 1864 and 1865.* (Campaigns of the Civil War, vol. 12.) New York: Charles Scribner's Sons, 1883.

Hyde, Thomas W. *Following the Greek Cross.* Boston and New York: Houghton, Mifflin & Co., 1894.

Jones, J. William. *Personal Reminiscences, Anecdotes, and Letters of Gen. Robert E. Lee.* New York: D. Appleton & Co., 1874.

King, W. C., and Derby, W. P. *Campfire Sketches and Battlefield Echoes.* Springfield, Mass.: W. C. King & Co., 1887.

Longstreet, James. *From Manassas to Appomattox.* Millwood, N.Y.: Kraus Reprint Co., 1976. First published in 1896.

McCarthy, Carlton. *Detailed Minutiae of Soldier Life in the Army of Northern Virginia 1861–1865.* Richmond: J. W. Randolph & English, 1888.

[McGuire, Judith W.]. *Diary of a Southern Refugee During the War.* New York: E. J. Hale & Son, 1867.

Our Women in the War. Charleston, S.C.: News and Courier Book Presses, 1885.

Owen, William Miller. *In Camp and Battle with the Washington Artillery.* Boston: Ticknor & Co., 1885. Second edition by Pelican Publishing Company, New Orleans, 1964.

Page, Charles A. *Letters of a War Correspondent.* Boston: L. C. Page & Co., 1899.

Pickett, George E. *The Heart of a Soldier.* New York: Seth Moyle, Inc., 1913.

Pollard, Edward A. *The Early Life, Campaigns, and Public Services of Robert E. Lee; with a Record of the Campaigns and Heroic Deeds of His Companions in Arms.* New York: E. B. Treat & Co., 1871.

——. *The Lost Cause.* New York: E. B. Treat & Co., 1866.

Porter, David D. *Incidents and Anecdotes of the Civil War.* New York: D. Appleton & Co., 1886.

Porter, Horace. *Campaigning with Grant.* New York: Century Co., 1897.

[Putnam, Sarah A.]. *Richmond During the War.* New York: G. W. Carleton & Co., 1867.

Sheridan, Philip H. *Personal Memoirs,* vol. 2. New York: Charles L. Webster & Co., 1888.

Stiles, Robert. *Four Years Under Marse Robert.* New York and Washington: Neale Publishing Co., 1903.

Swinton, William. *Campaigns of the Army of the Potomac.* New York: Charles Scribner's Sons, 1882.

Tenney, W. J. *The Military and Naval History of the Rebellion.* New York: D. Appleton & Co., 1865.

Townsend, George Alfred. *Campaigns of a Non-combatant.* New York: Blelock & Co., 1866.

Trobriand, P. Regis de. *Four Years with the Army of the Potomac.* Boston: Ticknor & Co., 1889.

Under Both Flags: A Panorama of the Great Civil War. Chicago: W. S. Reeve Publishing Co., 1896.

The War of the Rebellion: A Compilation of the Official Records of the Union and Confederate Armies, Series I, Volume XLVI. 3 vols. Washington, D.C.: Government Printing Office, 1894, 1895.

Wheeler, Richard. *Voices of the Civil War.* New York: Thomas Y. Crowell Co., 1976.

Supplementary References

Appomattox Court House, Handbook 109. Washington, D.C.: Division of Publications, National Park Service, U.S. Department of the Interior, 1980.

Badeau, Adam. *Military History of Ulysses S. Grant,* vol 3. New York: D. Appleton & Co., 1881.

Bill, Alfred Hoyt. *The Beleaguered City: Richmond 1861–1865.* New York: Alfred A. Knopf, 1946.

Blackford, W. W. *War Years with Jeb Stuart.* New York: Charles Scribner's Sons, 1945.

Cadwallader, Sylvanus. *Three Years with Grant.* Edited by Benjamin P. Thomas. New York: Alfred A. Knopf, 1955.

Calkins, Christopher M. *From Petersburg to Appomattox.* Farmville (Va.) Herald, 1983. Available through the Eastern National Park and Monument Association.

———. *Thirty-Six Hours Before Appomattox.* No publisher given, 1980. Available through the Eastern National Park and Monument Association.

Catton, Bruce. *The Army of the Potomac: A Stillness at Appomattox.* Garden City, New York: Doubleday & Co., 1953.

———. *Never Call Retreat: The Centennial History of the Civil War,* vol. 3. New York: Doubleday & Co., 1965.

Chamberlain, Joshua Lawrence. *The Passing of the Armies.* Dayton, Ohio: Morningside Bookshop, 1974. Facsimile of 1915 edition.

Commager, Henry Steele. *The Blue and the Gray.* Indianapolis and New York: The Bobbs-Merrill Co., 1950.

Coppée, Henry. *Grant and His Campaigns.* New York: Charles B. Richardson, 1866.

Dana, Charles A., and Wilson, J. H. *The Life of Ulysses S. Grant.* Springfield, Mass.: Gurdon Bill & Co., 1868.

Davis, Burke. *To Appomattox: Nine April Days, 1865.* New York and Toronto: Rinehart & Co., 1959.

Davis, Jefferson. *The Rise and Fall of the Confederate Government,* vol. 2. South Brunswick, N.J.: Thomas Yoseloff, 1958. Reprint of edition by D. Appleton & Co., 1881.

Eggleston, George Cary. *A Rebel's Recollections.* New York: Kraus Reprint Co., 1969. Reprint of 1905 edition.

Evans, Clement A. (ed.). *Confederate Military History: A Library of Confederate States History, in Twelve Volumes, Written by Distinguished Men of the South.* New York: Thomas Yoseloff, 1962. Reprint of edition by the Confederate Publishing Company, 1899.

Frassanito, William A. *Grant and Lee: The Virginia Campaigns, 1864–1865.* New York: Charles Scribner's Sons, 1983.

Freeman, Douglas Southall. *Lee's Lieutenants,* vol. 3. New York: Charles Scribner's Sons, 1944.

Goss, Warren Lee. *Recollections of a Private.* New York: Thomas Y. Crowell & Co., 1890.

Grant, Julia Dent. *Personal Memoirs.* Edited by John Y. Simon. New York: G. P. Putnam's Sons, 1975.

Harrison, Mrs. Burton. *Recollections Grave and Gay.* New York: Charles Scribner's Sons, 1911.

Hatcher, Edmund N. *The Last Four Weeks of the War.* Columbus, Ohio: Co-operative Publishing Co., 1892.

Holland, J. G. *The Life of Abraham Lincoln.* Springfield, Mass.: Gurdon Bill, 1866.

Jones, John B. *A Rebel War Clerk's Diary.* Edition condensed, edited, and annotated by Earl Schenck Miers. New York: Sagamore Press, 1958. First published in 1866.

Jones, Katharine M. *Ladies of Richmond.* Indianapolis and New York: Bobbs-Merrill Co., 1962.

Lee, Fitzhugh. *General Lee of the Confederate Army.* London: Chapman & Hall, 1895.

Lee, Captain Robert E. *Recollections and Letters of General Robert E. Lee.* New York: Doubleday, Page & Co., 1904.

Long, E. B., with Barbara Long. *The Civil War Day by Day.* Garden City, N.Y.: Doubleday and Co., 1971.

Lykes, Richard Wayne. *Campaign for Petersburg.* Washington, D.C.: National Park Service, U.S. Department of the Interior, 1970.

Manarin, Louis H. (ed.). *Richmond at War: The Minutes of the City Council, 1861–1865.* Chapel Hill: University of North Carolina Press, 1966.

Patrick, Rembert W. *The Fall of Richmond.* Baton Rouge: Louisiana State University Press, 1960.

Pember, Phoebe Yates. *A Southern Woman's Story: Life in Confederate Richmond.* Edited by Bell Irwin Wiley. Jackson, Tenn.: McCowat-Mercer Press, 1959. First published in 1879.

Pennypacker, Isaac R. *General Meade.* New York: D. Appleton & Co., 1901.

Pryor, Mrs. Roger A. *Reminiscences of Peace and War.* New York: Macmillan Co., 1904.

Richardson, Albert D. *A Personal History of Ulysses S. Grant.* Hartford, Conn.: American Publishing Co., 1868.

Rodick, Burleigh Cushing. *Appomattox: The Last Campaign.* New York: Philosophical Library, 1965.

Sherman, William T. *Memoirs,* vol 2. New York: D. Appleton & Co., 1875.

Stern, Philip Van Doren. *An End to Valor: The Last Days of the Civil War.* Boston: Houghton Mifflin Co., 1958.

Swinton, William. *The Twelve Decisive Battles of the War.* Dick & Fitzgerald, 1867.

Taylor, Walter H. *Four Years with General Lee.* New York: D. Appleton & Co., 1878.

Walker, Francis A. *History of the Second Army Corps in the Army of the Potomac.* New York: Charles Scribner's Sons, 1886.

Wright, Mrs. D. Giraud. *A Southern Girl in '61: The Wartime Memories of a Confederate Senator's Daughter.* New York: Doubleday, Page & Co., 1905.

Index